The EU Foreign Subsidies Regulation

Andreas Reindl

Isabelle Van Damme

Foreword by Dean Arancha González

Introduction by Frédéric Jenny

106 West 32nd Street, Suite 144 New York, NY, 10001, USA
www.concurrences.com
book@concurrences.com

First Printing, January 2024
978-1-939007-77-3 (Hardcover)
Library of Congress Control Number: 2024930945

Cover Design: Yves Buliard, www.yvesbuliard.fr
Book Design and Layout implementation: Nord Compo

Concurrences Books

Tributes

Eleanor M. Fox – Antitrust Ambassador to the World, *2021*

Herbert Hovenkamp – The Dean of American Antitrust Law, *2021*

Frédéric Jenny – Standing Up for Convergence and Relevance in Antitrust, (Vol. I & II), *2019 & 2021*

Albert Foer – A Consumer Voice in the Antitrust Arena, *2020*

Richard Whish – Taking Competition Law Outside the Box, *2020*

Douglas H. Ginsburg – An Antitrust Professor on the Bench (Vol. I & II), *2018 & 2020*

Wang Xiaoye – The Pioneer of Competition Law in China, *A. Emch, W. Ng (eds.), 2019*

Ian S. Forrester – A Scot without Borders (Vol. I & II), *A. Komninos (eds.), 2015*

William E. Kovacic – An Antitrust Tribute (Vol. I & II), *2013 & 2014*

Practical Books

Compendium of Antitrust Damages Action – International Chamber of Commerce (ICC) – 2nd edition, *John W.H. Denton AO, François Brunet, Sarina Williams, Caroline Inthavisay, 2023*

Pharmaceutical Antitrust: An Analysis of US and EU Law, *M. Thill-Tayara, G. Gordon, 2023*

Innovation Paradox in Merger Control, *G. Gurkaynak, 2023*

State Aid & National Enforcement, *J. Derenne, D. Jouve, C. Lemaire, F. Martucci (eds.), 2023*

Antitrust and the Digital Economy, *Y. Katsoulacos (ed.), 2023 (in collaboration with CRESSE)*

Judicial Review of Competition Cases, *D. Ginsburg, T. Eicke (eds.), 2023*

Competition Law Treatment of Joint Ventures, *B. Bleicher, N. Campbell, A. Hamilton, N. Hukkinen, A. Khan, A. Mordaunt (eds.), 2022 (in collaboration with the IBA)*

Information Exchange & Related Risks, *Z. Marosi, M. Soares (eds.), 2022 (in collaboration with the IBA)*

Rulemaking Authority of the US Federal Trade Commission, *D. Crane (ed.), 2022*

The International Competition Network at Twenty, *D. Anderson & P. Lugard (eds.), 2022*

Competition Case Law Digest – 5th Edition, *F. Jenny, N. Charbit (eds.), 2022*

Competition Inspections in 21 Jurisdictions – A Practitioner's Guide, *N. Jalabert-Doury (ed.), 2022*

Perspectives on Antitrust Compliance, *A. Riley, A. Stephan, A. Tubbs (eds.), 2022 (in collaboration with the ICC)*

Turkish Competition Law, *G. Gürkaynak, 2021*

Competition Law – Climate Change & Environmental Sustainability, *S. Holmes, D. Middelschulte, M. Snoep (eds.), 2021*

Merger Control in Latin America – A Jurisdictional Guide, *P. Burnier da Silveira, P. Sittenfeld (eds.), 2020*

Competition Inspections under EU Law – A Practitioner's Guide, *N. Jalabert-Doury, 2020*

Gun Jumping in Merger Control – A Jurisdictional Guide, *C. Hatton, Y. Comtois, A. Hamilton (eds.), 2019 (in collaboration with the IBA)*

Choice – A New Standard for Competition Analysis? *P. Nihoul (ed.), 2016*

PhD Theses

Abuse of Platform Power, *F. Bostoen, 2023*

Reform of Chinese State-Owned Enterprises, *X. Bai, 2023*

Competition & Regulation in Network Industries – Essays in Industrial Organization, *J-M. Zogheib, 2021*

The Role of Media Pluralism in the Enforcement of EU Competition Law, *K. Bania, 2019*

Buyer Power, *I. Herrera Anchustegui, 2017*

General Interest

Global Dictionary of Competition Law, *D. Healey, W. Kovacic, P. Trevisan, R. Whish, 2024*

Great Antitrust Enforcers, *W. E. Kovacic, 2023*

Competition – How to Speak Like an Expert, *E. Combe , 2023*

Women and Antitrust – Voices from the Field (Vol I & II), *E. Kurgonaite & K. Nordlander, 2020*

Conference Proceedings

Antitrust in Emerging and Developing Countries – (Vol I & II), *E. Fox, H. First, 2015 & 2016*

Global Antitrust Law – Current Issues in Antitrust Law and Economics, *D. Ginsburg, J. Wright, (eds.) 2015*

Competition Law on the Global Stage – David Gerber's Global Competition Law in Perspective, *D. Gerber, 2014*

e-Book versions available for **Concurrences+** subscribers

FOREWORD

ARANCHA GONZALEZ LAYA
Dean, Paris School of International Affairs, Sciences Po

Promoting fair competition is at the heart of the World Trade Organization (WTO) system. The principle of non-discrimination, whether the Most-Favoured Nation or the national treatment principle, is meant to ensure fair conditions for international trade.

The preamble of the WTO Agreement speaks of countries achieving its objectives by *"entering into reciprocal and mutually advantageous arrangements directed to the substantial reduction of tariffs and other barriers to trade and to the elimination of discriminatory treatment in international trade relations."*

The WTO rules on dumping, foreign subsidies, agriculture subsidies, non-discrimination on trade in services, intellectual property rights, or the plurilateral agreement on procurement are all translations of this principle in the different trade areas.

Fair competition is also a foundational principle of the EU's internal market, the idea being that tearing down barriers to trade between European nations had to be accompanied by the elimination of unfair practices between the Member States. The 1956 Spaak Report which served as a basis for the creation of the EU common market clearly identified the need to address State interventions that would distort competition as a priority. Today this principle is enshrined in Article 107 of the Treaty on the Functioning of the European Union according to which "any aid granted by a Member State or through State resources in any form whatsoever which distorts or threatens to distort competition by favouring certain undertakings or the production of certain goods shall, in so far as it affects trade between Member States, be incompatible with the internal market".

The legitimacy of openness lies in fairness. This explains why the EU has stringent rules on competition within the single market, as well as robust legislation on trade defence and government procurement. It also helps to understand why the EU has been a strong supporter of multilateral rules to guarantee fair competition in international trade: to align this external dimension with its own internal market.

When the last round of WTO trade negotiations – the Doha Round – was launched in 2001, the EU pushed for the inclusion of competition in the agenda of negotiations but ultimately it did not gather support for negotiating global rules on competition. Comprehensive rules on competition would have helped to better capture distorting policies and practices but since this avenue closed the EU turned its attention to tightening WTO rules on subsidies. Traditionally disciplines in this area had been the result of compromises between the two largest trading partners – the EU and the United States – each trying to preserve the ability to subsidise in their own way. But by 2015 a rising trading partner became a key actor in subsidisation: China. A trilateral dialogue was established between the EU, the US, and Japan – three like-minded large global traders - to tighten subsidy rules which resulted in 2020 in a joint blueprint to further limit the use of harmful subsidies and forced technology transfer provisions. Since then, negotiations in the WTO have shown limited progress.

At the same time, State aid and broader industrial policies have grown in importance worldwide, in particular in technology and around the climate and energy transitions in a context marked by a heightened rivalry between the US and China. The EU now faces additional pressures not only from China but also from the US, as evidenced by the measures included in the US Inflation Reduction Act.

Contextualising the EU's Foreign Subsidies Regulation is essential to understand its origins but also to place it in the wider context of a changing trading landscape. One with a new balance between security and efficiency, between markets and States, between action at the multilateral and the national stage. One where maintaining openness will require a more determined fight against unfairness.

This excellent book offers a rich analysis of the origins of this new EU trade instrument. More importantly, the publication is the first of its kind in providing a deep dive into the scope, application, and control mechanisms of the EU's Foreign Subsidies Regulation, as well as into compliance strategies. I commend the chapter concerning practical compliance with the Regulation as it provides businesses and practitioners with hands-on intelligence to navigate the Regulation's implementation. It can certainly contribute to helping businesses navigate the growing set of risks they face, particularly those stemming from a sharper geopolitical context.

I commend the authors for the timeliness of the publication and thank them for giving me the opportunity of contributing to what I am convinced will be an extremely useful publication.

Introduction

FREDERIC JENNY
Chairman of the OECD Competition Committee
Former Chairman of the WTO Working Group on Trade and Competition Policy
Emeritus Professor of Economics ESSEC Business School

Andreas Reindl and Isabelle Van Damme's book on Foreign Subsidies Regulation in Europe is being published as this new regulation comes into force and as some other countries are considering adopting similar legislation. This timely publication gives us the opportunity to reflect on three questions: What is the purpose of this type of regulation? Why was it not adopted earlier? Why is Europe leading the way in this area?

The late 1980s and the 1990s were characterised by a great confidence in the virtue of competitive market mechanisms to promote economic prosperity. The Berlin Wall fell in November 1989 and the economies of the Soviet bloc moved away from a socialist economic model and adopted liberal economic reforms. The Uruguay round of trade negotiations creating the WTO as a successor to the GATT was completed in 1994 and in December 2001 China became a member of the multilateral body. During the last two decades of the 20th century the growth of world trade averaged 6 percent per year, a growth rate which was twice as fast as that of the world output and hundreds of millions of people in developing countries (particularly in India and China) were lifted out of poverty. The number of countries which adopted competition laws (often a precondition for signing bilateral trade agreements) grew from about 50 to more than 100 (140 countries have a competition law today). As the import substitution models of development, which had been in vogue in the 1950s and the 1960s, had failed to provide a sound basis for economic development, a number of developing countries opted for an open economy and an export led type of growth model based on their comparative advantage (mineral resources and/or cheap labour).

However the consensus on the virtues of global economic liberalism to promote economic progress changed rapidly in the first two decades of the 21st century.

First, the financial and economic crisis of 2008 showed that competitive markets could fail and that in some sectors (for example, the financial sector) prone to systemic risks governmental regulation could be a useful complement to economic competition. Furthermore, the necessity to restart the economic engine following the financial crisis led a number of governments to adopt financial stimuli to help their businesses overcome the difficulties they faced due to the slowdown of their economies. In turn a number of countries started to take protectionist measures against the unfair competition of subsidised foreign products and to retaliate against protectionist measures adopted by their trade partners.

Second, starting in 2020, the Covid crisis added another layer of skepticism both on the virtues of the global economic value chain which had developed as a consequence of the rapid development of international trade and on the faith that could be attributed to free markets to self-correct sufficiently rapidly in cases of massive exogenous shocks. The notion that, at least for strategic products or services (but the list of what one could consider to be economically strategic was often a long, open-ended list) should be reoriented either at the national or the regional level to ensure the resilience of our economies became prevalent. Inevitably a combination of protectionism and distorting subsidies would be used to promote local value chains at least in the countries which had been the most open to international trade.

Third and simultaneously, most countries were faced with new realities which implied a massive reallocation of resources and required rapid technological developments. One of these issues, global warming (which had been discussed publicly since 1990 when the first GIEC report was published in 1990), finally became a hot political issue in many countries and required both the accelerated technical development of clean technologies and a rapid reallocation of resources toward clean technologies as they became available.

Another major issue is the development of digital technologies. This also required massive research and development in order for countries to seek to remain technologically independent and to benefit from these new services, which are likely to lead to important productivity gains and a reallocation of resources enabling the rapid diffusion of digital tools and techniques in businesses. In both cases the role of governments to accelerate economic progress through industrial policy is central as the European Union demonstrated when it adopted in 2020 "an industrial strategy that would support the twin transition to a green and digital economy, make EU industry more competitive globally, and enhance Europe's open strategic autonomy". The revival of industrial policy to face those challenges is not the monopoly of Europe as evidenced by an article published by the IMF, which states: "What is new is that the United States has joined China in an explicit embrace of industrial policies. China has been in the game at least since President Xi Jinping reasserted state control over the economy, moving away from the outward-oriented policies of Deng Xiaoping and his successors. The Made in China 2025 initiative, consisting of large subsidies to targeted industries, has given way to the idea of "dual circulation," focused on reducing external dependence by strengthening domestic sourcing by local firms, and the drive for self-sufficiency in key technologies. The United States began protecting the steel and aluminum industries, ostensibly on national security grounds, during the Trump administration. With the CHIPS Act and the Inflation Reduction Act, the US introduced subsidies to "reshore" production of semiconductors and adopted restrictive national content regulations for electric vehicles to ensure domestic production".

Lastly, the continued rapid development of globalisation, particularly in the first two decades of the current century (i.e. after the entry of China in the WTO), has not only fueled the discontent of significant portions of the electorate in a number of developed countries but has also raised the issue of the fairness of economic competition when firms coming from states with very different regulatory environments have to compete. The political opposition to economic globalisation is based on the fact that labour markets are not as flexible as assumed by economists, which means that the necessary reallocation of the workforce away from underachievers toward activities which have a comparative advantage does not take place seamlessly and requires enabling policies to increase the geographical mobility of workers and/or their acquisition of new skills. Most often such enabling policies are not implemented and some workers are displaced because of the international competition without any hope of finding new economic opportunities. The perception of unfairness of international competition is, of course reinforced when domestic firms fail to withstand the pressure of this competition because advantages have been conferred by foreign governments on foreign competitors (whether in the form of a subsidy or a protection against the risk of bankruptcy or a discriminatory access to financing) which the domestic firms could not benefit from in their own countries because those advantages would be considered illegal under their domestic laws.

The combination of these forces (i.e. the revival of industrial policy, the technological race between countries to guarantee their independence together with the growing importance of subsidies of various kinds in a world of liberalized trade between countries having quite different domestic regimes) is particularly problematic for the European Union which, on the one hand, has an open trade policy and is bound by its commitments in the WTO, and, on the other hand, prohibits its Member States from engaging in State aid to avoid the risk that a subsidy race between individual Member States might undermine the level playing field in the EU internal market and put at risk its core market integration policy. As the European Commission put it in its contribution to the OECD Competition Committee debate on Subsidies, Competition and Trade held in December 2022: "Increasing trade and investment flows have brought with them an increased risk of negative spillover effects through subsidies granted outside the EU".

State Aid in the European context is defined as any advantage granted by public authorities through state resources on a selective basis to any organizations that could potentially distort competition and trade in the European Union. Article 107(1) TFEU provides that State aid distorts the internal market, and negatively affects trade between Member States, and, as such, is therefore, prima facie, prohibited. Under Article 108 TFEU, the Commission is given the task to control State aid. The EU State aid policy purpose is to identify and avoid harmful support measures while allowing governments to continue to use State aid to facilitate the development of certain economic activities.

In the context of the WTO, the Agreement on Subsidies and Countervailing Measures regulates the actions countries can take to counter the effects of subsidies which adversely affect their interests. However this agreement is much weaker than the EU State aid policy in various ways. First, the agreement only applies to the production of goods and does not cover the provision of services unlike the European regulation of State aid. Second, whereas the European regulation of State aid prohibits EU Member States from providing subsidies which distort competition, such subsidies (except for export subsidies) are not prohibited under the WTO rules but negatively affected WTO Members can seek countervailing measures through the dispute settlement mechanism.

The perceived unfairness and disruptive effect of international competition in Europe comes thus from the fact that Europe has a very strict domestic regulation which prohibits European firms from benefitting from State aid while the international trade commitments of the European Union prevent it from refusing competition from foreign firms which in their home country benefit from more permissive regulations on subsidies.

Faced with this situation, and with little hope to force a change in the multilateral trading system, the European Commission has taken the lead and chosen boldly to "impose rules and procedures for investigating foreign subsidies that favour companies in a way that negatively affects competition in the EU internal market and for addressing such distortions. There is a particular focus on large concentrations and large public procurement procedures for which notifications are required, but the Commission can on its own initiative launch investigations in any other economic activity for which a distortive foreign subsidy was granted".

This regulation which is designed to fill a perceived gap in the European legal framework sits at the intersection between trade policy, industrial policy, market integration policy, and competition policy and tries to increase the consistency between these related EU policies.

Along somewhat similar lines (but with a scope which is different and more limited than the scope of the Foreign Subsidies Regulation), the U.S. Consolidated Appropriations Act passed in December 2022 calls for reporting certain subsidies in the context of notifications filed under the Hart-Scott-Rodino Antitrust Improvements Act. This reporting is limited to subsidies from "foreign entities of concern," rather than all foreign subsidies and the rules implementing these requirements have yet to be adopted.

Time will tell how this bold regulation will be enforced by the European Commission, whether it will be a source of inspiration for other jurisdictions, whether it will lead to protectionist retaliations or whether it will contribute to new efforts to strengthen the multilateral discipline on subsidies.

In the meanwhile we are guided in our exploration of this innovative regulation by the very able analysis and comments of Andreas Reindl and Isabelle Van Damme.

ACKNOWLEDGMENTS

This book on the Foreign Subsidies Regulation is the result of a close collaboration among lawyers at Van Bael & Bellis working in the fields of trade law, competition law, and public procurement law. Understanding the Foreign Subsidies Regulation and how it will operate in practice requires bringing together knowledge and practical experience in all of these fields. The team to be credited for contributing to this book consists of Jorren Garrez, Catherine Gordley, Emily Greenaway, Derya Kizil, Antigoni Matthaiou, Giovanni Pregno, Emmanuelle Rogiest, Steve Ross, Frenkchris Sinay, Pietro Stella and Valentina Zanda. The team is also grateful to Mario Di Carlo for his comments on an initial draft of the chapter setting out the FSR public procurement tool.

The Van Bael & Bellis team authoring this book wishes to thank Veerle Roelens for diligently and patiently editing the manuscript, and Carol Stephenson for her editorial assistance.

Finally, Van Bael & Bellis is grateful to Concurrences for its continuous support throughout the publication process. Special thanks go to Sébastien Gachot and Nicolas Charbit.

Andreas Reindl, Isabelle Van Damme, December 2023

Table of Contents

List of Abbreviations

Abbreviation	Full Reference
2021 Trade Policy Review	Communication from the Commission to the European Parliament, the Council, the European Economic and Social Committee and the Committee of the Regions, Trade Policy Review – An Open, Sustainable and Assertive Trade Policy COM (2021) 66 final
Basic Anti-Dumping Regulation	Regulation (EU) 2016/1036 of the European Parliament and of the Council of 8 June 2016 on protection against dumped imports from countries not members of the European Union [2016] OJ L176/21
Basic Anti-Subsidy Regulation	Regulation (EU) 2016/1037 of the European Parliament and of the Council of 8 June 2016 on protection against subsidised imports from countries not members of the European Union [2014] OJ L176/55
CJEU	Court of Justice of the European Union
Commission	European Commission
Commission Notice on the notion of State aid	Commission Notice on the notion of State aid as referred to in Article 107(1) of the Treaty on the Functioning of the European Union [2016] OJ C262/1
CTAR	Case Team Allocation Request
De Minimis Aid Regulation	Commission Regulation 1407/2013 on the application of Articles 107 and 108 of the Treaty on the Functioning of the European Union to *de minimis* aid [2013] OJ L352/1
ESPD	European Single Procurement Document
EU	European Union
EU Economic Security Strategy	Joint Communication to the European Parliament, the European Council and the Council on 'European Economic Security Strategy, JOIN (2023) 20 final
EUMR	EU Merger Regulation or Council Regulation (EC) 139/2004 of 20 January 2004 on the control of concentrations between undertakings [2004] OJ L24/1
European Wind Power Plan	Communication from the Commission to the European Parliament, the Council, the European Economic and Social Committee and the Committee of the Regions, European Wind Power Action Plan COM (2023) 669 final
FDI	Foreign direct investment
FDI Screening Regulation	Regulation (EU) 2019/452 of the European Parliament and of the Council of 19 March 2019 establishing a framework on the screening of foreign direct investments into the Union [2019] OJ LI79/1
FRAND	Fair, reasonable, and non-discriminatory
FSR	Regulation (EU) 2022/2560 of the European Parliament and of the Council of 14 December 2022 on foreign subsidies distorting the internal market [2022] OJ L330/1

Abbreviation	Full Reference
FSR FAQs	Frequently asked questions on the FSR, divided into FSR M&A FAQs, and FSR Public Procurement FAQs
FSR Impact Assessment	European Commission, Commission Staff Working Document Impact Assessment Accompanying the Proposal for a Regulation of the European Parliament and of the Council on foreign subsidies distorting the internal market SWD (2021) 99 final
FSR Implementing Regulation	Commission Implementing Regulation (EU) 2023/1441 of 10 July 2023 on detailed arrangements for the conduct of proceedings by the Commission pursuant to Regulation (EU) 2022/2560 of the European Parliament and of the Council on foreign subsidies distorting the internal market [2023] OJ L177/1, as corrected by Commission Implementing Regulation (EU) 2023/2414 of 25 October 2023 correcting Implementing Regulation (EU) 2023/1441 on detailed arrangements for the conduct of proceedings by the Commission pursuant to Regulation (EU) 2022/2560 of the European Parliament and of the Council on foreign subsidies distorting the internal market [2023] OJ L2414
FSR Proposal	Commission Proposal for a Regulation of the European Parliament and of the Council on foreign subsidies distorting the internal market, COM (2021) 223 final
GATT 1994	General Agreement on Tariffs and Trade 1994
GATS	General Agreement on Trade and Services
Guidelines on rescue and restructuring aid	Guidelines on State aid for rescuing and restructuring non-financial undertakings in difficulty
HR	Human resources
IPI	International Procurement Instrument
IPO	Initial public offering
IRA	Inflation Reduction Act
IRR	Internal rate of return
Jurisdictional Notice	Commission Consolidated Jurisdictional Notice under Council Regulation (EC) 139/2004 on the control of concentrations between undertakings (Jurisdictional Notice) [2008] OJ C95/1
JV	Joint venture
M&A	Mergers and acquisitions
MEOP	Market Economy Operator Principle
MEO test	Market Economy Operator Test
NASA	National Aeronautics and Space Administration
NPV	Net present value
OECD	Organisation for Economic Co-operation and Development
OECD Arrangement	OECD Arrangement on Officially Supported Export Credits

Abbreviation	Full Reference
Parliament	European Parliament
R&D	Research and development
RBI	Reserve Bank of India
Regulation 1/2003	Council Regulation (EC) 1/2003 of 16 December 2002 on the implementation of the rules on competition laid down in Articles 81 and 82 EC Treaty [2003] OJ L1/1 (as amended)
Regulation on subsidies in air transport	Regulation (EU) 2019/712 of the European Parliament and of the Council of 17 April 2019 on safeguarding competition in air transport, and repealing Regulation (EC) 868/2004 [2019] OJ L123/4
Remedies Notice	Commission Notice on remedies acceptable under the Council Regulation (EC) 139/2004 and under Commission Regulation (EC) 802/2004 [2008] OJ C267/1
RFI	Request for information
RMB	Renminbi
RSB	Regulatory Scrutiny Board
SASAC	State-owned Assets Supervision and Administration Commission of the State Council
SCM Agreement	Agreement on Subsidies and Countervailing Measures
SME	Small and medium-sized enterprises
SOEs	State-owned enterprises
TED	Tenders Electronic Daily
Temporary Framework	Temporary Crisis and Transition Framework for State Aid measures to support the economy following the aggression against Ukraine by Russia
TFEU	Treaty on the Functioning of the European Union
USDoD	US Department of Defence
White Paper	White Paper on levelling the playing field as regards foreign subsidies
WTO	World Trade Organization

List of Cited Cases Before the Court of Justice of the European Union and the General Court

List of cited cases before the Court of Justice of the European Union

Case C-272/23 P *Jushi Egypt for Fiberglass Industry v European Commission*
Case C-106/22 *Xella Magyarország* EU:C:2023:568
Case C-106/22 *Xella Magyarország* EU:C:2023:267, Opinion of AG Capeta
Case C-416/21 *Landkreis Aichach-Friedberg v J Sch Omnibusunternehme* EU:C:2022:689
Case C-672/20 P *European Commission v EFTA Surveillance Authority* EU:C:2023:561
Case C-331/20 P *Volotea SA v European Commission* EU:C:2022:886
Case C-933/19 P *Autostrada Wielkopolska SA v European Commission and Republic of Poland* EU:C:2021:905
Joined Cases C-885/19 P and C-898/19 P *Fiat Chrysler Finance Europe v European Commission and Ireland v European Commission* EU:C:2022:859
Case C-638/19 *European Commission v European Food SA and Others* EU:C:2022:50
Case C-598/19 *Conacee v Feacem* EU:C:2021:349, Opinion of AG Tanchev
Case C-425/19 P *European Commission v Italian Republic* EU:C:2021:154
Case C-362/19 P *European Commission v Fútbol Club Barcelona* EU:C:2021:169
Case C-10/18 P *Mowi ASA (formerly Marine Harvest ASA) v European Commission* EU:C:2020:149
Case C-706/17 *Achema AB and Others v Valstybinė kainų ir energetikos kontrolės komisija* EU:C:2019:407
Case C-633/16 *Ernst & Young P/S v Konkurrenceradet* EU:C:2018:371
Case C-579/16 P *European Commission v FIH Holding A/S* EU:C:2018:159
Case C-531/16 *Šiaulių regiono atliekų tvarkymo centras and 'Ecoservice projektai' UAB* EU:C:2018:324
Case C-349/16 T *KUP SAS v Belgische Staat* EU:C:2017:469
Case C-329/15 *ENEA SA v President of the Energy Regulatory Office* EU:C:2017:67
Case C-20/15 P *European Commission v World Duty Free Group SA* EU:C:2016:981
Case C-230/14 *Weltimmo sro v Nemzeti Adatvedelmi es Informacioszabadsag Hatosag* EU:C:2015:639
Case C-15/14 P *European Commission v MOL Magyar Olaj- és Gázipari Nyrt* EU:C:2015:362
Case C-518/13 R *(on the application of Eventech Ltd) v Parking Adjudicator* EU:C:2015:9
Joined Cases C-39/13 and C-40/13 and C-41/13 *Inspecteur van de Belastingdienst/Noord/kantoor Groningen v SCA Group Holding BV* EU:C:2014:1758
Case C-382/12 P *MasterCard Inc v European Commission* EU:C:2014:2201
Case C-262/12 *Association Vent De Colère! and Others* EU:C:2013:851
Case C-403/10 P *Mediaset SpA v European Commission* EU:C:2011:533
Joined Cases C-399/10 P and C-401/10 P *Bouygues SA v European Commission* EU:C:2013:175
Case C-81/10 P *France Télécom SA v European Commission* EU:C:2011:811

Joined Cases C-106/09 P and C-107/09 P *European Commission v Gibraltar* EU:C:2011:732
Joined Cases T-80/06 and T-182/09 *Budapesti Erőmű Zrt v European Commission* EU:T:2012:65
Case C-399/08 P *European Commission v Deutsche Post AG* EU:C:2010:481
Case C-538/07 *Assitur Srl v Camera di Commercio, Industria, Artigianato e Agricoltura di Milano* EU:C:2009:317
Case C-206/06 *Essent Netwerk Noord BV v Aluminium Delfzijl BV* EU:C:2008:413
Case C-206/06 *France v Ladbroke Racing Ltd* EU:C:2000:248
Case C-222/04 *Ministero dell'Economia e delle Finanze v Cassa di Risparmio di Firenze SpA* EU:C:2006:8
Case C-278/00 *Greece v Commission of the European Communities* EU:C:2004:239
Case C-280/00 *Altmark Trans GmbH v Nahverkehrsgesellschaft Altmark GmbH* EU:C:2003:415
Joined Cases C-328/99 and C-399/00 *Italy v Commission of the European Communities* EU:C:2003:252
Case C-482/99 *France v Commission of the European Communities (Stardust)* EU:C:2002:294
Joined Cases C-180/98 to 184/98 *Pavlov v Stichting Pensioenfonds Medische Specialisten* EU:C:2000:428
Case C-16/98 *Commission of the European Communities v French Republic* EU:C:2000:541
Case C-387/92 *Banco Exterior de España SA v Ayuntamiento de Valencia* EU:C:1994:100
Case C-41/90 *Höfner v Macrotron GmbH* EU:C:1991:161
Case C-196/87 *Steymann v Staatssecretaris van Justitie* EU:C:1988:475
Case 792/79 R *Camera Care Ltd v Commission of the European Communities* EU:C:1980:18
Case C-78/76 *Steinike & Weinlig v Federal Republic of Germany* EU:C:1977:52

List of cited cases before the General Court

Case T-744/20 *Airoldi Metalli SpA v European Commission* EU:T:2021:853
Case T-540/20 *Jushi Egypt for Fiberglass Industry v European Commission* EU:T:2023:91
Case T-451/20 *Meta Platforms Ireland Ltd v European Commission* EU:T:2023:276
Case T-609/19 *Canon Inc v European Commission* EU:T:2022:299
Case T-300/16 *Jindal Saw Ltd v European Commission* EU:T:2019:235
Case T-98/16 *Italian Republic and Others v European Commission* EU:T:2019:167
Case T-461/13 *Kingdom of Spain v European Commission* EU:T:2015:891
Case T-272/12 *Energetický a průmyslový holding as v European Commission* EU:T:2014:995
Case T-633/11 *Guangdong Kito Ceramics Co Ltd and Others v Council of the European Union* EU:T:2014:271
Case T-384/10 *Spain v European Commission* EU:T:2013:277
Case T-457/09 *Westfälisch-Lippischer Sparkassen- und Giroverband v European Commission* EU:T:2014:683
Case T-141/08 E.*ON Energie AG v European Commission* EU:T:2010:516
Case T-469/07 *Philips Lighting Poland SA and Philips Lighting BV v Council of the European Union* EU:T:2013:370

Case T-459/07 *Hangzhou Duralamp Electronics Co Ltd v Council of the European Union* EU:T:2013:369
Case T-1/07 *Apache Footwear Ltd and Apache II Footwear Ltd (Qingxin) v Council of the European Union* EU:T:2009:483
Case T-45/06 *Reliance Industries Ltd v Council of the European Union* EU:T:2008:398
Case T-184/01R IMS *Health Inc v Commission of the European Communities* EU:T:2001:200
Case T-267/97 *Broome & Wellington v Commission of the European Communities* EU:T:1998:108
Case T-134/95 *Dysan Magnetics Ltd and Review Magnetics (Macao) Ltd v Commission of the European Communities* EU:T:1996:38
Case T-44/90 *La Cinq SA v Commission of the European Communities* EU:T:1992:5
Case T-23/90 *Automobiles Peugeot SA v Commission of the European Communities* EU:T:1991:45

List of Cited Reports of the WTO Appellate Body and WTO Panels

WTO Appellate Body Report, *Brazil – Export Financing Programme for Aircraft*, WT/DS46/AB/R, adopted 20 August 1999, DSR 1999:III 1161 (*Brazil – Aircraft*)

WTO Appellate Body Report, *Canada – Measures Affecting the Export of Civilian Aircraft*, WT/DS70/AB/R, adopted 20 August 1999, DSR 1999:III 1377 (*Canada – Aircraft*)

WTO Appellate Body Report, *European Communities – Definitive Anti-Dumping Measures on Certain Iron or Steel Fasteners from China*, WT/DS397/AB/R, adopted 28 July 2011, DSR 2011:VII 3995 (*EC – Fasteners (China)*)

WTO Appellate Body Report, *European Communities and Certain Member States – Measures Affecting Trade in Large Civil Aircraft*, WT/DS316/AB/R, adopted 1 June 2011, DSR 2011:I 7 (*EC and certain member States – Large Civil Aircraft*)

WTO Appellate Body Report, *Mexico – Definitive Anti-Dumping Measures on Beef and Rice, Complaint with Respect to Rice*, WT/DS295/AB/R, adopted 20 December 2005, DSR 2005:XXII 10853 (*Mexico – Anti-Dumping Measures on Rice*)

WTO Appellate Body Report, *United States – Tax Treatment for 'Foreign Sales Corporations'*, WT/DS108/AB/R, adopted 20 March 2000, DSR 2000:III 1619 (*US – FSC*)

WTO Appellate Body Report, *United States – Countervailing Duties on Certain Corrosion-Resistant Carbon Steel Flat Products from Germany*, WT/DS213/AB/R and Corr.1, adopted 19 December 2002, DSR 2002:IX 3779 (*US – Carbon Steel (India)*)

WTO Appellate Body Report, *United States – Final Countervailing Duty Determination with Respect to Certain Softwood Lumber from Canada*, WT/DS257/AB/R, adopted 17 February 2004, DSR 2004:II 571 (*US – Softwood Lumber IV*)

WTO Appellate Body Report, *United States – Countervailing Duty Investigation on Dynamic Random Access Memory Semiconductors (DRAMS) from Korea*, WT/DS296/AB/R, adopted 20 July 2005, DSR 2005:XVI 8131 (*US – Countervailing Duty Investigation on DRAMs*)

WTO Appellate Body Report, *United States – Definitive Anti-Dumping and Countervailing Duties on Certain Products from China*, WT/DS379/AB/R, adopted 25 March 2011, DSR 2011:V 2869 (*US – Anti-Dumping and Countervailing Duties (China)*)

WTO Appellate Body Report, *United States – Measures Affecting Trade in Large Civil Aircraft (Second Complaint)*, WT/DS353/AB/R, adopted 23 March 2012, DSR 2012:I 7 (*US – Large Civil Aircraft (2nd complaint)*)

WTO Appellate Body Report, *United States – Countervailing Duty Measures on Certain Products from China*, WT/DS437/AB/RW, adopted 15 August 2019 (*US – Countervailing Measures (China) (Article 21.5 – China)*)

WTO Panel Report, *Brazil – Export Financing Programme for Aircraft*, WT/DS46/R, adopted 20 August 1999, as modified by Appellate Body Report WT/DS46/AB/R, DSR 1999:III 1221 (*Brazil – Aircraft*)

WTO Panel Report, *Brazil – Export Financing Programme for Aircraft – Recourse by Canada to Article 21.5 of the DSU*, WT/DS46/RW, adopted 4 August 2000, as modified by Appellate Body Report WT/DS46/AB/RW, DSR 2000:IX 4093 (*Brazil – Aircraft (Article 21.5 – Canada)*)

WTO Panel Report, *European Communities – Countervailing Measures on Dynamic Random Access Memory Chips from Korea*, WT/DS299/R, adopted 3 August 2005, DSR 2005:XVIII 8671 (*EC – Countervailing Measures on DRAM Chips*)

WTO Panel Report, *European Communities and Certain Member States – Measures Affecting Trade in Large Civil Aircraft*, WT/DS316/R, adopted 1 June 2011, as modified by Appellate Body Report, WT/DS316/AB/R, DSR 2011:II 685 (*EC and certain member States – Large Civil Aircraft*)

WTO Panel Report, *Japan – Countervailing Duties on Dynamic Random Access Memories from Korea*, WT/DS336/R, adopted 17 December 2007, as modified by Appellate Body Report WT/DS336/AB/R, DSR 2007:VII 2805 (*Japan – DRAMS (Korea)*)

WTO Panel Report, *Korea – Anti-Dumping Duties on Imports of Certain Paper from Indonesia*, WT/DS312/R, adopted 28 November 2005, DSR 2005:XXII 10637 (*Korea – Certain Paper*)

WTO Panel Report, *Korea – Measures Affecting Trade in Commercial Vessels*, WT/DS273/R, adopted 11 April 2005, DSR 2005:VII 2749 (*Korea – Commercial Vessels*)

WTO Panel Report, *United States – Sections 301-310 of the Trade Act of 1974*, WT/DS152/R, adopted 27 January 2000, DSR 2000:II 815 (*US – Section 301 Trade Act*)

WTO Panel Report, *United States – Tax Treatment for 'Foreign Sales Corporations'*, WT/DS108/R, adopted 20 March 2000, as modified by Appellate Body Report WT/DS108/AB/R, DSR 2000:IV 1675 (*US – FSC*)

WTO Panel Report, *United States – Preliminary Determinations with Respect to Certain Softwood Lumber from Canada*, WT/DS236/R, adopted 1 November 2002, DSR 2002:IX 3597 (*US – Softwood Lumber VII*)

WTO Panel Report, *United States – Measures Affecting Trade in Large Civil Aircraft (Second Complaint)*, WT/DS353/R, adopted 23 March 2012, as modified by Appellate Body Report WT/DS353/AB/R, DSR 2012:II 649 (*US – Large Civil Aircraft (2nd complaint)*)

WTO Panel Report, *United States—Countervailing Measures on Softwood Lumber from Canada*, WT/DS533R, circulated 24 August 2020 (*US – Softwood Lumber VII*)

INDEX

A

B

C

D

E

F

G

H

I

J

L

M

N

O

P

R

S

T

U

V

W

Chapter I
Introduction

1. Introduction

The Foreign Subsidies Regulation (FSR) is a new instrument through which the European Union (EU) seeks to ensure a level playing field in the internal market.[1] The FSR came about as a result of concerns about the effects of, especially, Chinese subsidies on markets in the EU that could not be remedied through existing remedies under EU trade remedies legislation and the WTO Agreement on Subsidies and Countervailing Measures (SCM Agreement).[2]

The FSR, reflecting these concerns, is a far-reaching instrument that subjects foreign subsidies to EU review regardless of the third country granting them, and confers extensive powers on the European Commission (Commission) to investigate and, if necessary, remedy the distortive effects of foreign subsidies on competition in the internal market. The FSR also imposes considerable administrative burdens on companies[3] seeking to merge with or acquire EU companies or to participate in public procurement projects[4] in the EU (and which, in this context, must file FSR notifications). Moreover, under the FSR, the Commission enjoys broad discretion to investigate, on its own motion, foreign subsidies and remedy their effects on any economic activity in the EU. In essence, nothing in the FSR precludes the Commission from using the powers under the new instrument to pursue the EU's industrial policy goals.

In its design, the FSR is a hybrid instrument. This also explains why its legal bases are Article 114 of the Treaty on the Functioning of the European Union (TFEU) (internal market harmonisation) and Article 207 TFEU (common commercial policy). The FSR draws on existing concepts and practices under EU merger control, EU State aid law, EU trade remedies legislation, EU procurement law, and the SCM Agreement. At the same time, the FSR must be understood as a response to perceived gaps in the control and the remedies available under these existing instruments. That feature also explains why, as this book illustrates, there is

---

1 Regulation (EU) 2022/2560 of the European Parliament and of the Council of 14 December 2022 on foreign subsidies distorting the internal market (FSR Regulation 2022/2560) [2022] OJ L330/1, recital 6.

2 WTO Agreement on Subsidies and Countervailing Measures 1994 (SCM Agreement) <www.wto.org/english/docs_e/legal_e/24-scm.pdf> accessed 18 December 2023.

3 Throughout this book, we have avoided using the term 'undertaking' (unless quoting an official EU text), which is less familiar to readers outside the EU, and instead refer to a 'company', 'entity', or 'control group'. We appreciate that these terms do not have the same exact meaning as the EU's term 'undertaking', which refers to any entity engaged in an 'economic activity'. See, eg, Joined Cases C-180/98 to 184/98 *Pavlov v Stichting Pensioenfonds Medische Specialisten* EU:C:2000:428, paras 74–75; Case C-41/90 *Höfner v Macrotron GmbH* EU:C:1991:161, para 21. But we hope that this convention will improve the readability of our text.

4 To ensure consistency and improve readability, this text refers to procurement 'projects'.

considerable uncertainty about how the FSR will be applied. In turn, this also affects the compliance obligations of companies and the preparatory steps that they must undertake to notify transactions or otherwise anticipate the initiation of a Commission investigation into the distortive effects of foreign subsidies on competition in the internal market.

This chapter focuses on the FSR's origin and legislative history, its objectives, main features, and its interaction with related areas of regulation of subsidies and foreign investments.

2. The Origin, Legislative History and Objectives of the FSR

A. State Aid Control as a Key Component of the Internal Market

From its inception, the EU considered the internal market as a fundamental pillar of European integration, and recognised the importance of protecting undistorted competition for the functioning of the internal market. Protecting undistorted competition in the internal market required rules governing private firm behaviour. At the same time, when the (now) EU was established, there was an additional concern that certain Member States would trigger a 'race to the bottom' by excessively subsidising domestic businesses with lasting effects on competition in the internal market.

To address these concerns, the EU – unlike other major trading partners granting subsidies – created an elaborate State aid control mechanism, which prohibits the granting of aid by the Member States, unless authorised by the Commission under (now) Article 107 TFEU.

With aid granted by Member States already – at least in principle, and mostly from a historic perspective – tightly controlled under EU law, the focus more recently shifted to subsidies granted by third countries and their effects on competition in the internal market.

B. Origins of the FSR and its Legislative Process

In 2017, the European Parliament (Parliament) issued a resolution on the EU industrial strategy, noting that the existing global rulebook on distortive foreign subsidies was incomplete.[5] The Parliament asked the Commission to 'pay more attention to the role of

---

[5] European Parliament resolution of 5 July 2017 on building an ambitious EU industrial strategy as a strategic priority for growth, employment and innovation in Europe [2017] OJ C334/124 <https://eur-lex.europa.eu/legal-content/EN/TXT/?uri=CELEX%3A52017IP0305&qid=1701454926216> accessed 18 December 2023.

foreign-based State-owned enterprises (SOEs) that are supported and subsidised by their governments in ways that EU internal market rules prohibit for EU entities'.[6] In 2019, the European Council also called on the Commission to identify gaps in EU law and how to fill these gaps for the purpose of addressing the distortive effects of foreign subsidies. In particular, it noted that '[f]air competition should be ensured within the single market and globally, both to protect consumers and to foster economic growth and competitiveness, in line with the long-term strategic interests of the Union'.[7]

In response to these calls for regulating foreign subsidies, in March 2020, the Commission communicated, in its '*New Industrial Strategy for Europe*', the objective of upholding a global level playing field. The Commission noted that although the EU industry is 'highly integrated in global value chains and operates globally', it must be protected against 'threats to fair competition and trade'.[8] As part of this strategy, the Commission committed to strengthening the EU anti-subsidies mechanisms and preparing a white paper on distortive foreign subsidies.

A few months later, in June 2020, the Commission published the '*White Paper on Levelling the Playing Field as Regards Foreign Subsidies*' (White Paper) which examined available options for addressing the material impact of foreign subsidies on competition in the internal market and, particularly, on the acquisition of EU targets and EU public procurement. The White Paper analysed existing legal instruments, identified the regulatory gaps, and proposed new tools to address the distortive effects of foreign subsidies.

The White Paper was premised on the Commission's narrative that '[o]penness to trade and investment is part of the economy's resilience, but it must go hand in hand with fairness and predictable rules'.[9] The broader policy objective underpinning the EU's choice to address foreign subsidies was that of ensuring the European economy's resilience by pursuing a model of 'open strategic autonomy'.[10] The Commission presented open strategic autonomy as a policy direction that would allow the EU to reap the full benefits of global trade. According to the Commission, the concept of open strategic autonomy entails shaping a new system of global economic governance through developing mutually beneficial bilateral trade relations and protecting the EU internal market from unfair and abusive practices.

The Commission emphasised the potential impact on the EU of third-country markets with a limited degree of openness. It noted that beneficiaries of third-country subsidies facing little or no competition in their domestic market are placed in a privileged position,

---

6 ibid, para 19.

7 European Council, European Council meeting (21 and 22 March 2019) – Conclusions (22 March 2019) 2 <https://data.consilium.europa.eu/doc/document/ST-1-2019-INIT/en/pdf> accessed 18 December 2023.

8 Commission Communication to the European Parliament, the European Council, the Council, the European Economic and Social Committee and the Committee of the Regions, 'A New Industrial Strategy for Europe' COM (2020) 102 final 6 <https://eur-lex.europa.eu/legal-content/EN/TXT/PDF/?uri=CELEX:52020DC0102> accessed 18 December 2023.

9 European Commission, 'White Paper on Levelling the Playing Field as Regards Foreign Subsidies' (White Paper) COM (2020) 253 final 4 <https://competition-policy.ec.europa.eu/system/files/2021-06/foreign_subsidies_white_paper_en.pdf> accessed 18 December 2023.

10 See also Commission Communication to the European Parliament, the European Council, the Council, the European Economic and Social Committee, and the Committee of the Regions, 'Europe's Moment: Repair and Prepare for the Next Generation' COM (2020) 456 final 12–13.

and might enjoy undue advantages over companies that compete with them in the EU internal market. In particular, the White Paper referred to 'foreign subsidies' as promoting and facilitating aggressive market conduct or acquisitions in the EU.[11] In that context, the Commission referred by way of example to the Sino-CEEF fund, which is a ten-billion-euro investment fund 'especially created for investments in the EU'.[12]

Following the publication of the White Paper, most respondents seemed to welcome the initiative.[13] However, some stakeholders voiced concerns about the heavy administrative burden that might come with the adoption of a new legal instrument.[14] At the same time, the Regulatory Scrutiny Board (RSB) issued a positive opinion with reservations on the Commission's preference for a new legal instrument. Among others, the RSB took the position that the Commission did not clearly establish when foreign subsidies would be problematic, how the balancing test of the positive effects of foreign subsidies would precisely operate, or how a new regulation would specifically interact with other EU regimes.[15]

Against this background, on 5 May 2021, the Commission adopted a proposal for a new regulation in which it reiterated the broader policy objective of promoting a 'strong, open and competitive single market' (FSR Proposal).[16] In the FSR impact assessment accompanying the FSR Proposal, the Commission highlighted the geopolitical context of the proposed instrument, referring to growing evidence that certain trade partners of the EU 'actively [pursue] industrial policies with the declared aim of achieving global leadership in key industrial sectors'.[17] According to the Commission, those industrial policies involve large volumes of subsidies that produce distortive effects in the EU

11 White Paper COM (2020) 253 final (n 9) 8.

12 ibid, fn 10.

13 Following the White Paper, the Commission received 150 contributions in total from the EU Member States, from third-country stakeholders and governments, business/industry associations and individual businesses, as well as law firms, academic institutions, trade unions, NGOs and citizens. The outcome of the consultations on the White Paper on Foreign Subsidies is available at <https://competition-policy.ec.europa.eu/system/files/2021-06/foreign_subsidies_white_paper_en.pdf> accessed 18 December 2023. In addition, on 6 October 2020, the Commission published an Inception Impact Assessment that further outlined various policy options, which sparked more feedback. The outcome of those consultations is available at <https://ec.europa.eu/info/law/better-regulation/have-your-say/initiatives/12621-Trade-investment-addressing-distortions-caused-by-foreign-subsidies/public-consultation_en> accessed 18 December 2023.

14 Taking into account these consultations, the Inception Impact Assessment accompanying the FSR proposal sets out four possible options to address distortive foreign subsidies: (i) taking no action, (ii) publishing guidance on existing EU legislation, (iii) amending existing EU rules, or (iv) adopting a new legal instrument, see European Commission, 'Commission Staff Working Document Impact Assessment Accompanying the Proposal for a Regulation of the European Parliament and of the Council on foreign subsidies distorting the internal market' (FSR Impact Assessment) SWD (2021) 99 final 38.

15 European Commission, Regulatory Scrutiny Board, 'Impact assessment/Addressing distortions caused by foreign subsidies' (Opinion) 2021 1 at <https://competition-policy.ec.europa.eu/system/files/2021-06/foreign_subsidies_scrutiny_board_opinion.pdf> accessed 18 December 2023.

16 European Commission, 'Proposal for a Regulation of the European Parliament and of the Council on foreign subsidies distorting the internal market' (FSR Proposal) COM (2021) 223 final 1. See also FSR Impact Assessment SWD (2021) 99 final (n 14). The Commission also issued an executive summary of this Impact Assessment: European Commission, 'Commission Staff Working Document Executive Summary of the Impact Assessment Report accompanying the Commission staff working document impact assessment Proposal for a Regulation of the European Parliament and of the Council on foreign subsidies distorting the internal market' SWD (2021) 100 final.

17 FSR Impact Assessment (n 14) 5.

internal market.[18] In that context, the Commission emphasised the need to address the potential distortive effects of China's industrial policies through the adoption of the FSR. For example, the Commission highlighted in its FSR impact assessment that:

> 'the Chinese industrial strategy 'Made in China 2025' aims to make the country an industrial leader by providing favourable conditions for growth to a number of industrial and hi-tech sectors such as robotics, electric vehicles, medical equipment, aerospace, maritime and railways. Studies indicate that public financial support is an important part of this strategy and that Chinese direct and indirect subsidies to SOEs have amounted to 1.3 – 1.6% of annual GDP in recent years, with the total subsidy figure in fact likely being higher as private firms receive about a third of total direct subsidies (2018).'[19]

In its FSR Proposal, the Commission also relied on the findings of the European Court of Auditors that certain subsidies granted by China could constitute State aid under EU law if the same subsidies would have been granted by an EU Member State.[20] In particular, the Commission focused on the European Court of Auditors' finding that the absence in China of rules similar to EU State aid rules amounts to a 'difference in treatment' that 'can distort competition in the EU's internal market'.[21]

In the course of the legislative negotiations,[22] the scope of the FSR was broadened, the role of interested parties in FSR proceedings was strengthened, while the timeframe available to the Commission for investigating foreign subsidies was shortened.[23]

On 30 June 2022, the Council and the Parliament reached an agreement on the proposed FSR.[24] The final text was adopted on 10 November 2022 by the Parliament[25] and on 28 November 2022 by the Council.[26]

---

18 ibid 5 and 34.

19 ibid 5.

20 ibid 7.

21 European Court of Auditors, *The EU's Response to China's State-Driven Investment Strategy* (2020) 15 <www.eca.europa.eu/Lists/ECADocuments/RW20_03/RW_EU_response_to_China_EN.pdf> accessed 18 December 2023.

22 The negotiations between the Parliament, the Council, and the Commission commenced after the Council adopted its negotiating mandate on 4 May 2022. See FSR Proposal COM (2021) 223 final (n 16).

23 The Parliament negotiators ensured that State-owned companies were also included in the scope of the proposed regulation and insisted that (non-monetary) support measures should also be considered as financial contributions. They also included the possibility for interested parties to inform the Commission about the existence of potential distortive subsidies and shortened the timeframe for the Commission to investigate subsidies in public procurement procedures. Moreover, the time accorded to the Commission to retrospectively investigate subsidies was shortened from 10 to 5 years. The Parliament negotiators also required the Commission to issue guidelines on how it will assess the distortive nature of a subsidy, and to provide more details on the balancing test.

24 European Commission, Press Release, 'Foreign Subsidies: Commission welcomes political agreement on Regulation on distortive foreign subsidies' (30 June 2022) <https://ec.europa.eu/commission/presscorner/detail/e%20n/ip_22_4190> accessed 18 December 2023.

25 European Parliament, Press Release, 'Parliament approves new tool to ensure fair competition on the single market' (10 November 2022) <www.europarl.europa.eu/news/en/press-room/20221107IPR49609/parliament-approves-new-tool-to-ensure-fair-competition-on-the-single-market> accessed 18 December 2023.

26 European Council, Press Release, 'Council gives final approval to tackling distortive foreign subsidies on the internal market' (28 November 2022) <www.consilium.europa.eu/en/press/press-releases/2022/11/28/council-gives-final-approval-to-tackling-distortive-foreign-subsidies-on-the-internal-market/> accessed 18 December 2023.

C. *Implementing Legislation*

The FSR was published in the Official Journal on 23 December 2022 and entered into force on 12 January 2023. The FSR applied as of 12 July 2023, which means that the Commission has had the ability to start ex officio investigations from that date onwards. The notification obligations for transactions and public procurement projects applied as of 12 October 2023.[27] These tight deadlines left the Commission only approximately six months to adopt implementing rules.

On 6 February 2023, the Commission published the draft FSR Implementing Regulation, which laid out details about the enforcement process and the notification process.[28] As the extensive reporting requirements under the two notification tools became more concrete, concerns about the administrative burden imposed by the FSR intensified. The feedback on the draft FSR Implementing Regulation was therefore overwhelmingly negative. Numerous stakeholders raised concerns about the broad scope of the notification and reporting obligations under the M&A and public procurement tools, resulting in part from the FSR's broad definition of a 'financial contribution' and the use of many concepts that lacked an objective definition.[29]

On 10 July 2023, after an intense exchange with stakeholders, the Commission adopted the final version of Implementing Regulation 2023/1441 (FSR Implementing Regulation), in which the Commission attempted to address at least some of these concerns.[30] The FSR Implementing Regulation contains two annexes with notification forms detailing the information that parties must provide to fulfil their notification obligations under the M&A and public procurement tools.

Finally, on 6 June 2023, the Commission launched two FAQs webpages (one focused on the M&A tool, the other one on the public procurement tool) with answers to the most frequently asked questions on the FSR (FSR FAQs). The Q&A pages have since then been regularly updated.[31]

---

27 FSR Regulation 2022/2560 [2022] OJ L330/1 (n 1), art 54.

28 The outcome of this feedback is available at <https://ec.europa.eu/info/law/better-regulation/have-your-say/initiatives/13602-Distortive-foreign-subsidies-procedural-rules-for-assessing-them_en> accessed 18 December 2023.

29 As Chapter 2 further explains, this would mean that every purchase or supply relationship with a third country government or company with conduct attributable to a third country government would become subject to the FSR notification obligations, even when a transaction would be on market terms.

30 Commission Implementing Regulation (EU) 2023/1441 of 10 July 2023 on detailed arrangements for the conduct of proceedings by the Commission pursuant to Regulation (EU) 2022/2560 of the European Parliament and of the Council on foreign subsidies distorting the internal market (FSR Implementing Regulation) [2023] OJ L177/1, as corrected by Commission Implementing Regulation (EU) 2023/2414 of 25 October 2023 correcting Implementing Regulation (EU) 2023/1441 on detailed arrangements for the conduct of proceedings by the Commission pursuant to Regulation (EU) 2022/2560 of the European Parliament and of the Council on foreign subsidies distorting the internal market [2023] OJ L2414.

31 FSR M&A FAQs <https://competition-policy.ec.europa.eu/foreign-subsidies-regulation/questions-and-answers_en> accessed 18 December 2023; FSR Public Procurement FAQs <https://single-market-economy.ec.europa.eu/single-market/public-procurement/foreign-subsidies-regulation/questions-and-answers_en> (accessed 18 December 2023).

3. Main Features of the FSR

The FSR – although in many respects inspired by related areas of EU law (as further detailed in the next section of this chapter) – introduces a completely new enforcement regime with its own distinct objectives, legal concepts, enforcement processes, and remedial powers.

The FSR's policy objective is to prevent distortions caused by foreign subsidies received by operators engaged in economic activity in the EU's internal market. This policy objective is reflected in key elements that define the scope of the FSR and the boundaries of the Commission's enforcement powers. These include the concepts of a 'financial contribution' and a 'subsidy', the factors informing the distortion analysis, and the considerations underlying the balancing test involving an assessment of the foreign subsidy's distortion against its positive effects on the internal market (see Chapter II).

The new enforcement regime introduced by the FSR is organised around three 'tools' for the Commission to investigate the distortive effects of foreign subsidies. Under the ex officio tool, the Commission may investigate the distortive effects of foreign subsidies on the internal market on its own initiative, regardless of the level of the subsidy or the economic activity in the EU possibly affected by the subsidies (see Chapter VI). In addition, the FSR provides for two notification-based tools: the M&A tool and the public procurement tool (see, respectively, Chapters III and IV). Under these two tools, concentrations and participation in a public procurement tender must be notified to the Commission under certain conditions, and the Commission may also request notification when notifications are not mandatory. Compliance with these novel notification requirements will require significant preparations and investment in due diligence (see Chapter V).

In the context of the ex officio tool, the FSR defines the structure of investigations, the Commission's investigatory powers and its powers to impose fines, and rights of defence (see especially Chapter VII). The same rules apply in principle horizontally across all investigatory tools, although they are sometimes complemented (or replaced) by rules specific to each notification-based tool.

4. Related Regimes

A. *Introduction*

Existing EU trade and competition policy instruments were not designed to address the distortive effects of foreign subsidies. State aid control under Article 107 TFEU does not cover subsidies granted by authorities other than the Member States' authorities.

Likewise, trade defence instruments, such as the Basic Anti-Subsidy Regulation,[32] do not discipline subsidised investments, services, or financial flows. Accordingly, the Commission observed in its FSR impact assessment accompanying the proposed FSR, that '[w]hile the existing EU toolbox includes some rules to deal with foreign subsidies in certain market circumstances, these rules are not sufficient, leaving a "*regulatory gap*"'.[33]

To fill the perceived regulatory gap, the FSR underlines that its objective is that of 'establishing a harmonised framework to address distortions caused, directly or indirectly, by foreign subsidies, with a view to ensuring a level playing field, contributing to the resilience of the internal market and thereby EU's open strategic autonomy'.[34] The FSR further clarifies that it is without prejudice to the application of EU competition law,[35] the Anti-Subsidy Regulation,[36] the Foreign Direct Investment (FDI) Screening Regulation,[37] the International Procurement Instrument (IPI),[38] and Regulation 2019/712 (the Regulation on subsidies in air transport).[39] In addition, the FSR explicitly confirms that '[t]his Regulation should be applied and interpreted in light of the relevant Union legislation, including that relating to State aid, mergers and public procurement'.[40]

The following sections address the relationship between the FSR and EU State aid law, as well as the SCM Agreement and EU anti-subsidy law. Moreover, they address the relationship between the FSR and other related regimes that might influence its operation, such as EU legislation on subsidies in air transport and FDI screening.[41]

B. The FSR and EU State Aid Law

EU State aid rules form a strict framework applicable to financial support provided by the Member States that intends to protect the internal market against Member State interventions that distort competition.

---

32 Regulation (EU) 2016/1037 of the European Parliament and of the Council of 8 June 2016 on protection against subsidised imports from countries not members of the European Union (Basic Anti-Subsidy Regulation) [2016] OJ L176/55.

33 FSR Impact Assessment SWD (2021) 99 final (n 14) 29 (emphasis added).

34 FSR Regulation 2022/2560 [2022] OJ L330/1 (n 1), recital 7 and art 1.

35 To cover rules on antitrust, mergers, services of general economic interest, and State aid, FSR art 44(1) lists TFEU arts 101, 102, 106, 107 as well as Council Regulation (EC) 1/2003 of 16 December 2002 on the implementation of the rules on competition laid down in Articles 81 and 82 of the Treaty [2003] OJ L1/1 and Council Regulation (EC) 139/2004 of 20 January 2004 on the control of concentrations between undertakings (EUMR Regulation 139/2004) [2004] OJ L24/1.

36 FSR Regulation 2022/2560 [2022] OJ L330/1 (n 1), art 44(2).

37 ibid, art 44(3).

38 FSR art 44(5) refers to Regulation (EU) 2022/1031 of the European Parliament and of the Council of 23 June 2022 on the access of third-country economic operators, goods and services to the Union's public procurement and concession markets and procedures supporting negotiations on access of Union economic operators, goods and services to the public procurement and concession markets of third countries (International Procurement Instrument – IPI) [2022] OJ L173/1.

39 FSR art 44(7) refers to Regulation (EU) 2019/712 of the European Parliament and of the Council of 17 April 2019 on safeguarding competition in air transport, and repealing Regulation (EC) 868/2004[2019] OJ L123/4.

40 FSR Regulation 2022/2560 [2022] OJ L330/1 (n 1), recital 9.

41 Given a paucity of practice since the IPI's recent entry into force, this section does not discuss the relationship between the FSR and the IPI.

Article 107 TFEU applies to 'State aid', which is in principle any aid granted by a Member State. A number of conditions must be met to identify State aid, namely:

- State origin: the aid must be of public origin, that is, support must be granted, directly or indirectly, through State resources and be attributable to a Member State;
- advantage: the recipient of the aid must have obtained an economic benefit it would not have obtained under normal market conditions;
- selectivity: the aid must selectively benefit certain companies or categories of companies; and
- effects on trade and competition: the economic activity exercised by the recipient distorts or threatens to distort competition and affects trade between the Member States.[42]

Recital 9 FSR states that the definition of a 'foreign subsidy' under the FSR must be interpreted in light of EU law, including the notion of 'State aid'. Although the concepts used in EU State aid law can inform the interpretation of similar concepts under the FSR, there remain important differences between the two regimes. These differences relate to: (i) the object of the notification, (ii) the coverage of private law entities' financial contributions, (iii) the notion of 'distortion of competition', (iv) the balancing test, and (v) the burden to notify.

First, under EU State aid law, every instance of State aid is notifiable to the Commission unless certain aid is exempted from notification under Article 108(3) TFEU.[43] But this also means that a financial relationship with a Member State that does not meet the conditions of State aid is not notifiable.

Second, a difference exists with respect to private law entities and State origin. EU State aid law is relatively strict on attributing aid from a private law entity to a Member State.[44] In contrast, when determining if a financial contribution is granted by a third country, Article 1 FSR requires 'taking into account all relevant circumstances'. These circumstances include the legal and economic environment that prevails in that country.[45]

Third, another main difference between EU State aid law and the FSR relates to the question of whether there is 'distortion of competition' in the internal market. In light of the fact that State aid is deemed to distort competition in the internal market, the

---

42 In synthesising the case-law, the Commission categorises those conditions in Sections 3, 4, 5, and 6 in the Commission Notice on the notion of State aid as referred to in the Treaty on the Functioning of the European Union [2016] OJ C262/1, art 107(1) (Commission Notice on the notion of State aid). Certain cases separated the effects on trade and competition and incorporated 'selectivity' into the 'advantage' analysis, see, eg, Case C-399/08 P *European Commission v Deutsche Post AG* EU:C:2010:481, para 39; Case C-280/00 *Altmark Trans GmbH v Nahverkehrsgesellschaft Altmark GmbH* EU:C:2003:415, para 75.

43 See, eg, Commission Regulation (EU) 651/2014 of 17 June 2014 declaring certain categories of aid compatible with the internal market in application of Articles 107 and 108 of the Treaty [2014] OJ L187/1, based on TFEU art 108(4). See also Council Regulation (EU) 2015/1589 of 13 July 2015 laying down detailed rules for the application of Article 108 of the Treaty on the Functioning of the European Union (codification) [2015] OJ L248/9, art 2.

44 Case C-425/19 *European Commission v Italian Republic* EU:C:2021:154.

45 Thus, attribution under the FSR is closer to attribution under the SCM Agreement. See Chapter I 3.C.

assessment of distortion of competition tends to be rather cursory in EU State aid cases. The Commission Notice on the notion of State aid states, for example, that '[p]ublic support is liable to distort competition even if it does not help the recipient undertaking to expand and gain market share'.[46] In practice, the existence of an economic advantage and of competition on or for the market is enough to establish that there is a distortion under EU State aid law.

The FSR's distortion analysis will require a more detailed effects-based analysis. Given the FSR's broad scope, it can be expected that numerous subsidies that a notifying party might have received from third countries and might need to notify will have limited, if any, effects on the internal market. Many of these subsidies, for example, will likely have mostly local effects. This could even apply to subsidies that the FSR considers presumptively distortive.[47]

Moreover, under the M&A and public procurement tools, the FSR requires the Commission to establish that a foreign subsidy facilitated an acquisition or resulted in an unduly advantageous tender. In both cases, the Commission will be required to support its findings with a body of consistent and persuasive evidence, a more demanding task than the 'distortion of competition' analysis prevailing in State aid cases. The Commission will thus likely face a challenge when it must establish that foreign subsidies have a material impact on competition in the internal market.[48]

Fourth, the factors to be considered in applying the balancing test under the FSR are different, compared to the practice under EU State aid law.

Under both EU State aid law and the FSR, the Commission may balance a subsidy's negative effects against its positive effects. The negative effect is the distortion of competition in the internal market. In EU State aid control, the compatibility analysis (and more specifically the balancing test) under Article 107(3) TFEU focuses in essence on the extent to which the aid achieves an EU legitimate objective, balanced against the distortion of competition in the internal market and the effects on trade.[49] To that end, the Commission evaluates whether the objective of common interest is well-defined, whether the aid is designed to achieve that objective, and whether the distortion of competition and effects on trade are limited.

---

46 Commission Notice on the notion of State aid [2016] OJ C262/1 (n 42), para 189. The Commission stated that '[a] measure granted by the State is considered to distort or threaten to distort competition when it is liable to improve the competitive position of the recipient compared to other undertakings with which it competes', see para 187.

47 See Chapter V B.1.2.1.

48 FSR Regulation 2022/2560 [2022] OJ L330/1 (n 1), art 4(1) provides that '[a] distortion in the internal market shall be deemed to exist where a foreign subsidy is liable to improve the competitive position of an undertaking in the internal market and where, in doing so, that foreign subsidy actually or potentially negatively affects competition in the internal market'.

49 The differences between the subparagraphs of art 107(3) are not discussed at length in this contribution. According to settled case-law, art 107(3) gives the Commission discretion to make economic and social assessments in a Union context, regardless of whether the assessment is to take place under subparagraph (b) or subparagraph (c). See, eg, Case T-457/09 *Westfälisch-Lippischer Sparkassen- und Giroverband v European Commission* EU:T:2014:683 (not appealed).

Similarly, Article 6(2) FSR envisages that there is no need to remedy the distortive effects of a foreign subsidy if that subsidy results in 'positive effects on the development of the relevant subsidised economic activity on the internal market' or 'other positive effects of the foreign subsidy such as the broader positive effects in relation to the relevant policy objectives, in particular those of the Union'. Yet, the manner in which the Commission will exercise the discretion to balance between positive and negative effects is expected to differ on a case-by-case basis.[50]

Fifth, the FSR imposes on companies a much higher burden than State aid law. Under EU State aid law, the EU Member State intending to grant aid must in principle notify that specific instance of aid. The FSR notification burden under the M&A and public procurement tools is more expansive in two respects. First, the FSR requires recipients to notify financial contributions for a period spanning multiple years that have been received from any third country. Second, the recipient of financial contributions is responsible for filing notifications, instead of the public authority that granted them. However, the latter will typically hold much of the information relevant to the notification.

Finally, if financial contributions are equivalent to permissible State aid, they arguably cannot be remedied under the FSR. As increasing amounts of aid are authorised under EU State aid law, the scope of financial contributions that can be remedied under the FSR is bound to shrink.

C. The FSR, the Basic Anti-Subsidy Regulation and the SCM Agreement

EU anti-subsidy law and the SCM Agreement are also relevant for interpreting the FSR. At the multilateral level, the basic rules governing subsidies are set out in Articles VI and XVI of the General Agreement on Tariffs and Trade 1994 (GATT 1994).[51] These rules are further elaborated in the SCM Agreement.[52] At the EU level, anti-subsidy action is governed by Council Regulation (EU) 2016/1037 (Basic Anti-Subsidy Regulation).[53] According to recital 3 Basic Anti-Subsidy Regulation, this regulation 'reflect[s]' the rules of the SCM Agreement 'to the best extent possible'. Moreover, the General Court has noted that the Basic Anti-Subsidy Regulation is deemed to be identical to the SCM Agreement.[54]

The Basic Anti-Subsidy Regulation and Part V of the SCM Agreement allow the EU to take countervailing action through the imposition of countervailing duties on imports of subsidised goods into the EU that cause or threaten to cause material injury to EU industry. Although the notion of a 'subsidy' under the Basic Anti-Subsidy Regulation and

---

50 See Chapter II 4.

51 General Agreement on Tariffs and Trade (GATT) 1994 (15 April 1994).

52 SCM Agreement 1994 (n 2).

53 Regulation (EU) 2016/1037 [2016] OJ L176/55 (n 32).

54 See, eg, Case T-300/16 *Jindal Saw Ltd v European Commission* EU:T:2019:235, paras 99, 101.

Part V of the SCM Agreement entails, similar to the notion of a 'foreign subsidy' under the FSR,[55] a financial contribution that confers a (specific) benefit, the Basic Anti-Subsidy Regulation and Part V of the SCM Agreement permit countervailing action only in respect of imports of (subsidised) goods in the EU. In other words, these instruments are limited to addressing the impact of subsidisation on imports of goods into the EU. They do not address potentially distortive effects of subsidies granted by third countries on services, investments, or other financial flows in the internal market. This is also recognised by the FSR, which states that '[t]rade defence instruments enable the Commission to act when subsidised goods are imported into the Union, but not when foreign subsidies take the form of subsidised investments, or when services and financial flows are concerned'.[56]

As acknowledged by the Commission, '[u]nder the [SCM Agreement], the Union has the possibility to initiate State-to-State dispute settlement against certain foreign subsidies granted by WTO members'.[57] WTO dispute settlement under the SCM Agreement is available to the EU in relation to, first, prohibited export performance and import substitution subsidies granted by WTO Members;[58] and, second, actionable subsidies, such as domestic production subsidies, that are specific to an enterprise or industry or group of enterprises or industries.

Although Article XV of the General Agreement on Trade and Services (GATS) recognises the potential distorting effects of subsidisation on trade in services, WTO Members have not yet agreed on subsidies rules to cover trade in services. Moreover, the multilateral trading regime continues to offer limited responses to subsidisation. This applies despite efforts at the multilateral level to strengthen disciplines on industrial subsidies, in order to cover, for example, excessively large subsidies, subsidies that support uncompetitive firms and prevent their exit from the market, subsidies creating massive manufacturing capacity, without private commercial participation, or subsidies distorting capacity.[59]

Against this background, the FSR offers means to redress (foreign) subsidies which are not already captured by existing EU and WTO subsidies regimes. Recital 69 FSR explicitly states that '[t]he implementation of this Regulation by the Union should comply with [...] the WTO Agreement' and that it 'should complement the Union effort to improve multilateral rules on addressing distortive subsidies'.[60] In the absence of progress in reforming multilateral disciplines on subsidies, the FSR already provides the EU with an opportunity to collect information about the incidence and magnitude of subsidies worldwide.[61] The

---

55 See Chapter II 2.

56 FSR Regulation 2022/2560 [2022] OJ L330/1 (n 1), recital 5.

57 ibid, recital 5.

58 See SCM Agreement (n 2), art 3. These are subsidies that are contingent, in law or in fact, on export performance and subsidies that are contingent, in law or in fact, upon the use of domestic over imported goods.

59 USTR, 'Joint Statement of the Trilateral Meeting of the Trade Ministers of the EU, Japan and the United States' (Washington, DC, 9 January 2019) <https://ustr.gov/about-us/policy-offices/press-office/press-releases/2019/january/joint-statement-trilateral-meeting> accessed 18 December 2023; USTR, 'Joint Statement of the Trilateral Meeting of the Trade Ministers of Japan, the United States and the EU' (Washington, DC, 14 January 2020) <https://ustr.gov/about-us/policy-offices/press-office/press-releases/2020/january/joint-statement-trilateral-meeting-trade-ministers-japan-united-states-and-european-union> accessed 18 December 2023.

60 See Chapter V.

61 See similarly S Li and X Tu, 'Reforming WTO Subsidy Rules: Past Experiences and Prospects' (2020) 54(6) *Journal of World Trade* 853.

FSR further allows the EU to experiment with what might (or might not) become clear, justifiable, and practical rules on these subsidies. As such, the EU may intend to start building a critical mass among the WTO Membership for the approach reflected in the FSR and ultimately gain leverage in negotiations on multilateral reform. In effect, the FSR might prompt other WTO Members to re-evaluate the adequacy of the current SCM Agreement.

Article 44(2) FSR also provides that the FSR 'is without prejudice to the application of' the Basic Anti-Subsidy Regulation. Moreover, Article 44(9) FSR sets out a conflict rule which clarifies that '[a]n investigation pursuant to this Regulation shall not be carried out and measures shall not be imposed or maintained where such investigation or measures [...] amount to a specific action against a subsidy within the meaning of Article 32.1 of the [SCM Agreement] and granted by a third country which is a [WTO Member]'.[62]

Consequently, the EU may not impose remedies under the FSR with respect to a subsidy that can be countervailed under the Basic Anti-Subsidy Regulation and Part V of the SCM Agreement, or where the EU can initiate WTO dispute settlement proceedings against a subsidy granted by a WTO Member.

In practice, this means that the FSR is relevant in situations where either a foreign subsidy does not fall within the scope of application of the EU and WTO subsidies regimes, or where the effects caused by a foreign subsidy cannot be redressed through countervailing action or recourse to WTO dispute settlement. Nevertheless, even if subsidies fall under the EU and WTO regimes, they would still be 'in scope' and considered notifiable financial contributions under the FSR's M&A and public procurement tools. However, the Commission cannot remedy these subsidies, even if they must be reported under the FSR.

Despite the intention to distinguish between the scope of application of the EU and WTO subsidies regimes and the FSR, the conflict rule introduced in Article 44(9) FSR could be undermined by the lack of clarity in respect of the scope of application of the Basic Anti-Subsidy Regulation and the SCM Agreement in the context of so-called cross-border, or transnational, subsidies.

Even where subsidisation leads to adverse effects on trade in goods within the meaning of the Basic Anti-Subsidy Regulation and the SCM Agreement, it remains uncertain whether transnational subsidies, namely subsidies granted by a third country to companies established outside that country's jurisdiction (but not based in the EU), fall within the scope of the existing EU and WTO subsidies regimes.

Under the SCM Agreement, a subsidy exists if there is a financial contribution by a government or any public body 'within the territory of a Member'.[63] Moreover, an actionable subsidy is specific when it is limited to an enterprise or industry or group of enterprises or industries 'within the jurisdiction of the granting authority'.[64] Although the use of the qualifications 'within the territory of' and 'within the jurisdiction of' seems

---

62 See, eg, on the fact that WTO law restricts unilateral measures covering conduct subject to WTO law, WTO Panel Report, *US – Section 301 Trade Act 1974* (2000), WT/DS152/R.

63 SCM Agreement (n 2), art 1.1.

64 ibid, art 2.1.

to imply a territorial link, it has not been clarified in WTO dispute settlement whether only subsidies granted to beneficiaries within the territory/jurisdiction of the subsidising Member are covered by the SCM Agreement.[65]

Similarly, under the Basic Anti-Subsidy Regulation, a subsidy exists if there is a financial contribution by a government 'in the country of origin or export', while it is countervailable when it is specific to an enterprise or industry or group of enterprises or industries 'within the jurisdiction of the granting authority'.[66]

In past anti-subsidy investigations, the Commission considered that transnational subsidies do not fall within the scope of the Basic Anti-Subsidy Regulation.[67] However, in 2020, the Commission countervailed Chinese subsidies by imposing countervailing duties on imports of continuous filament glass fibre products originating in Egypt. The products at issue were produced by Egyptian subsidiaries of Chinese SOEs that had received subsidies from the Chinese Government. Although the subsidies at issue were granted by the Chinese Government, the Commission imposed countervailing duties against imports from Egypt on the grounds that the Chinese subsidies at issue were attributable to the government of Egypt under the principles of State responsibility under international law.[68] The Commission's decision was later upheld by the General Court.[69] However, an appeal against that judgment is currently pending before the Court of Justice of the European Union (CJEU).[70]

---

65 In the context of discussing development aid, a note by the WTO Secretariat on the Expert Group Meeting on Trade Financing stated that it is not entirely clear whether the SCM Agreement applies where the recipient of the subsidy is not within the territory of the subsidising country, see WTO General Council, Working Group on Trade, Debt and Finance, 'Expert Group meeting on Trade Financing' (16 March 2004). See also GN Horlick, 'An Annotated Explanation of Articles 1 and 2 of the WTO' (2013) 8(9) *Global Trade and Customs Journal* 297; M Tokas, 'Playing the Game: The EU's Proposed Regulation on Foreign Subsidies' (2022) 56(5) *Journal of World Trade* 779; M Frank, 'The EU's New Foreign Subsidies Regulation on Collision course with the WTO' (2023) 60 CML Rev 925. On 24 January 2023, Indonesia requested consultations in connection with the EU's imposition of countervailing duties on imports or stainless steel and cold-rolled flat products originating in India and Indonesia. Indonesia argues, among others, that the EU countervailing duties on imports from Indonesia are inconsistent with the SCM Agreement because of the EU's attribution to the Government of Indonesia of financial contributions provided by Chinese grantors to Indonesian producers. A Panel was composed to hear the dispute on 13 September 2023. See WTO, *European Union – Anti-Dumping and Countervailing Duties on Stainless Steel Products from Indonesia*, Request for Consultations by Indonesia (26 January 2023).

66 See Regulation (EU) 2016/1037 [2016] OJ L176/55 (n 32), arts 3(1), 4(2) and recital 5.

67 Recitals 396 and 399 of Commission Implementing Regulation (EU) 2017/969 of 8 June 2017 imposing definitive countervailing duties on imports of certain hot-rolled flat products of iron, non-alloy or other alloy steel originating in the People's Republic of China and amending Commission Implementing Regulation (EU) 2017/649 imposing a definitive anti-dumping duty on imports of certain hot-rolled flat products of iron, non-alloy or other alloy steel originating in the People's Republic of China [2017] OJ L146/17.

68 See, Commission Implementing Regulation (EU) 2020/379 of 5 March 2020 imposing a provisional countervailing duty on imports of continuous filament glass fibre products originating in Egypt [2020] OJ L69/14; Commission Implementing Regulation (EU) 2020/870 of 24 June 2020 imposing a definitive countervailing duty and definitively collecting the provisional countervailing duty imposed on imports of continuous filament glass fibre products originating in Egypt, and levying the definitive countervailing duty on the registered imports of continuous filament glass fibre products originating in Egypt [2020] OJ L201/10. See also Commission Implementing Regulation (EU) 2022/433 of 15 March 2022 imposing definitive countervailing duties on imports of stainless-steel cold-rolled flat products originating in India and Indonesia and amending Implementing Regulation (EU) 2021/2012 imposing a definitive anti-dumping duty and definitively collecting the provisional duty imposed on imports of stainless-steel cold-rolled flat products originating in India and Indonesia [2022] OJ L88/24.

69 Case T-540/20 *Jushi Egypt for Fiberglass Industry v European Commission* EU:T:2023:91.

70 Case C-272/23 P *Jushi Egypt for Fiberglass Industry v European Commission*.

D. The FSR and the Regulation on Subsidies in Air Transport

The Regulation on Subsidies in Air Transport[71] aims to safeguard competition in air transport which might be affected by 'practices' of a third country or a third-country entity. These concerns include both discrimination between EU and non-EU carriers as well as the subsidisation of airlines. Similar to other instruments, this instrument exists to ensure a level playing field.

As the Commission noted in its FSR impact assessment, unfair practices in international air transport are not regulated by the WTO/GATS framework. Nor are there specific WTO rules dealing with subsidies for services.[72] To that end, the Regulation on Subsidies in Air Transport establishes the power of the Commission to investigate any distortions and to adopt redressive measures in that sector.

Under the Regulation on Subsidies in Air Transport, a Member State, one or more EU air carriers, or an association of carriers may submit a written complaint alleging that a third-country practice injures or threatens to injure one or more EU carriers, which requires the Commission to initiate an investigation. The Commission may also initiate an ex officio investigation. However, the Commission may suspend the investigation if it is more appropriate to address the distortive practice exclusively under dispute settlement procedures agreed by the EU. These procedures are typically found in a clause in an applicable air transport or air services agreement, but could also be included in a different type of agreement. Moreover, an investigation is to be suspended if the relevant Member State has notified its intention to use these dispute settlement procedures.

Under the Regulation on Subsidies in Air Transport, the determination of injury or threat of injury includes the consideration of both: (i) the situation of the EU air carriers concerned, and (ii) the general situation of the affected air transport services markets. On the one hand, the EU air carriers' situation is evaluated through indicators such as the frequency of services, the use of capacity, network effects, sales, market share, profits, return on capital, investment and employment. On the other, the affected air transport services markets are evaluated through indicators such as the level of fares or rates, capacity, and frequency of air transport services, or use of the network.

The Commission anticipated the risk of a potential overlap or conflict between the Regulation on Subsidies in Air Transport and the FSR in respect of the Commission's powers and analysis of the distortion of competition. These concerns stem from the fact that both Regulations enable the Commission to address foreign subsidies that distort competition in (ultimately) the internal market in a specified situation.

---

71 Regulation (EU) 2019/712 [2019] OJ L123/4 (n 39).

72 European Commission, Commission Staff Working Document, 'Impact Assessment accompanying the Document for a Proposal for a Regulation of the European Parliament and of the Council on safeguarding competition in air transport, repealing Regulation (EC) 868/2004' SWD (2017) 182 final 38 <https://eur-lex.europa.eu/legal-content/EN/TXT/PDF/?uri=CELEX:52017SC0182> accessed 18 December 2023.

When it published its FSR Proposal, the Commission explained that 'Regulation 2019/712 (…) allows the Commission to conduct investigations if it finds evidence of a practice distorting competition among EU air carriers and in the air transport services markets. It also covers subsidies to third-country air carriers, but not to other actors of the aviation chain and does not contain any specific rules on public procurement or subsidised acquisitions of EU targets.'[73]

Therefore, the FSR is not applicable to cases that strictly fall within the scope of the Regulation on Subsidies in Air Transport. Conversely, the Commission could use the FSR for subsidised tenders or acquisitions by air carriers, and with respect to services provided by other actors in the aviation sector.

The Regulation on Subsidies in Air Transport has not been used to date. Even though the Commission does not comment on its investigative powers to initiate proceedings on its own initiative, the Commission has stressed that the Regulation on Subsidies in Air Transport has remained untested mainly because the Commission has not yet received complaints.[74] It is unclear why European carriers have not more actively made use of the Regulation on Subsidies in Air Transport, after complaining for many years about distortions of competition resulting from subsidies provided by third countries to their carriers. One reason might be that several European carriers received massive subsidies during the COVID-19 pandemic, making complaints about subsidies granted to non-EU rivals less attractive.

E. The FSR and the FDI Screening Regulation

Both the FSR and the FDI Screening Regulation[75] are applicable to transactions involving European targets.[76] In screening investments for risks to national security and public order, the FDI Screening Regulation states that the Member States and the Commission should be able to take into account significant funding, including foreign subsidies.[77] It also provides that information pertaining to foreign subsidies must be made available by the Member State.[78]

According to Article 44(3) FSR, both the FSR and the FDI Screening Regulation may be applied in parallel, and an investigation under one instrument does not exclude an investigation under the other. This means that Member State authorities may investigate,

---

73 On this point see the Legislative and Financial Statement in FSR Proposal COM (2021) 223 final (n 16) 53.

74 FSR Impact Assessment SWD (2021) 99 final (n 14) 33.

75 Council Regulation (EU) 2019/452 of the European Parliament and of the Council of 19 March 2019 establishing a framework on the screening of foreign direct investments into the Union (FDI Screening Regulation) [2019] OJ LI79/1.

76 Joint Commission Communication to the European Parliament, the European Council and the Council on 'European Economic Security Strategy' JOIN (2023) 20 final 8 <https://eur-lex.europa.eu/legal-content/EN/TXT/PDF/?uri=CELEX:52023JC0020> accessed 18 December 2023.

77 FDI Screening Regulation 2019/452 [2019] OJ LI79/1 (n 75), recital 13.

78 ibid, recital 23.

for example, a transaction under their national FDI control regimes, while the Commission investigates the same transaction under the FSR.

A Member State must inform the Commission when it has opened a national screening procedure.[79] Likewise, Article 10 FSR requires the Commission to inform that Member State of the start of the preliminary review of a foreign subsidy.

5. The FSR as a Tool in an Evolving Geopolitical Context

In its 2021 Trade Policy Review, the EU signalled that it would reshape its trade policy to include new tools to achieve its objectives in external relations, in particular to level the playing field in international trade.[80] In recent times, the interaction between trade and geopolitics has not gone unnoticed, as recent litigation relating to the FDI Screening Regulation has demonstrated.[81] In a similar vein, an instrument such as the FSR might have a much broader geopolitical reach than initially anticipated.

Three important themes might inform the Commission's potential use of the FSR.

First, the EU explicitly situates foreign subsidies within its Economic Security Strategy.[82] The EU considers that its economic dependency on trading partners might pose risks to its economic security and thus its autonomy. As President von der Leyen has noted, Europe has become 'the first major economy to set out a strategy on economic security', adding that this strategy 'will ensure Europe's sovereignty, security, and prosperity in the years to come'.[83] The priorities of the EU Economic Security Strategy centre around: (i) promoting the EU's competitiveness, (ii) protecting the EU from commonly identified economic security risks, and (iii) partnering with like-minded countries.[84] Among the identified economic securities risks, the EU Economic Security Strategy identifies

---

79 ibid, art 6.

80 See in particular Commission Communication to the European Parliament, the Council, the European Economic and Social Committee and the Committee of the Regions, 'Trade Policy Review – An Open, Sustainable and Assertive Trade Policy' COM (2021) 66 final, s 3.2.6 (2021 Trade Policy Review).

81 In Case C-106/22 *Xella Magyarország* EU:C:2023:568, the CJEU interpreted the FDI Screening Regulation, which is based on Article 207 TFEU. Advocate-General Capeta recently commented on the geo-political context underpinning the EU's adoption and implementation of legislative instruments falling within the scope of the CCP. In discussing the policy context underpinning the adoption of the FDI Screening Regulation and EU trade policy at large, the Advocate-General noted that: '[t]he world has changed, as every EU citizen has seen and felt, whether in the form of empty supermarket shelves or higher energy bills. Indeed, the Russian aggression in Ukraine has laid painfully bare the dangers of the dependency on the goodwill of yesterday's trading partners. Accordingly, and particularly when presented with measures that arguably represent a step backwards in the openness of the EU's internal market vis-à-vis trade with third countries, one should not jump to conclusions too quickly: tomorrow's strategic geopolitical interests have the potential to influence today's commitments to free trade', see Case C-106/22 *Xella Magyarország* EU:C:2023:267, Opinion of AG Capeta, para 5.

82 European Economic Security Strategy JOIN (2023) 20 final (n 76).

83 European Commission, Press Release, 'An EU Approach to Enhance Economic Security' <https://ec.europa.eu/commission/presscorner/detail/en/IP_23_3358> accessed 18 December 2023.

84 European Economic Security Strategy JOIN (2023) 20 final (n 76) 2–3.

foreign subsidies as threats to the EU internal market and stresses that the Commission 'is ready to deploy' the FSR to address the 'weaponisation of economic dependencies'.[85]

Second, various reports signal that the Commission might use the FSR to focus on sectors of economic activity that are central to the EU's sustainability efforts. The title of the 2023 Strategic Foresight Report stresses that sustainability is at the heart of the EU's open strategic autonomy. The report argues that 'to achieve open strategic autonomy, including economic security', the EU should make 'better and more strategic use of (…) the regulation on foreign subsidies' whereby the EU ensures 'strong linkages between market access and high sustainability standards'.[86]

Similar to its climate-recalibrated enforcement of EU State aid rules,[87] the Commission might focus on foreign subsidies that distort the EU internal market in view of the EU's ambitions related to climate, environmental protection, and energy.

The European Wind Power Action Plan[88] further signals how the Commission might use the FSR. In addition to activating its trade defence instruments, the Commission announced that it would use the FSR tools to counter any foreign subsidisation of wind-related products on the EU market.[89] To that end, the Commission has explicitly encouraged the European wind industry to submit further evidence on foreign subsidies granted to their competitors.

Third, apart from China, the Commission has closely monitored other major subsidisers, including the United States. On 18 July 2023, Executive Vice-President Dombrovskis signalled that the EU might adopt trade defence measures in respect of imports of US-originating goods subsidised under the Inflation Reduction Act (IRA).[90] The statement of Commissioner Dombrovskis indicates that the EU is ready to recalibrate its common commercial policy instruments to protect its interests against any effect on trade and, ultimately, distortion in the internal market, including effects resulting from the commercial policies of its trade partners, such as the United States. Some in the EU might therefore want to see an aggressive application of the FSR where trade defence measures (such as the Basic Anti-Subsidy Regulation) cannot address the material impact of foreign subsidies on the EU internal market.

However, in recent years the EU and its Member States have also decided to make massive amounts of State aid available that far exceed subsidies available under the IRA in order to pursue industrial policy goals. This casts doubt on the underlying

85 ibid 7–8.

86 Commission Communication to the European Parliament and the Council, '2023 Strategic Foresight Report: Sustainability and people's wellbeing at the heart of Europe's Open Strategic Autonomy' COM (2023) 376 final.

87 Commission Communication Guidelines on State aid for Climate, Environmental Protection and Energy [2022] OJ C80/1.

88 Commission Communication to the European Parliament, the Council, the European Economic and Social Committee and the Committee of the Regions, 'European Wind Power Action Plan' COM (2023) 669 final <https://eur-lex.europa.eu/legal-content/EN/TXT/PDF/?uri=CELEX:52023DC0669> accessed 18 December 2023.

89 ibid 17 (Action 12).

90 European Commission, 'Statement by Executive Vice-President Dombrovskis at the ECON Committee of the European Parliament on the EU's reaction to the US Inflation Reduction Act (IRA)' (18 July 2023) <https://ec.europa.eu/commission/presscorner/detail/en/STATEMENT_23_3926> accessed 18 December 2023.

narrative behind the FSR, namely that State aid rules prevent European companies from receiving government support while financial support to companies in third countries goes unchecked.

Moreover, another idea behind the FSR might have been to fend off political pressure of certain Member States (and parts of the Commission) to soften the strict application of competition (including State aid) rules, which some perceived as harming European competitiveness. The FSR Proposal could be seen as an attempt to reduce that pressure, by introducing a new instrument targeting foreign subsidies instead of loosening the strict application of competition law.

If that was one of the motives for (some in) the Commission to propose the FSR, the initiative has come too late. The global subsidies race has gained momentum in recent years. The EU's participation in the global subsidies race limits the remedial scope of the FSR and undermines the general and undifferentiated narrative underlying the FSR that strict EU State aid control puts European companies at a disadvantage.

Chapter II
The Scope of the FSR

1. Introduction

Article 1(1) FSR specifies that the FSR is an instrument that 'lays down rules and procedures for investigating foreign subsidies that distort the internal market and for redressing such distortions'.[91] This section elaborates on the horizontal concepts that shape the scope of application of the FSR, namely the notion of a 'foreign subsidy' (Section 2 below) distorting the internal market (Section 3 below).

As explained in Chapter I, recital 9 FSR states that the FSR should be applied and interpreted in light of EU legislation relating to State aid, mergers and acquisitions. Moreover, the key elements of the notion of a 'foreign subsidy', as set out in Article 3(1) FSR, mirror the elements of a 'subsidy' within the meaning of the EU and WTO subsidies regimes. Therefore, the Commission can be expected to draw from the extensive practice under the EU and WTO subsidy regimes in its interpretation and application of the notion of a 'foreign subsidy' under the FSR, in addition to concepts developed in EU State aid law.

The FSR's starting point is not the concept of a subsidy, but the wider concept of a 'financial contribution', to which this chapter will turn first. As discussed in Chapters III and IV, the notion of a financial contribution is the reference point that determines notification obligations and, to some extent, reporting obligations. Even though the concept of a financial contribution is central, the FSR merely provides a list of illustrative examples and no clear definition. Practice taken from the EU and WTO subsidies regimes and EU State aid law might be used when trying to determine what constitutes a financial contribution.

This approach creates one of the core problems of the FSR, especially under the FSR's M&A and public procurement notification regimes. In international trade law and State aid cases, the EU will assess and establish whether a financial contribution exists, and whether it can be characterised as a subsidy or as State aid, in the context of a typically very targeted investigation. In investigations under the Basic Anti-Subsidy Regulation and the SCM Agreement, for example, the 'financial contribution' concept is applied on a case-by-case basis, in light of a list of criteria developed in the decisional practice. The EU Courts may review, and agree or disagree with, the Commission's assessment, in light of multifactor tests that are interpreted in light of the specific facts of a particular case. This process can take several years. This also applies in State aid investigations, where, moreover, typically one specific contribution is the subject of an investigation.

---

91 FSR Regulation 2022/2560 [2022] OJ L330/1 (n 1), art 1(1).

The FSR's approach is unsuitable for notification regimes. Companies must identify relevant financial contributions (potentially in a large number of third countries) when determining whether they are subject to notification obligations, and when preparing a notification. For this exercise, they must rely on the FSR's loose description of a financial contribution, which incorporates by reference concepts developed and applied in international trade law and EU State aid law on a case-by-case basis. The same concerns apply to other key concepts of the FSR, such as the definition of a 'public body,' or of a private entity of which the financial contributions are attributable to a State.

This approach leads to a significant administrative burden, and is bound to create considerable uncertainty, for companies seeking to comply with the notification obligations under the FSR.[92] Yet, they must in the end still be able to certify that their notification is accurate and complete.

Against this background, this chapter elaborates on the meaning of the FSR concept of a 'foreign subsidy' by taking into consideration the interpretative practice under EU State aid law as well as the Basic Anti-Subsidy Regulation and the SCM Agreement. Chapter V seeks to make these concepts operational for companies assessing their notification obligations and preparing notifications.

2. The Definition of a 'Foreign Subsidy'

Foreign subsidies are support measures provided by third countries to companies active in the EU. More specifically, Article 3(1) FSR states that a foreign subsidy is deemed to exist 'where a third country provides, directly or indirectly, a financial contribution which confers a benefit on an undertaking engaging in an economic activity in the internal market and which is limited, in law or in fact, to one or more undertakings or industries'. Recital 11 FSR further explains that a foreign subsidy, for the purpose of the FSR, should be understood 'as a financial contribution which is provided directly or indirectly by a third country, which confers a benefit and which is limited to one or more undertakings or industries'.

A 'foreign subsidy' within the meaning of the FSR exists if four cumulative conditions are met

- a financial contribution
- granted, directly or indirectly, by a third country
- which confers a benefit to a company engaging in an economic activity in the internal market
- which is specific, namely limited, in law or in fact, to one or more companies or industries

[92] See Chapter II 2.A.1, and V 5.A.

A. A 'Financial Contribution'

A.1 The Link between a 'Financial Contribution' and the FSR Notification Obligations

The notion of a 'financial contribution' is central to the notification obligations under the FSR. The definition of a 'financial contribution' (and not that of a subsidy) determines whether the contribution thresholds triggering notification obligations under the FSR are met and, in the context of a public procurement project meeting the FSR's value threshold, whether bidders must submit a notification or declaration.[93] This is because the FSR requires companies to calculate the relevant notification thresholds by taking into account all 'financial contributions' received in the three years prior to a notification (ie, irrespective of whether the financial contributions resulted in any advantage).

The reporting obligations in M&A and procurement notifications are more targeted and cover mostly subsidies, ie, financial contributions conferring an advantage on the recipient. In both notification forms annexed to the FSR Implementing Regulation, financial contributions at market rates, with the exception of financial services, as well as certain generally applicable tax measures, are exempted from reporting requirements.[94]

A.2 The Definition of a 'Financial Contribution'

The FSR does not spell out the constituent elements of a financial contribution. Instead, Article 3(2) FSR sets out a non-exhaustive list of circumstances in which a financial contribution is deemed to exist, namely where there is:

- a 'transfer of funds or liabilities', which includes 'capital injections, grants, loans, loan guarantees, fiscal incentives, the setting off of operating losses, compensation for financial burdens imposed by public authorities, debt forgiveness, debt to equity swaps or rescheduling';
- the 'foregoing of revenue that is otherwise due', which includes 'tax exemptions or the granting of special or exclusive rights without adequate remuneration'; or
- the 'provision of goods or services' or the 'purchase of goods or services'.

In essence, a 'financial contribution' under the FSR largely corresponds to the concept of a 'financial contribution' under the EU and WTO subsidies regimes, and to that of a 'transfer of State resources' under EU State aid law. In its FSR impact assessment, the Commission identified the above types of financial contribution on the basis of the

93 As explained in more detail in Chapter III, FSR Regulation 2022/2560 [2022] OJ L330/1 (n 1), art 20 imposes a notification requirement in relation to certain large concentrations involving substantial foreign financial contributions before the concentration is put into effect. Likewise, FSR Regulation 2022/2560 [2022] OJ L330/1 (n 1), art 29 requires the notification (or a declaration) of certain foreign financial contributions in the context of public procurement procedures above certain thresholds before the contract is awarded. See Chapter IV.

94 These exemptions are not applicable if a declaration must be filed in connection with public procurement projects. See Chapter IV 2 and IV 3.

most common types of subsidy countervailed under the Basic Anti-Subsidy Regulation.[95] Similar to the FSR, under Article 3(1) Basic Anti-Subsidy Regulation and Article 1.1(a)(1) SCM Agreement, a 'financial contribution' includes:

- 'a direct transfer of funds (such as grants, loans, and equity infusion), potential direct transfers of funds or liabilities (for example, loan guarantees)';
- 'government revenue that is otherwise due foregone or not collected (for example fiscal incentives such as tax credits)'; or
- the 'provis[ion of] goods or services other than general infrastructure', or the 'purchases of goods'.

It follows that the concept of a 'financial contribution' under the FSR is very wide. It does not require that the financial relationship with the third country,[96] has conferred any potential advantage – selective or not – on a company.

The definition of 'State resources' is wide. As noted in the Commission Notice on the notion of State aid,[97] 'the transfer of State resources may take many forms, such as direct grants, loans, guarantees, direct investment in the capital of companies and benefits in kind'.[98] It thus covers any form of aid,[99] including all resources of the public sector, irrespective of the level and type or degree of autonomy of the public entity providing the aid.[100]

As a matter of EU State aid law, resources of public entities may also constitute State resources where the State has 'public control' over the resources at issue.[101] Exceptionally, resources pertaining to private bodies may be considered State resources if the Member State exercises public control over those resources. In this regard, case-law has confirmed that the origin of the resources is not relevant, provided that the Member State exercises public control over those resources.[102] In fact, even if sums corresponding to the aid are not permanently held by the Member State, the fact that they constantly remain under public control, and are therefore available to the competent national authorities, is sufficient for them to be categorised as 'State resources'.[103]

The Commission Notice on the notion of State aid provides a relatively detailed list of examples of forms of transfer of State resources.[104] But that list is not exhaustive. Article 107(1) TFEU establishes that State aid may be granted 'in any form whatsoever'.

---

95 FSR Impact Assessment (n 14) 28, fn 123.

96 See Chapter II 2.B below as regards the imputability of the financial contribution to a third country.

97 Commission Notice on the notion of State aid [2016] OJ C262/1 (n 42).

98 ibid, para 51.

99 See Chapter I 1, and I 2.A above.

100 Commission Notice on the notion of State aid [2016] OJ C262/1 (n 42), para 48.

101 Case C-482/99 *France v Commission of the European Communities (Stardust)* EU:C:2002:294, para 38. See also Case C-278/00 *Greece v Commission of the European Communities* EU:C:2004:239, paras 53 and 54; Joined Cases C-328/99 and C-399/00 *Italy v Commission of the European Communities* EU:C:2003:252, paras 33 and 34.

102 See, eg, Case C-206/06 *Essent Netwerk Noord BV v Aluminium Delfzijl BV* EU:C:2008:413, para 70; Case C-83/98 P *France v Ladbroke Racing Ltd* EU:C:2000:248, para 50.

103 Case C-262/12 *Association Vent De Colère! and Others* EU:C:2013:851, para 21; Case C-329/15 *ENEA SA v President of the Energy Regulatory Office* EU:C:2017:671, para 25 and the case-law cited therein.

104 Commission Notice on the notion of State aid [2016] OJ C262/1 (n 42), paras 51–53.

Therefore, considering that the FSR will also be interpreted taking into account EU State aid law, a foreign subsidy under the FSR – and hence the underlying financial contribution – might also take 'any form whatsoever'.

Likewise, a State aid resource does not require a positive transfer of funds. Foregoing State revenue is sufficient.[105] According to the Commission Notice on the notion of State aid, this latter category may also include situations in which public authorities or public entities provide goods or services at a price below market rates, invest or grant access to a public domain or natural resources, or grant special or exclusive rights. It is important to remember that, for the calculation of the FSR notification thresholds and, to some extent, reporting requirements, it does not matter whether these transactions were carried out at market terms, because the concept of 'financial contribution' is wider than the concepts of 'subsidy' and 'State aid'.

A.3 The Relevant Timing of a 'Financial Contribution'

Recital 15 FSR explains that a foreign subsidy, and thus a financial contribution, should be considered granted from the moment the beneficiary obtains an entitlement to receive the financial contribution. The actual disbursement of that financial contribution is not a necessary condition for it to fall within the scope of the FSR.

The same concept applies under EU State aid law. For example, in *Bouygues and Bouygues Télécom v Commission*, the CJEU found that the Commission was right in determining that an offer of a shareholder loan by the French State to France Telecom was State aid.[106] Specifically, although the offer was not signed by the company – and thus the loan was not provided – the Commission and the CJEU concluded that it provided an immediately available credit line in favour of the company. Hence, the offer created the concrete risk of imposing an additional burden on the State, which was sufficient to treat it as a transfer (more correctly, foregoing) of State resources within the meaning of Article 107(1) TFEU. If the same reasoning is applied under the FSR, a financial contribution will be found to exist even when payments have not (yet) been provided to the company (but only guaranteed), provided that the payments are not subject to further conditions.

The FSR's rule on the relevant time of a financial contribution could be particularly relevant in the context of notifications, because the determination of whether thresholds have been met and of the reporting obligations in notifications cover only financial contributions received in the three years prior to the notification. Taking the *Bouygues* case as an example, if a State guarantee was offered prior to the three year period, not only would the guarantee fall outside the scope of notification obligations, but any payments made by the State according to that guarantee would not be considered relevant financial contributions (unless they were conditional on certain events), even if these payments occurred during the three-year period.

---

105 ibid, para 51.

106 Joined Cases C-399/10 P and C-401/10 P *Bouygues SA v European Commission* EU:C:2013:175, paras 137–139.

The FSR FAQs reflect these principles, but also clarify that they apply only if payments under a grant are unconditional.[107] When the recipient is entitled to payments only after specific conditions are met, a financial contribution will exist only when the conditions have materialised and the recipient is entitled to the payment (not when the payment is actually made).[108]

This interpretation can be relevant when a company has won a government contract in a third country prior to the three-year period, but receives payments under the contract during the three-year period. If the payments are unconditional payments in regular instalments, the financial contribution will exist at the time of the contract award and the amount will be determined by the value of the entire contract. If the contract award was prior to the three-year period, it will not result in a financial contribution for FSR notification purposes. However, if payments under the contract are conditioned on the contractor achieving certain milestones, each payment is to be considered a financial contribution which occurs when the conditions triggering a payment obligation have been met.

These principles are also relevant, for example, when a company obtains insurance from a public entity. In this scenario, the payment of insurance rates is considered a financial contribution. However, the insured amount as such, is in principle not to be considered a financial contribution because any payments under the insurance contract are contingent on the occurrence of the insured event. The payout by the insurer is also a financial contribution, but only if the insured event occurred.

Main features of a financial contribution

- wider concept than a 'subsidy' or 'State aid' (includes financial relationships at market rates)
- government transfer of funds, including government revenue foregone
- no formal requirements
- entitlement (to a financial contribution) is sufficient (actual disbursement of funds not required) and determines the timing of the financial contribution

107 See FSR M&A FAQs, question 7 (n 31).

108 ibid.

Examples of a financial contribution

- transfer of funds or liabilities
  - capital injections
  - grants
  - loans loan guarantees
  - fiscal incentives
  - setting off of operating losses
  - compensation for financial burdens imposed by public authorities
  - debt forgiveness
  - debt to equity swaps or rescheduling
- foregoing of revenue that is otherwise due
  - tax exemptions
  - granting of special or exclusive rights without adequate remuneration
- provision/purchase of goods or services

A.4 Types of Financial Contribution

A.4.1 Transfer of Funds or Liabilities

The first type of financial contribution listed in Article 3(2)(a) FSR is the 'transfer of funds or liabilities'. The term 'funds and liabilities' indicates that this type of financial contribution is broader than a transfer of money. Transactions involving financial resources or other financial claims also fall within the broad category of 'transfer of funds or liabilities'. In particular, according to the FSR, 'a transfer of funds or liabilities' includes, but is not limited to, 'capital injections, grants, loans, loan guarantees, fiscal incentives, the setting off of operating losses, compensation for financial burdens imposed by public authorities, debt forgiveness, debt to equity swaps or rescheduling'.[109]

Financial contributions in the form of transfers or funds or liabilities have frequently been countervailed in the context of anti-subsidy investigations[110] or found to be State aid within the meaning of Article 107(1) TFEU. These forms of financial contributions include:

- *capital injections*, often referred to as equity infusions, equity injections or equity investments, taking the form of *provision of equity capital* in return for the acquisition of full shareholding rights,[111] or in exchange for future equity shares.[112] The key characteristic of these financial contributions is that the

---

109 FSR Regulation 2022/2560 [2022] OJ L330/1 (n 1), art 3(2)(a).

110 Van Bael & Bellis, *EU Anti-Dumping and Other Trade Defence Instruments* (6th edn, Wolters Kluwer 2019) 646.

111 Regulation (EU) 2021/2012 [2022] OJ L88/24 (n 68). State aid: SA.59913 (France) [2021] OJ C2401, para 24; *COVID-19—Aid to Lufthansa* (Case COMP/SA.57153) (Germany) [2020] OJ C397/1, paras 40–42.

112 Commission Implementing Regulation (EU) 2020/776 of 12 June 2020 imposing definitive countervailing duties on imports of certain woven and/or stitched glass fibre fabrics originating in the People's Republic of China and Egypt and amending Commission Implementing Regulation (EU) 2020/492 imposing definitive

government makes an investment in the recipient company, and will be entitled to the dividends or any capital gains attributable to that investment.[113] The return on the investment will depend on the success of the recipient company. At the time when the government provides the capital, it does not know how the recipient will perform. The government, thus, enjoys a return on its capital to the extent the enterprise succeeds, and suffers losses in capital to the extent it fails.[114] Participation in an initial public offering (IPO) would most likely be treated like an equity infusion.[115] Moreover, *debt-to-equity swaps* have been found to constitute a form of equity infusion where outstanding debt is cancelled in return for equity.[116]

- *joint ventures* might, under certain circumstances, present characteristics which are analogous to an equity infusion. For example, where the joint venture partners operate as equity investors, equity contributions can constitute a financial contribution in the form of a transfer of funds.[117] *United States – Large Civil Aircraft (second complaint)* illustrates this point. In that case, the US Department of Defence (USDoD) and the National Aeronautics and Space Administration (NASA) concluded procurement contracts and assistance instruments with Boeing. As part of those transactions, USDoD and NASA provided Boeing with funding and access to governmental facilities, equipment and employees for research and development (R&D) projects. These arrangements were deemed to be akin to a joint venture and having characteristics analogous to equity infusions. In particular, the funding and access were provided in the expectation of a (non-financial) return in the form of scientific and technical information, discoveries, and data expected to result from the research performed. On that basis, USDoD and NASA were seen to operate as equity investors, in the sense that at the time of committing to provide funding and access to Boeing, they had no certainty that the research would be successful. Moreover, they were exposed to a risk equal to the amount of capital they contributed, and the opportunity cost of the access provided.[118]

---

anti-dumping duties on imports of certain woven and/or stitched glass fibre fabrics originating in the People's Republic of China and Egypt [2020] OJ L189/1; Commission Implementing Regulation (EU) 2018/1690 of 9 November 2018 imposing definitive countervailing duties on imports of certain pneumatic tyres, new or retreaded, of rubber, of a kind used for buses or lorries and with a load index exceeding 121 originating in the People's Republic of China and amending Commission Implementing Regulation (EU) 2018/1579*)* [2018] OJ L283/1, recital 330. State aid: *COVID-19—Aid to Lufthansa* (Case COMP/SA.57153) (Germany) [2020] OJ C397/1 (n 112), paras 54–64.

113 WTO Appellate Body Report, *US – Large Civil Aircraft (2nd complaint)* (2006), WT/DS353/AB/R, para 622.

114 ibid.

115 In contrast, the purchase of publicly traded shares by a government or public entity on a stock exchange or other trading platform would not be considered a financial contribution to the company.

116 Commission Implementing Regulation (EU) 2019/688 of 2 May 2019 imposing a definitive countervailing duty on imports of certain organic coated steel products originating in the People's Republic of China following an expiry review pursuant to Article 18 of the Regulation (EU) 2016/1037 of the European Parliament and of the Council [2019] OJ L116/39, recital 119. See also WTO Panel Report, *Korea – Commercial Vessels* (2005), WT/DS273/R, paras 7.411–7.413, 7.420. State aid: *Training aid for Cyprus Airways* (Case COMP/SA.38225) (Cyprus) [2015] OJ L179/83, para 34; *Restructuring program of Cimos dd* (Case COMP/SA.37792) (Slovenia) [2016] OJ L59/168, paras 97–109.

117 *US – Large Civil Aircraft (2nd complaint)* (n 113), paras 621 and following.

118 ibid, para 623.

- *grants*, namely situations where money or money's worth is given by a third country to a company, normally without an obligation or expectation that anything will be provided to the government in return.[119] Grants can take many forms, such as payments in the form of bonds,[120] purchases of corporate bonds,[121] and tax refunds.[122] Grants are also found to exist in the context of rescheduling of debt.[123] This would apply, for example, to modifications of loan repayment terms, including extensions of the maturities of existing loans, reductions of the interest rates on existing loans, or conversion of interest to principal.[124] In certain cases, grants might be conditional. This was the case, for example, in *Certain Pneumatic Tyres (China)*, where the Commission found that a RMB 500 million grant provided to the recipient to 'promote global production capacity cooperation under the "One Belt, one Road Initiative"', was a form of financial contribution.[125] Moreover, forms of debt forgiveness, such as the assumption of an investigated exporter's debt, for example, by purchasing bonds, when it is highly unlikely whether the funds provided will be recuperated, are considered by the Commission to constitute grants.[126] In addition, debt-to-equity swaps have been considered to amount to debt forgiveness in the form of grants, where the relevant State-owned bank would not have converted its debt to equity under normal market conditions without further compensation.[127]
- *loans*, where a government lends money or money's worth on the basis that the principal, along with interest as might be agreed, is repaid.[128] The provision of credit is also considered a form of loan.[129] For example, in *Electric Bicycles (China)*, the Commission considered that bank acceptances, namely forms of credit whereby banks take over supplier account payables from buyers and transfer an agreed amount to the suppliers at an agreed date, amount to *de facto* loans (as well as bank guarantees) on the grounds that the payment date for the buyer to transfer the same amount to the bank was posterior to the payment term agreed with the supplier.[130]

---

119 WTO Panel Report, *US – Softwood Lumber VII* (2004), WT/DS533R, para 7.618.

120 WTO Panel Report, *Brazil – Aircraft* (1999), WT/DS46/R, para 7.72; WTO Panel Report, *Brazil – Aircraft (Article 21.5 – Canada)* (2000), WT/DS46/AB/RW, para 6.17.

121 Anti-subsidy: WTO Panel Report, *EC – Countervailing Measures on DRAM Chips* (2006), WT/DS299/R, para 7.93. State aid: *COVID-19*: *Capital-strengthening measures for medium-sized companies* (Case COMP/SA.57289) (Italy) [2020] OJ C269/1, paras 28–34.

122 Implementing Regulation (EU) 2020/776 [2020] OJ L189/1 (n 112), recital 587. State aid: *Partial refund of excise duties* (Case COMP/SA.30812) (Czechia) [2009] OJ C26/5, para 2 and following; *Refund of Social Security Contributions of Seafarers* (Case COMP/SA.19574) (Ireland) OJ 2007 C90/1, para 3 and following.

123 Anti-subsidy: see, eg, WTO Panel Report, *Japan – DRAMS (Korea)* (2010), WT/DS336/AB/R, paras 7.439–7.446. State aid: *Restructuring program of Cimos dd* [2016] OJ L59/168 (n 116), paras 97–102.

124 WTO Panel Report , *Japan – DRAMs (Korea)* (n 123), para 7.439.

125 Implementing Regulation (EU) 2018/1690 [2018] OJ L283/1 (n 112), recital 335.

126 Commission Regulation (EC) 708/2003 of 23 April 2003 imposing a provisional countervailing duty on imports of certain electronic microcircuits known as DRAMs (dynamic random access memories) originating in the Republic of Korea [2003] OJ L102/7, recital 66.

127 Implementing Regulation (EU) 2020/776 [2020] OJ L189/1 (n 112), recitals 420, 422 and 425.

128 Anti-subsidy: *US – Large Civil Aircraft (2nd complaint)* (n 113), para 616. State aid: *Rescue aid in favour of Complexul Energetic Oltenia SA* (Case COMP/SA.56250) (Romania) [2020] OJ C112/1, paras 10–11.

129 Implementing Regulation (EU) 2020/776 [2020] OJ L189/1 (n 112), recitals 345–357.

130 Implementing Regulation (EU) 2019/72 of 17 January 2019 imposing a definitive countervailing duty on imports of electric bicycles originating in the People's Republic of China [2019] OJ L16/5, recital 304.

- *loan guarantees*, where a government makes a legally binding promise to repay the outstanding balance of a loan when the loan recipient defaults on its repayments. The promise to repay an outstanding loan in the event of default is the financial contribution (ie, the potential direct transfer of funds), not the funds that might be transferred in the future in the event of default.[131] For example, in *Biodiesel (United States)*, the Commission found that the 'advanced biofuels loan guarantees' programme providing loan guarantees up to $250 million to assist in the development of new and emerging technologies for advanced biofuels (including biodiesel), renewable chemicals, and biobased products (up to 80% of the total eligible project costs) was a financial contribution.[132] Another example is *Salmon (Norway)*, where the Commission found that loan guarantees provided by the Norwegian Industrial and Regional Development Fund loan programme amounted to a financial contribution to salmon growers.[133]

When is a transfer of funds or liabilities considered a financial contribution?

- the term 'funds and liabilities' is broader than a transfer of money
- covers transactions involving financial resources, as well as other financial claims
- includes, but is not limited to, capital injections, grants, loans, loan guarantees, fiscal incentives, the setting off of operating losses, compensation for financial burdens imposed by public authorities, debt forgiveness, debt to equity swaps or rescheduling

A.4.2 Foregoing of Revenue that is Otherwise Due

The second type of financial contribution listed in Article 3(2)(b) FSR relates to the foregoing of revenue that is otherwise due. Identifying this type of financial contribution can raise particularly challenging questions. This has already been confirmed during the first months of application of the FSR, as in particular the characterisation of third country fiscal measures have regularly led to questions by the Commission in the context of M&A notifications.

The FSR's express reference to the foregoing of revenue that is otherwise due as a form of financial contribution implies that a financial contribution can be found even if the government has not incurred a cost. The same concept applies in the State aid regime, as well as under the SCM Agreement and the Basic Anti-Subsidy Regulation.

---

131 Anti-subsidy: WTO Panel Report, *EC and Certain Member States – Large Civil Aircraft* (2019), WT/DS316/R, paras 7.302, 7.304, and 7.1495. State aid: *Granting aid in the form of loan payment guarantees - large enterprises* (Case COMP/SA.41289) (Poland) [2017] OJ C193/4, para 17 and following; State Aid: *COVID-19: Loan guarantee scheme* (Case COMP/SA.56843) (Malta) [2020] OJ C125/1, para 4 and following.

132 Implementing Regulation (EU) 2021/1266 of 29 July 2021 imposing a definitive anti-dumping duty on imports of biodiesel originating in the United States of America following an expiry review pursuant to Article 11(2) of Regulation (EU) 2016/1036 of the European Parliament and of the Council [2021] OJ L277/34, recitals 88–92.

133 Council Regulation (EC) 1891/97 of 26 September 1997 imposing a definitive countervailing duty on imports of farmed Atlantic salmon originating in Norway [1997] OJ L267/19, recitals 45–46.

As mentioned above, the Commission Notice on the notion of State aid clarifies that '[w]aiving revenue which would otherwise have been paid to the State constitutes a transfer of State resources'. In particular a 'shortfall in tax and social security revenue due to exemptions or reductions in taxes or social security contributions granted by the Member State, or exemptions from the obligation to pay fines or other pecuniary penalties, fulfils the State resources requirement of Article 107(1) of the Treaty'.[134] In fact, the risk of imposing an additional burden on the State in the future, by a guarantee or by a contractual offer, is sufficient for the purposes of Article 107(1) TFEU.

This also corresponds to the understanding of the concept of a financial contribution under the SCM Agreement and the Basic Anti-Subsidy Regulation. Before the entry into force of the SCM Agreement, the Commission took the view that subsidy programmes that did not cost the government any money were not countervailable subsidies. This restrictive approach has since been abandoned. Under the Basic Anti-Subsidy Regulation, a countervailable subsidy can be found not only where there is a direct transfer of funds, but also where revenue otherwise due is forgone or not collected. This approach was confirmed by the Appellate Body in *Canada – Aircraft* which ruled that the cost to the government is irrelevant for determining whether a subsidy under Article 1 SCM Agreement exists.[135]

The first example of a financial contribution in the form of (government) revenue forgone, provided in Article 3(2)(b) FSR, relates to tax exemptions. Revenue could be forgone by all forms of exemptions of taxation, such as internal taxes, covering direct (raised on income) and indirect (raised on products) taxes, and import duties (tariffs). The second example refers to the granting of special or exclusive rights without adequate remuneration.

In order to assess whether, through tax exemptions or similar measures, there is government revenue foregone, the Commission should compare the tax treatment granted to a company with the ordinary system of taxation chosen and applied by the third country.[136] On this basis, the Commission should conclude whether the third country did not collect government revenue that should have been collected according to the ordinary system of taxation. Tax exemptions or similar measures resulting in revenue foregone would constitute a financial contribution irrespective of whether they applied selectively.

In assessing the first example under Article 3(2)(b) FSR, the Commission might be guided by the practice under WTO law in determining when government revenue is foregone. Under the SCM Agreement, the 'foregoing' of revenue implies that less revenue is raised by the government than would have been raised in a different situation and that the government has given up an entitlement to raise revenue that it could 'otherwise' have raised. This cannot, however, be an entitlement in the abstract, because governments, in theory, could tax *all* revenues.[137] The term 'otherwise due' thus refers to the situation

134 Commission Notice on the notion of State aid [2016] OJ C262/1 (n 42), para 51.

135 WTO Panel Report, *Brazil – Aircraft (Article 21.5 – Canada) (2000)*, WT/DS46/AB/RW, para 156.

136 Joined Cases C-885/19 P and C-898/19 P *Fiat Chrysler Finance Europe* v *European Commission and Ireland v European Commission* EU:C:2022:859.

137 WTO Appellate Body Report, *US – FSC* (2000), WT/DS108/AB/R, para 90.

that would prevail *but for* the measure at issue.[138] A mere change in the tax base or rate is not sufficient to conclude that there is a financial contribution. Instead, a comparison must be made between the tax treatment resulting from the measure and the ordinary tax system of the third country.[139]

The Commission also considers accelerated depreciation as a tax reduction.[140] In that regard, the Commission's views follow the interpretation adopted by the Appellate Body. However, it is important to note that the notion of a financial contribution under the FSR is wider than that established by the Appellate Body, as the Commission assumes that even generally applicable depreciation rules (or loss-carry-forward rules) constitute financial contributions under the FSR. This follows from the instructions to Table 1 in Forms FS-CO and FS-PP, which expressly exempt generally applicable depreciation rules from reporting obligations (confirming the default rule whereby generally applicable depreciation rules are considered financial contributions under the FSR). Thus, even generally applicable exemptions from tax measures are relevant when determining whether a company meets FSR contribution thresholds. Reporting requirements, however, are more limited.

In anti-subsidy investigations, the Commission has considered that tax exemptions, including exemptions from income or sales taxes, and import duty exemptions are financial contributions in the form of government revenue foregone, due to the non-paid tax or duty that otherwise would be due.[141] Tax exemptions might also take the form of favourable income tax rates for certain enterprises active in certain industries.[142] However, exemptions from non-definitive duties, such as excise and additional customs duties, which, if paid, could be used as a credit for future duty liabilities, have not been considered a financial contribution in the form of revenue forgone.[143]

---

138 ibid, para 7.45.

139 See FSR Public Procurement FAQs, question 6 (n 31). Unfortunately, there is no bright line test to determine what the 'ordinary tax regime' is, and this question has led to considerable litigation in EU State aid cases. See, eg, Joined Cases C-885/19 P and 898/19 P, *Fiat Chrysler Finance Europe v European Commission* and *Ireland v European Commission* EU:C:2022:859. In this judgment, the CJEU emphasised that it is the prerogative of the Member States to determine what constitutes the 'normal' tax regime, and this determination cannot be second-guessed by the Commission.

140 Commission Decision 284/2000/ECSC of 4 February 2000 imposing a definitive countervailing duty on imports of certain flat rolled products of iron or non-alloy steel, of a width of 600 mm or more, not clad, plated or coated, in coils, not further worked than hot-rolled, originating in India and Taiwan and accepting undertakings offered by certain exporting producers and terminating the proceeding concerning imports originating in South Africa [2000] OJ L31/44, recital 110. See also Van Bael & Bellis (n 110), 646.

141 Implementing Regulation (EU) 2020/776 [2020] OJ L189/1 (n 112), recital 587; Commission Regulation (EU) 1261/2010 of 22 December 2010 imposing a provisional countervailing duty on imports of certain stainless steel bars originating in India [2010] OJ L343/57, recital 72; Commission Implementing Regulation (EU) 2022/433 of 15 March 2022 imposing definitive countervailing duties on imports of stainless steel cold-rolled flat products originating in India and Indonesia and amending Implementing Regulation (EU) 2021/2012 imposing a definitive anti-dumping duty and definitively collecting the provisional duty imposed on imports of stainless steel cold-rolled flat products originating in India and Indonesia [2022] OJ L88/24, recitals 193, 194 and 199; Implementing Regulation (EU) 2018/1690 [2018] OJ L283/1 (n 112), recital 558.

142 Commission Implementing Regulation (EU) 2022/72 of 18 January 2022 imposing definitive countervailing duties on imports of optical fibre cables originating in the People's Republic of China and amending Implementing Regulation (EU) 2021/2011 imposing a definitive anti-dumping duty on imports of optical fibre cables originating in the People's Republic of China [2022] OJ L12/34, recital 472.

143 Regulation 1261/2010 [2010] OJ L343/57 (n 140), recital 73.

In the context of FSR notifications, the time dimension of accelerated depreciation rules would also be relevant. The question would be whether accelerated depreciation that was granted before the three-year period would still be relevant where the period of depreciation continues into the three-year period. While the Commission has not provided any guidance on this issue, it can be expected that accelerated depreciation should be regarded as a benefit in the three-year period, provided that the depreciation costs that can be deducted within the three-year period are higher than the rates normally applied to the relevant depreciation costs. Accordingly, notification would be required even if depreciation has started before the three-year period.

When is the 'foregoing of revenue that is otherwise due' considered a financial contribution?

- not linked to whether the government has incurred a loss
- includes tax exemptions, the granting of special or exclusive rights without adequate renumeration and accelerated depreciation

A.4.3 Provision of Goods or Services or Purchase of Goods or Services

Finally, the third type of financial contribution listed in Article 3(2)(c) FSR concerns the provision of goods or services or the purchase of goods or services. Under the FSR, the provision of goods or services, or the purchase of goods or services, constitutes a financial contribution, irrespective of whether or not it has been provided at market rates.

A sell/purchase relationship between the State and a private actor can exist in a broad set of circumstances, as the practice under the EU and WTO subsidies regimes as well as the EU State aid regime demonstrates.

In the EU and WTO subsidies regimes, a government provision of goods or services is listed among the types of financial contribution that may give rise to a 'subsidy' if it has the potential to *artificially* lower the cost of producing a product by providing inputs having a financial value to a company.[144] Similarly, a purchase of goods (but not of services) is captured by the Basic Anti-Subsidy Regulation and the SCM Agreement because it has the potential to artificially increase the revenues gained from selling the products.[145] A 'purchase of goods or services' also covers a transaction where a government purchases goods from an enterprise and this transaction has the potential to artificially increase the revenues gained from selling the product at issue.[146]

As a result, a financial contribution in the form of a provision of services could exist, for example, if a third country would provide training concerning technical skills related to the production of a certain type of product, management skills, or marketing skills

---

144 WTO Appellate Body Report, *US – Softwood Lumber IV* (2005), WT/DS257/AB/R, para 53.

145 ibid.

146 ibid.

to a company's employees.[147] This would apply even if the company pays market rates for the training. The training would become a subsidy if it were offered for free or at below market rates. Similarly, a financial contribution would exist if a third country leases a building to a company for its exclusive use for a certain period of time.[148]

Moreover, under the EU and WTO subsidies regimes, the provision of intangible rights by a government which has the effect of making goods or services available also amounts to a provision of goods or services.[149] For example, the Appellate Body in *US – Softwood Lumber IV* considered that the granting of an intangible right to harvest standing timber can be equated with the act of providing that standing timber. The Appellate Body noted that '[b]y granting a right to harvest, the provincial governments [of Canada] put particular stands of timber at the disposal of timber harvesters and allow those enterprises, exclusively, to make use of those resources'.[150]

Likewise, from a State aid perspective, the transfer of State resources relevant under Article 107(1) TFEU can also take the form of the provision of goods or services to a company. The Commission Notice on the notion of State aid explains that '[i]f public authorities or public undertakings provide goods or services at a price below market rates or invest in an undertaking in a manner that is inconsistent with the market economy operator test […], this implies foregoing State resources (as well as the granting of an advantage)'.[151]

Moreover, a transaction can be considered State aid if the purchase did not meet an actual need of the public authority. For instance, in *Aid to Ryanair Montpellier Airport*, the Commission found that a marketing service purchased by the Association for the Promotion of Tourist and Economic Flow from a Ryanair subsidiary in connection to the Montpellier airport constituted State aid because the purchase did not meet a real need but was in fact intended to subsidise Ryanair flights from and to Montpellier airport.[152]

When is the 'provision of goods or services', or 'purchase of goods or services' considered a financial contribution?

- the provision of goods or services, or purchase of goods or services, constitutes a financial contribution, irrespective of whether it has been provided under normal market conditions
- examples: government contracts, the leasing of a building, free training concerning technical skills related to production

---

147 See WTO Appellate Body Report, US – *Large Civil Aircraft (2nd complaint) (2006) Recourse to article 21.5 of the DSU by the European Union*, WT/DS353/AB/R, paras 7.584–7.585.

148 ibid, para 7.587.

149 See WTO Appellate Body Report, US – *Softwood Lumber IV* (2005), WT/DS257/AB/R, paras 68–75; see also WTO Appellate Body Report, *EC and Certain Member States – Large Civil Aircraft* (2019), WT/DS316/AB/R, paras 964–967.

150 See WTO Appellate Body Report, US – *Softwood Lumber IV* (2005), WT/DS257/AB/R, paras 75.

151 Commission Notice on the notion of State aid [2016] OJ C262/1 (n 42), para 52.

152 *Aid to Ryanair Montpellier airport* (Case COMP/SA.47867) (France) [2020] OJ L388/1, para 180.

B. Which is 'Provided Directly or Indirectly by a Third Country'

B.1 Introduction

Only financial contributions provided, directly or indirectly, by a third country fall within the scope of the FSR. Article 3(3) FSR specifies that a financial contribution is considered to have been provided by a third country if it is provided by an entity falling within any of the following three categories:

- the central government and public authorities at all other levels;
- a foreign public entity of which the actions can be attributed to the third country, taking into account, for example, the characteristics of the entity and the legal and economic environment prevailing in the State in which the entity operates, including the government's role in the economy; or
- a private entity of which the actions can be attributed to the third country, taking into account all relevant circumstances.

This section analyses these three categories identified in the FSR, in view of the available practice in EU State aid law and the EU and WTO subsidies regimes.

When is a financial contribution a government financial contribution?

- the central government
- public authorities at all other (decentralised) levels (regional, local, and municipal public authorities)
- a foreign public entity of which the actions can be attributed to a third country
- a private entity of which the actions can be attributed to a third country

B.2 The Central Government and Public Authorities at All Other Levels

Article 3(2) FSR establishes that all financial contributions provided by the central government and public authorities at all other levels must be considered imputable to a (third) country. In general, all public authorities at any level, such as the central government, as well as federal, regional, local or municipal institutions, fall within the scope of the central government and public authorities at all other levels.

Neither the FSR, nor any other instrument, provides specific definitions of what is a public authority of a third country. They only refer to central governments and any decentralised public authority. In line with principles of general international law, the definition of public authority of a foreign country under the FSR includes any person or entity which has that status in accordance with the internal law of that State.[153]

B.3 A Public Company/Body

Under Article 3(2) FSR, a financial contribution is considered imputable to a third country when the contribution is provided by a foreign public entity of which the actions can be attributed to the third country at issue. Recital 12 FSR states that a case-by-case assessment is needed to determine whether a public entity provides a financial contribution, taking into account various elements such as the characteristics of the relevant entity, the legal and economic environment prevailing in the third country in which the entity operates and the government's role in the economy of that country.[154]

Such a case-by-case assessment is problematic under the FSR, and specifically the notification-based M&A and public procurement tools. Under the FSR, companies (not authorities in specific investigations) must self-assess whether a public entity in any third country has provided a financial contribution when determining whether they are subject to a notification obligation, and when preparing a notification. The FSR's approach – referring to a case-by-case analysis, which has to be applied in multiple jurisdictions with different legal frameworks, but without providing clear guidance – will lead to a significant administrative burden and create considerable uncertainty for companies seeking to comply with the notification obligations under the FSR.

As a matter of State aid law, aid is imputable to the State where a public authority grants the aid or a public or private body is tasked by the State to administer the aid.[155] Additionally, a measure might be imputable to the State when the aid is granted by a public entity. In *Stardust*, the CJEU held that the imputability to the State of an aid measure taken by a public entity may be inferred from a set of indicators arising from the circumstances of the case and the context in which that measure was taken. Those circumstances, which are non-exhaustive, include: the fact that the body in question could not take the decision at issue (such as the fixing of a tariff) without taking account of the requirements of the public authorities,[156] the integration of that body into the structures of the public administration, the nature of its activities, the legal status of that body (in the sense of being subject to public law or ordinary company law) or the intensity of the supervision exercised by public authorities over the management of the entity.[157]

The fact that an entity has been constituted in the form of a private company is not a sufficient reason to exclude the imputability of the aid to the State.[158] Otherwise, the prohibition to grant aid could easily be circumvented by administering the aid through a private company.

---

153 See Draft Articles on the Responsibility of States for Internationally Wrongful Acts 2001 art 4(2).

154 The explicit reference in the FSR to the fact that 'the government's role in the economy' should be taken into account when determining whether a certain financial contribution should be considered as 'foreign', indicates that the Commission is likely to apply a broad reading of the concept of government or public entity in the context of the FSR, in particular when it comes to non-market economies such as China.

155 Case 78/76 *Steinike & Weinlig v Federal Republic of Germany* EU:C:1977:52, para 21.

156 *Stardust* (n 101), para 55.

157 ibid .

158 ibid, para 57.

Following the guidance provided by the EU Courts, the Commission's Notice on the notion of State aid includes a non-exhaustive list of possible indicators to establish whether a measure is imputable to a State.[159] The list includes the following factors:

- the fact that the body in question could not take the contested decision without taking account of the requirements of the public authorities;
- the presence of factors of an organic nature which link the public entity to the State;
- the fact that the entity had to take account of directives issued by governmental bodies;
- the integration of the public entity into the structures of the public administration;
- the nature of the public entity's activities and their exercise on the market in normal conditions of competition with private operators;
- the legal status of the entity (whether it is subject to public law or ordinary company law); the mere fact that a public entity has been constituted in the form of a capital company under ordinary company law cannot be regarded as sufficient reason to exclude imputability, having regard to the autonomy which that legal form confers on it;
- the degree of supervision that the public authorities exercise over the management of the entity; and
- any other indicator showing the involvement of public authorities in adopting the aid measure in question or the unlikelihood of those authorities not being involved, taking account of the scope of the measure, its content or the conditions it contains.

Under the EU and WTO subsidies regimes, Article 2(b) Basic Anti-Subsidy Regulation and Article 1.1(a)(1) SCM Agreement define the term 'government' as 'a government or any public body within the territory of the country of origin or export'. However, neither the Basic Anti-Subsidy Regulation nor the SCM Agreement defines the term 'public body'. In essence, the criteria used in trade law cases are not so different from those used in State aid law.

In *DRAMs (dynamic random access memories) (Korea)*, the Commission identified two broad criteria for determining whether a company is a 'public body': (i) the pursuance of public policy objectives which go beyond the normal remit of a private organisation, and (ii) government control going beyond ownership. These criteria reflect the consideration 'that a public body is an institution authorised to act on behalf of a community as a government entity, as distinct from a private body which is presumed to act in the interests of its owners'.[160]

---

159 Commission Notice on the notion of State aid [2016] OJ C262/1 (n 42), para 43.

160 Council Regulation (EC) 1480/2003 of 11 August 2003 imposing a definitive countervailing duty and collecting definitively the provisional duty imposed on imports of certain electronic microcircuits known as DRAMs (dynamic random access memories) originating in the Republic of Korea [2003] OJ L212/1, recital 13.

The first criterion (ie, 'the pursuance of public policy objectives which go beyond the normal remit of a private organisation') includes, for example, a requirement to take account of national or regional economic interests, or the promotion of social objectives. As stated by the Commission, this criterion may be 'non-commercial, in the sense that [it] compromise[s] the normal objective of profit maximisation'.[161]

The second criterion refers to 'government control going beyond ownership'. Determining whether that condition is satisfied may involve demonstrating 'government influence in appointments, the right of the government to review results and to determine objectives, and the extent to which the government has to be involved in individual investment or business decisions'.[162] With respect to government ownership, the Commission accepts that even 100% government ownership does not in itself mean that a company is a public body. It has further stated that government ownership, irrespective of its level, does not create a 'rebuttable presumption' that the government-owned company is a 'public body'.[163] However, according to the Commission, 'the level of government ownership is an important, in some cases the most important, component of a determination of whether a public body exists'. In that regard, the Commission has highlighted that '[t]he higher the government ownership, the more likely it is that control exists'. As regards 100% privately-owned companies and companies in which the government is not the shareholder, the Commission has considered that 'it will normally be difficult to establish that a company is a public body, unless convincing evidence to the contrary exists'.[164]

To illustrate those points, in *DRAMs (dynamic random access memories) (Korea)*, the Commission found that the Korea Development Bank was a 'public body' within the meaning of Article 2 Basic Anti-Subsidy Regulation on the basis that the Korea Development Bank was:

- 100% owned by the Government of Korea and founded as 'a special purpose bank to supply long-term credit for industries to stabilise the economy and promote industrial rehabilitation';
- required to undertake its business in accordance with Government-set objectives;
- benefitting from compensation of its annual losses by the Government of Korea, which also regularly injected capital into the bank; and
- publicly recognised as having a special relationship with the Government of Korea, as well as 'a special policy public role in the Korean economy".[165]

---

161 ibid, recital 14.
162 ibid, recitals 11 and 14.
163 ibid, recital 11.
164 ibid, recital 12.
165 ibid, recital 36, referring to Regulation 708/2003 [2003] OJ L102/7 (n 126), recitals 55–59.

Using these criteria,[166] the Commission has considered, for example, State-owned steel producers,[167] State-owned banks[168] and a State-owned insurance company[169] to fall within the definition of 'public bodies' under Article 2 Basic Anti-Subsidy Regulation.[170]

The fact that the third country in which the entity is established and operates is a non-market economy is likely to facilitate the Commission's determination that that entity is a public body. This is exemplified by the practice under the EU and WTO subsidies regimes.

For example, the Commission found in *Coated Fine Paper (China)* that loans granted to Chinese coated paper producers by Chinese 'policy and state-owned banks' were financial contributions granted by public bodies. In view of those banks' relations with the government, the Commission considered that 'the lending practices of these entities are directly attributable to the government'. In particular, the Commission noted that the 'policy and state-owned banks' were:

- 'more than 50% State-owned and are thus considered controlled by the government';
- 'effectively exercise[d] government authority since [...] there is a clear intervention by the State [...] in the way commercial banks take decisions on interest rates for loans granted to Chinese companies'; and
- required to pursue 'government industrial policies'.[171]

In subsequent anti-subsidy investigations, the Commission has focused its 'public body' determinations on the criteria developed by the Appellate Body in *United States – Anti-Dumping and Countervailing Duties (China)*. According to the Appellate Body, to determine if an entity may be considered as a 'public body' within the meaning of Article 1.1(a)(1) SCM Agreement, it must be assessed whether the entity 'possesses, exercises, or is vested with government authority', and whether the entity performs functions which are ordinarily considered part of governmental functions in the legal order of the country under investigation.[172] Although the meaningful exercise of formal government control or ownership might suggest that an entity possesses government authority, the WTO Appellate Body has cautioned that the investigating authority must also determine whether that control was in fact exercised by the government over the entity.[173]

---

166 See, Van Bael & Bellis (n 110) 629–630.

167 See, eg, Council Implementing Regulation (EU) 215/2013 of 11 March 2013 imposing a countervailing duty on imports of certain organic coated steel products originating in the People's Republic of China [2013] OJ L73/16, recitals 45–73.

168 See, eg, Certain pneumatic tyres, new or retreaded, of rubber, of a kind used for buses or lorries and with a load index exceeding 121 (China), Implementing Regulation (EU) 2018/1690 [2018] OJ L283/1 (n 112), recitals 168–208.

169 See, eg, Implementing Regulation (EU) 2019/72 [2019] OJ L16/5 (n 130), recitals 176–217.

170 Van Bael & Bellis (n 110) 629-630.

171 Council Implementing Regulation (EU) 452/2011 of 6 May 2011 imposing a definitive anti-subsidy duty on imports of coated fine paper originating in the People's Republic of China [2011] OJ L128/18, recital 90.

172 WTO Appellate Body Report, *US – Anti-Dumping and Countervailing Duties (China)* (2011), WT/DS379/AB/R, paras 290, 297 and 317.

173 WTO Appellate Body Report, *US – Carbon Steel (India) (2002)*, WT/DS213/AB/R and Corr.1, para 4.54.

In view of the criteria developed by the Appellate Body in *United States – Anti-Dumping and Countervailing Duties (China)*, the Commission has found that a series of Chinese State-owned banks possess, are vested with, and exercise, governmental authority and, thus, are 'public bodies' within the meaning of Article 2 Basic Anti-Subsidy Regulation. The Commission reached this conclusion, taking into account the high degree of State ownership (through shareholding) in those banks, the government guarantees for those banks' cheap access to capital, and the instructions for them to grant loans in accordance with government plans and objectives.[174]

In essence, the assessment of whether an entity is a 'public body' under the Basic Anti-Subsidy Regulation and the SCM Agreement focuses on whether the relevant entity shares a 'degree of commonality or overlap in [its] essential characteristics' with the 'government (in the narrow sense)'.[175] As noted by the Appellate Body in *US – Countervailing Measures (China) (Article 21.5 – China)*,[176] similarly to a government, 'all conduct' of an entity established to be a public body 'shall be attributable to the [State] concerned for purposes of Article 1.1(a)(1)' SCM Agreement.[177]

How to determine whether a public entity's financial contribution may be attributed to a third country?

- State ownership or control rights (although not in itself determinative)
- government entities exercise control
- involvement of the government in decision granting the financial contribution
- public entity acts to promote the government's interests/does not clearly act only to maximise shareholder value

B.4 Private Entities whose Actions May Be Attributed to a Third Country

Under the FSR, a financial contribution may also be granted through a private entity, provided the actions of that private entity 'can be attributed to the third country'.

174 See, eg, Council Implementing Regulation (EU) 1239/2013 of 2 December 2013 imposing a definitive countervailing duty on imports of crystalline silicon photovoltaic modules and key components (ie cells) originating in or consigned from the People's Republic of China [2013] OJ L325/66, recitals 158–168 and 225–235; Commission Implementing Regulation (EU) 471/2014 of 13 May 2014 imposing definitive countervailing duties on imports of solar glass originating in the People's Republic of China [2014] OJ L142/23, recitals 71–87. In view of similar factual findings in anti-subsidy investigations concerning imports from India, the Commission has concluded that the Reserve Bank of India is a 'public body' within the meaning of Article 2 EU Anti-Subsidy Regulation. See, eg, Council Regulation (EC) 713/2005 of 10 May 2005 imposing a definitive countervailing duty on imports of certain broad-spectrum antibiotics originating in India [2005] OJ L121/1.

175 WTO Appellate Body Report, *US – Countervailing Measures (China) (Article 21.5 – China)* (2019), WT/DS437/AB/RW, para 5.100.

176 ibid.

177 ibid, para 5.103. This applies equally under Regulation (EU) 2016/1037 [2016] OJ L176/55 (n 32), art 2.

A common understanding of State aid law is that State aid 'covers all aid granted by a Member State or through State resources without it being necessary to make a distinction whether the aid is granted directly by the State or by public or private bodies established or appointed by it to administer the aid'.[178] This broad understanding is intended to counteract a risk of under-inclusion, because otherwise there would be a risk of circumventing the prohibition to provide State aid. On the other hand, the decision to include in the scope of Article 107(1) TFEU advantages granted by bodies distinct from the State gives rise to a specific risk of over-inclusion, as observed by the General Court in *Italy v Commission.*[179]

In *Italy v Commission*, Italy challenged a decision of the Commission finding that the 2014 rescue intervention of a consortium of banks governed by private law in favour of a private equity bank was incompatible State aid. In its judgment, the General Court found that the Commission had not proved that the Italian public authorities were involved in the adoption of the measure at issue and, consequently, that the measure was imputable to the State.[180] According to the General Court, where aid is provided by a private entity, the Commission is under an 'even more important obligation to specify and substantiate the reasons which justify its conclusion that the resources used are under public control and the measures are imputable to the State'.[181] Moreover, the Commission must prove a sufficient degree of State involvement in granting the measure at issue by showing that: (i) the State is able to exercise a dominant influence over the private entity granting the aid, and (ii) the State was in a position to exercise that control in the circumstances of the particular case.[182]

Turning to the guidance that might be taken from the trade defence regime, Article 3(1)(iv) Basic Anti-Subsidy Regulation and Article 1.1(a)(1)(iv) SCM Agreement provide that a financial contribution is attributable to a government, when that government 'entrusts or directs a private body' to carry out the functions which amount to granting a 'financial contribution', and 'which would normally be vested in the government and the practice, in no real sense, differs from practices normally followed by governments'.[183]

As explained by the Appellate Body in *US – Countervailing Duty Investigation on DRAMs*, the concepts of 'entrustment' and 'direction' in Article 1.1(a)(1)(iv) SCM Agreement identify 'the instances where seemingly private conduct may be attributable to a government for purposes of determining whether there has been a financial contribution'.[184] 'Entrustment' occurs where a government gives responsibility to a private entity to undertake functions amounting to the granting of a 'financial contribution'. 'Direction' refers to situations where the government exercises its authority over a private body.[185]

---

178 *Steinike & Weinlig* (n 155), para 21.
179 Case T-98/16 *Italian Republic and Others v European Commission* EU:T:2019:167, para 65.
180 ibid, para 132.
181 ibid, para 67.
182 ibid, para 69. The judgment of the General Court was upheld on appeal, see *European Commission v Italian Republic* (n 44).
183 See, Van Bael & Bellis (n 110) 630–632.
184 WTO Appellate Body Report, *US – Countervailing Duty Investigation on DRAMS* (2005), WT/DS296/AB/R, para 108.
185 ibid, paras 106–116.

Contrary to the assessment of whether an entity is a 'public body', the assessment of whether an entity is 'entrusted or directed' by a government or a public body focuses on the conduct giving rise to a financial contribution. As noted by the Appellate Body in *US – Countervailing Measures (China) (Article 21.5 – China)*:

> '[W]hen it is alleged that the conduct of a private body gives rise to a financial contribution, an investigating authority must establish an additional 'link between the government and *that conduct*' in the form of 'entrustment or direction'. [...] By contrast, if it is established that an entity is a public body within the domestic system of a Member, then the conduct of that entity is *directly* attributable to the Member concerned'.[186]

For example, in *DRAMs (dynamic random access memories) (Korea)*,[187] the Commission noted that 'direction' exists where the government requires a private body to carry out functions amounting to the granting of a financial contribution that are normally vested in the government. According to the Commission, it is not sufficient 'to show that a government merely encouraged or facilitated such actions, although such encouragement or facilitation may be a factor to be considered'. The factors considered by the Commission to reach a finding of 'direction' in *DRAMs (dynamic random access memories) (Korea)* with respect to new loans, debt-to-equity swaps and similar instruments made available by commercial Korean banks in the context of the recipient's restructuring, included:

- the fact that, under commercial considerations, the relevant banks would not have provided the relevant loans etc. In particular, the Commission relied on the alarming financial situation of the recipient, including the fact that its credit rating was poor, while some of the previous loans it had received remained unpaid;
- the majority ownership stake of the Government of Korea in some of the banks at issue, permitting the Government of Korea to appoint the Directors of those banks and influence their operations through its voting power; and
- the government influence over the business decisions of some of the banks at issue taking into account that several banks received capital injections for recovering from the Korean financial crisis and were themselves in a period of restructuring.

The Panel that subsequently examined the Commission's findings in *DRAMs (dynamic random access memories) (Korea)* explained that 'entrustment or direction' exists, among others, where a government has intervened to have a bank's credit ceiling extended by the financial supervisory authority in order to facilitate lending to an indebted company beyond binding prudential lending limits. Likewise, it exists where, in response to the Commission's enquiry, a financial institution refused to provide information about its involvement in the restructuring of an indebted company under a programme of 'doubtful commercial reasonableness'.[188]

---

186 WTO Appellate Body Report, *US – Countervailing Measures (China) (Article 21.5 – China) (2019)*, WT/DS437/AB/RW, para 5.103. (emphasis original)

187 Regulation 1480/2003 [2003] OJ L212/1 (n 160), recital 15.

188 WTO Panel Report, *EC – Countervailing Measures on DRAM Chips (2006)*, WT/DS299/R, paras 7.97–7.109. See also, Van Bael & Bellis (n 110) 631.

Another example is *Broad spectrum antibiotics (India)*, a case in which the Commission found that preferential export credits granted by commercial banks constituted a financial contribution by the government because those banks were 'directed' by the Reserve Bank of India (RBI), which was found to be a 'public body'. The Commission considered that the RBI directed the commercial banks at issue because those 'banks are bound by the conditions, inter alia, the maximum ceilings for interest rates on export credits mandated in the RBI Master Circulars and the RBI provisions that commercial banks have to provide a certain amount of their net bank credit towards export finance'. According to the Commission, this form of 'direction obliges commercial banks to carry out functions mentioned in [...] the basic Regulation, in this case loans in the form of preferential export financing'.[189]

The interpretation of the concepts of 'entrustment' and 'direction' in the Commission's anti-subsidy investigations likely will inform the Commission's understanding of 'attribution' under the FSR. However, the Commission might interpret the concept of 'attribution' in Article 3(2)(c) FSR more broadly. In particular, the Commission might consider whether (intense) encouragement without evidence of official direction may be sufficient to make actions of private actors attributable to the State.

How to determine whether a private entity's financial contributions may be attributed to a third country?

- verify whether government entities exercise control over a private entity
- determine whether government entities confer responsibility on a private entity to grant financial contributions
- assess whether government entities direct the actions of a private entity

C. Which Confers a 'Benefit' to an 'Undertaking Engaging in Economic Activity in the Internal Market'

C.1 The Financial Contribution Must Confer a Benefit

C.1.1 The Legal Framework of the Concept of a Benefit

Article 3(1) FSR states that a foreign subsidy exists where a third country provides a financial contribution which confers a benefit on a company engaging in an activity in the internal market:

> 'For the purposes of this Regulation, a foreign subsidy must be deemed to exist where a third country provides, directly or indirectly, a financial contribution

189 Regulation 713/2005 [2005] OJ L121/1 (n 174), recital 113.

> which confers a benefit on a company that is engaged in an economic activity in the internal market and which is limited, in law or in fact, to one or more companies or industries.'

The preamble to the FSR provides further guidance on what is meant by the concept of a benefit conferred on a company engaging in an economic activity. Recital 13 states that:

> 'A financial contribution should confer a benefit on an undertaking engaging in an economic activity in the internal market. A financial contribution should be considered to confer a benefit on an undertaking if it could not have been obtained under normal market conditions. The existence of a benefit should be determined on the basis of comparative benchmarks, such as the investment practice of private investors, financing rates obtainable on the market, a comparable tax treatment, or the adequate remuneration for a given good or service. If no directly comparable benchmarks are available, existing benchmarks could be adjusted or alternative benchmarks could be established based on generally accepted assessment methods. Benefits can, for example, be conferred in the context of the relationship established between public authorities and public undertakings, if such a relationship, and in particular any financing by the public authorities to public undertakings does not comply with normal market conditions. The provision or purchase of goods or services carried out following a competitive, transparent and non-discriminatory tender procedure, is presumed to be in line with normal market conditions. A financial contribution to an undertaking engaging in an economic activity in the internal market should not be considered as conferring a benefit when the benchmark assessment shows that the undertaking would have obtained that benefit under normal market conditions. Transfer pricing in the context of goods and services exchanged within an undertaking can confer a benefit if that transfer pricing is not in line with normal market conditions. The benefit conferred by a financial contribution may be passed to an undertaking engaging in an economic activity in the Union.'

C.1.2 The Concept of 'Normal Market Conditions' under the FSR and the State Aid and EU Trade Defence Regimes

The assessment of whether a benefit could not have been obtained under normal market conditions requires using comparative benchmarks. Those benchmarks include the investment practice of private investors with respect to, for example, capital injections, financing rates obtainable on the market for loans or other forms of financing, a comparable tax treatment in relation to tax exemptions, or the adequate remuneration for a given good or service.

The consideration that a subsidy entails a benefit is not unique to the FSR. Likewise, under EU State aid law, Article 107(1) TFEU applies to aid conferring a benefit (that is, an 'advantage') to its recipient. That benefit or advantage refers to any economic benefit conferred on the recipient which it could not have obtained under normal market conditions, ie, in the absence of State intervention.[190]

---

190 Commission Notice on the notion of State aid [2016] OJ C262/1 (n 42), para 66.

If no directly comparable benchmarks are available, the assessment is to rely on either existing benchmarks that are to be adjusted or alternative benchmarks established based on generally accepted assessment methods. These concepts are comparable to those used in EU State aid law. Existing benchmarks refer to the assessment of the compliance of a transaction with market conditions in the light of the terms of comparable transactions carried out by comparable private operators in comparable situations, adjusted according to the specific features of the State transaction. Alternatively, compliance with market conditions may also be established on the basis of a generally accepted, standard assessment methodology, such as the calculation of the internal rate of return (IRR) or the net present value (NPV) of investments.

Under EU State aid law, the concept of an advantage includes 'not only positive benefits, such as subsidies, but also interventions which, in various forms, mitigate the charges which would normally be included in the budget of the recipient undertaking or undertakings and which, therefore, are of the same character as subsidies and have the same effect'.[191] The determination of an 'advantage' focuses on the effects of the measure.[192] The causes or objectives of the measure are not relevant for deciding whether the measure grants an advantage to one or more companies and, more broadly, whether it is to be classified as State aid.[193] Nor is the form of the measure relevant.[194]

The assessment of whether a company could have obtained the advantage under normal market conditions is generally carried out by applying the market economy operator principle (also known as MEOP).[195] Practically speaking, to assess whether that principle is satisfied, the Commission carries out a test ie, the market economy operator test (MEO test) with the purpose of evaluating whether a Member State has granted an advantage to the recipient by not acting like a market economy operator with regard to a certain transaction. That test is typically carried out on an ex-ante basis – ie, having regard to the information available at the time the intervention was decided upon.[196] In addition, it is typically applied only when the State has acted as an economic operator, and not when its decisions were driven by public policy reasons.[197]

Relying on the MEO test involves using various specific tests which aim to compare, in the most appropriate manner possible, the measure at issue with a measure that might have been adopted by a private operator in a situation that is as alike as possible and acting under normal market conditions.[198] These include the private investor, private debtor,

---

191 Case C-387/92 *Banco Exterior de España SA v Ayuntamiento de Valencia* EU:C:1994:100, para 13; Case C-362/19 P *European Commission v Fútbol Club Barcelona* EU:C:2021:169, para 59.

192 *Steinike & Weinlig* (n 153), para 21; Case C-706/17 *Achema AB and Others v Valstybinė kainų ir energetikos kontrolės komisija* EU:C:2019:407, para 50; Case C-331/20 P *Volotea SA v European Commission* EU:C:2022:886, para 105.

193 Case C-81/10 P *France Télécom SA v European Commission* EU:C:2011:811, para 17, Case C-638/19 P *European Commission v European Food SA and Others* EU:C:2022:50, para 122.

194 *Altmark Trans GmbH* (n 42), para 84; Case C-212/19 *Ministre de l'Agriculture et de l'Alimentation v Compagnie des pêches de Saint-Malo* EU:C:2020:726, para 39.

195 Case C-579/16 P *European Commission v FIH Holding A/S* EU:C:2018:159, para 45; Case C-933/19 P *Autostrada Wielkopolska SA v European Commission and Republic of Poland* EU:C:2021:905, para 105.

196 Commission Notice on the notion of State aid [2016] OJ C262/1 (n 42), para 78.

197 ibid, paras 76–77.

198 *Volotea SA* (n 192), para 109 and case-law cited therein.

private creditor and private vendor tests,[199] depending on whether the State invested, borrowed or lent money, or sold goods to a beneficiary. All these tests correspond essentially to a different practical implementation of the same principle.

The Commission Notice on the notion of State aid clarifies that, when applying the MEO test, it is useful to distinguish between situations in which the transaction's compliance with market conditions can be directly established through transaction-specific market data and situations in which, due to the absence of that data, the transaction's compliance with market conditions has to be benchmarked on the basis of other available methods.[200]

Compliance with market conditions can be directly established through transaction-specific market information:

- when the transaction is carried out under the same terms and conditions (and therefore with the same level of risk and rewards) by public bodies and private operators who are in a comparable situation (a 'pari-passu' transaction);[201] or
- when the transaction concerns the sale and purchase of assets, goods and services (or other comparable transactions) carried out through a competitive, transparent non-discriminatory and unconditional tender procedure.[202]

In case no private operator in a comparable situation exists or the transaction has not been completed through a tender, the transaction may be assessed:

- using the terms of comparable transactions carried out by comparable private operators in comparable situations (benchmarking);[203] or
- through a generally accepted, standard assessment methodology, based on available, objectively verifiable and reliable data, which should reflect the economic situation of the market at the time when the transaction was decided. This assessment is normally based on the calculation of the IRR or the NPV calculation.[204]

Transfer of property-related assets from FIH to the FSC illustrates the practical application of these principles. In that case, the Commission assessed a complex transfer of assets from a Danish bank with liquidity issues to a new subsidiary, which also entailed Denmark's commitment to provide funding and recapitalisation of the new subsidiary.[205] To assess whether this transaction was in line with the MEOP, the Commission examined: (i) whether a private investor was initially willing to finance the measures on the same terms and conditions as Denmark, (ii) if so, what was the return on investment which the private investor demanded in comparison with the return for Denmark, and (iii) in the absence of private interest, whether the overall return of the measures in favour of the bank was

---

199 ibid, para 110 and case-law cited therein.

200 Commission Notice on the notion of State aid [2016] OJ C262/1 (n 42), para 83.

201 ibid, paras 86–88.

202 ibid, paras 89–96.

203 ibid, paras 98–100.

204 ibid, paras 101–105.

205 *The transfer of property-related assets from FIH to the FSC* (Case COMP/SA.34445) (Denmark) [2020] OJ L261/16, recitals 25–33.

equal to or higher than the expected return that a hypothetical private investor would have demanded in order to make that investment under normal market economy conditions.[206] Relying on expert advice, the Commission calculated that a private operator would have required a significantly higher remuneration compared to that accepted by Denmark. Therefore, no market economy operator would have been willing to invest on terms and conditions equivalent to those of the share purchase agreement. As a result, the measures at issue were not in line with the MEOP and conferred an advantage.[207]

Similar principles apply under the Basic Anti-Subsidy Regulation, which provides that a benefit is considered to be conferred when the provision of goods or services is made for less than adequate remuneration. This comparison is based on the 'prevailing market conditions for the product or service in question in the country of provision [...], including price, quality, availability, marketability, transportation and other conditions of purchase and sale'.[208]

There is a distinction between the situation where the goods or services are provided by the government in competition with other suppliers and where the government is the monopoly supplier or the predominant supplier of the goods or services.[209]

Where goods or services are provided by the government under competitive conditions, the amount of the subsidy involved is the difference between: (i) the price actually paid for the goods or services, and (ii) the normal market price for the goods and services in question. This comparison can only be made if the goods and services are also supplied by private operators on the domestic market of the country concerned.

Where the government is the monopoly supplier or the predominant supplier of the goods or services, the Commission may compare the price paid for the goods or services by the recipient company with the price paid for the same goods by other companies:

- if the recipient company has benefitted from *preferential pricing*, the amount of the benefit is the difference between: (i) the preferential price, and (ii) the price paid by other companies to the government;
- if the comparison does not reveal preferential pricing, *the price actually paid is compared with the price charged* in relation to the 'prevailing market conditions' for the product or service in question in the country of provision or purchase; and
- if there are no 'prevailing market conditions' in the country of provision of the goods or services which can be used as appropriate benchmark, the Commission has considered that private prices are likely distorted if the government is the monopolist or the predominant supplier. A case-by-case assessment is undertaken to determine whether the relevant market operates on market conditions. If the Commission concludes that this is not the case, it will establish the benchmark by either *adjusting the terms and conditions* prevailing in

206 ibid, recital 87.
207 ibid, recital 84–102.
208 Regulation (EU) 2016/1037 [2016] OJ L176/55 (n 32), art 6(d).
209 Van Bael & Bellis (n 110) 654–655.

> the country concerned on the basis of actual costs, prices and other factors by an appropriate amount which reflects normal market terms and conditions, *or relying on an external benchmark.*[210]

For example, land prices from Taiwan have been used as external benchmarks when assessing the benefit conferred by financial contributions in the form of the provision of land-use rights in China.[211] Moreover, in an anti-subsidy investigation pertaining to the provision of certain steel products from State-owned Chinese enterprises, the Commission used a constructed benchmark on the basis of the *world market prices* published in specialised steel journals.[212]

However, external benchmarks are not used by the Commission when determining whether financial contributions in the form of loans provide a benefit. According to Article 6(b) Basic Anti-Subsidy Regulation, in the case of financial contributions in the form of loans, the comparison is made between the interest rate actually paid for the loan and the interest rate for a comparable commercial loan. In such an assessment, *interest rates in third countries do not play any role.* As explained in the Commission's guidelines for the calculation of the amount of subsidy in countervailing duty investigations, '[i]f there are no comparable commercial lending practices on the domestic market of the exporting country, the interest rate on a commercial loan may be estimated with reference to indicators of the economic situation prevailing at the time, (notably the inflation rate) and the situation of the company concerned'.[213]

Finally, the question arises whether a quantitative assessment should be carried out in order to conclude that a benefit exists. According to the Commission, a subsidy must confer a 'net' benefit to the recipient in order to be regarded as countervailable. For example, the Commission has considered that where a financial contribution had the effect of offsetting the negative effects of the devaluation of a certain currency, it did not confer a benefit and thus, did not amount to a subsidy.[214]

---

210 See Implementing Regulation (EU) 215/2013 [2013] OJ L73/16 (n 167), recitals 81–82, in which the Commission considered it impractical to adjust costs and prices in any meaningful way because it considered that the whole of the Chinese steel market was distorted. Therefore, reference was made to an external benchmark, consisting of a constructed benchmark on the basis of the world market prices published in specialised steel journals.

211 Implementing Regulation (EU) 2018/1690 [2018] OJ L283/1 (n 112), recitals 494–495; Implementing Regulation (EU) 2017/969 [2017] OJ L146/17 (n 67), recitals 281–310; Commission Implementing Regulation (EU) 1379/2014 of 16 December 2014 imposing a definitive countervailing duty on imports of certain filament glass fibre products originating in the People" Republic of China and amending Council Implementing Regulation (EU) No 248/2011 imposing a definitive anti-dumping duty on imports of certain continuous filament glass fibre products originating in the People's Republic of [2014] OJ L367/22, recitals 200–204; Implementing Regulation (EU) 471/2014 [2014] OJ L142/23 (n 174), recitals 190–191; Implementing Regulation (EU) 452/2011 [2011] OJ L128/18 (n 169), recital 261. See also Case T-444/11 *Gold East Paper (Jiangsu) Co Ltd and Gold Huasheng Paper (Suzhou Industrial Park) Co Ltd v Council of the European Union* EU:T:2014:773.

212 Implementing Regulation (EU) 215/2013 [2013] OJ L73/16 (n 167), recitals 81–82.

213 See, Information from the Commission - Guidelines for the calculation of the amount of subsidy in countervailing duty investigations [1998] OJ C394/6.

214 Implementing Regulation (EU) 2020/870 [2020] OJ L201/10 (n 68), recitals 287–288. See also, Council Regulation (EC) 584/2006 of 10 April 2006 amending Regulation (EC) 1480/2003 imposing a definitive countervailing duty and collecting definitely the provisional duty imposed on imports of certain electronic microcircuits known as DRAMs (dynamic random access memories) originating in the Republic of Korea [2006] OJ L103/1, recital 75.

In contrast, the FSR does not refer to a 'net' benefit: conduct by a third country that results in the setting-off of operations losses is listed in Article 3(2) FSR among the types of financial contributions covered under the FSR.

C.1.3 Indirect Benefits and Passing-On of Benefits

In various scenarios, the question will arise of whether financial contributions or subsidies granted to another entity could become relevant under the FSR because they are considered to indirectly benefit a notifying party or the target of an investigation. Recital 13 FSR confirms that the benefit conferred by a financial contribution to a company not active in the internal market may be passed on to an entity engaging in an economic activity in the EU.

The possibility of passing on the benefit conferred by a subsidy is relevant in, at least, three different scenarios: (i) internal transfers within a control group, (ii) government payments made with the purpose of indirectly benefitting a specific recipient, and (iii) benefits granted to independent entities in a supply chain.

C.1.3.1 *Intra-Group Transfers*

Recital 13 FSR, addressing the issue of passing-on a benefit, gives the specific example of transfer pricing in the context of goods and services exchanged within a group of companies. Thus, subsidies passed on within a control group can be considered to benefit the entire group and its individual members.

This is consistent with the Commission's approach in trade defence cases, where the Commission has found that financial contributions granted in relation to products other than the product concerned in the anti-subsidy investigation at issue may reduce the overall financing costs of the exporting producer and thus benefit that producer.[215] In *Broad-spectrum antibiotics (India)*, the Commission stated that it is sufficient to establish a direct link between the subsidy and the manufacturing company because, in that case, the domestic subsidy will lead to lower priced export transactions and therefore benefit from that subsidy.[216] Furthermore, in *Graphite electrode systems (India)*, the Commission found that it is not relevant that the subsidy scheme was targeted at a unit of the company that did not itself produce the product concerned. Any benefit to one of the units of the company is considered to be sufficient.[217]

This scenario, focusing on indirect benefits through transfers within a control group, is most likely to raise issues in ex officio investigations (similar to the trade defence cases summarised above).[218]

---

215 Council Regulation (EC) 1599/1999 of 12 July 1999 imposing a definitive countervailing duty and collecting definitively the provisional duty imposed on stainless steel wires with a diameter of 1 mm or more originating in India and terminating the proceeding concerning imports of stainless steel wires with a diameter of 1 mm or more originating in the Republic of Korea [1999] OJ L189/1, recital 48.

216 Regulation 713/2005 [2005] OJ L121/1 (n 174), recital 135.

217 Council Regulation (EC) 1628/2004 of 13 September 2004 imposing a definitive countervailing duty and collecting definitively the provisional duty imposed on imports of certain graphite electrode systems originating in India [2004] OJ L295/4, recital 19.

218 See Chapter VI.

The other two FSR tools approach this issue differently. For investigations using the M&A tool, Articles 22(4) and 23 FSR expressly state that all financial contributions to the entire control group will always be in scope. By contrast, the public procurement tool takes a narrower view of the group of entities that are considered potential recipients of relevant financial contributions.[219] For example, for the main bidder, only the economic operator submitting a bid, its subsidiaries without commercial independence, and its parents would be considered relevant recipients of financial contributions. Contributions to corporate affiliates outside this group do not fall within the scope of public procurement notifications. Moreover, for main suppliers and subcontractors, only contributions to the entity entering into a contract with the main bidder would be in scope, but not contributions to the main supplier's or subcontractor's corporate affiliates.[220] These rules on in-scope entities preclude consideration of intra-group transfers of subsidies from an entity that is out of scope to an entity that is considered a potential recipient of relevant financial contributions, subject to the FSR's anti-circumvention rules.[221]

C.1.3.2 *Indirect Benefits for a Specific Recipient*

With respect to the second scenario, EU State aid law has confirmed that an advantage can be conferred on companies even if State resources are only indirectly transferred to them. Essentially, an indirect advantage exists when the measure is neutral on its face, but is designed in such a way that, in practice, it benefits identifiable recipients or a group of recipients even though they are not the direct recipients of government funds.

For instance, in *Mediaset*, the Court agreed with the Commission that the grant by Italy of a subsidy to final consumers for the purchase of certain digital terrestrial decoders constituted State aid because it conferred an indirect advantage to digital terrestrial broadcasters offering pay-for-TV services and to digital cable pay-for-TV operators, as compared with satellite broadcasters.[222]

C.1.3.3 *Pass-through of Benefits in a Supply Chain*

What position the Commission will take in respect of the third scenario remains uncertain. State aid law has confirmed that the expansive interpretation of what constitutes an 'indirect benefit' must be distinguished from the mere secondary economic effects of a measure. According to the Commission Notice on the notion of State aid, State measures might, for example, result in an increased output (which should also lead to lower prices). This would not be considered State aid, unless the measure was designed to channel its secondary effects towards identifiable recipients.[223] Applied to the FSR, this approach would mean that where a notifying party has purchased products or services at low prices reflecting subsidies that the supplier has received in a third country (not

---

219 FSR Regulation 2022/2560 [2022] OJ L330/1 (n 1), art 28(1)(b).

220 ibid, art 29(6).

221 See Chapter VII.

222 Case C-403/10 P *Mediaset SpA v European Commission* EU:C:2011:533, paras 73–77.

223 Commission Notice on the notion of State aid [2016] OJ C262/1 (n 42), para 116 and fn 181.

specifically targeting the notifying party), these advantages should not be attributable to the notifying party.

By contrast, in anti-subsidy investigations a benefit arising from financial contributions granted to upstream producers of goods passed through to downstream purchasers might, in certain circumstances, be considered relevant at the downstream level. For example, in *Certain rainbow trout (Türkiye)*,[224] the Commission considered that a direct subsidy to producers of trout also benefitted exporting producers that did not produce trout (and did not receive the subsidy) but that purchased trout for processing. For that purpose, the Commission relied on the fact that the purchase price of live or chilled trout was below the cost of farming.[225] By comparison, in *Biodiesel (USA)*, regional tax exemption schemes were found by the Commission not to be countervailable as they granted benefits only to consumers, rather than to the manufacturers, producers, exporters or transporters of biodiesel.[226] However, in the same case, with respect to another scheme, the Commission found that a company 'indirectly received benefits' because it used a factoring system to outsource the blending activity (which established the eligibility to claim the so-called blender's credit) to an unrelated company that claimed the credit and then paid the money back to the outsourcer.[227]

Adopting this broad approach in investigations triggered by M&A or public procurement notifications seems untenable because it would make the FSR notification mechanism impracticable: the administrative burden and legal uncertainty created for notifying parties would undermine the effectiveness of the FSR's entire notification and control system. At the same time, the Commission might consider adopting a broad view of benefits passing through in a supply chain in ex officio investigations, where concerns about the administrative burden, predictability and legal certainty might be less relevant. However, should the Commission take that position in ex officio investigations, it would mean that different understandings of the pass-through effects would be applied under each of the three tools envisaged by the FSR. This might mean that a more restrictive view in the context of the notification tools would restrict the Commission's interpretative flexibility in ex officio investigations.

---

224 Commission Implementing Regulation (EU) 1195/2014 of 29 October 2014 imposing a provisional countervailing duty on imports of certain rainbow trout originating in Turkey [2014] OJ L319/1, recitals 52–58.

225 See, Van Bael & Bellis (n 110) 635.

226 Commission Regulation (EC) 194/2009 of 11 March 2009 imposing a provisional countervailing duty on imports of biodiesel originating in the United States of America [2009] OJ L67/50, recitals 97 and 134, and Council Regulation (EC) 598/2009 of 7 July 2009 imposing a definitive countervailing duty and collecting definitively the provisional duty imposed on imports of biodiesel originating in the United States of America [2009] OJ L179/1, recital 68. [2009] OJ L179/1.

227 ibid, recitals 97 and 134; Regulation 598/2009 [2009] OJ L179/1, recital 60.

How to determine whether a financial contribution conferred a benefit?

- assess whether the financial contribution was obtained under normal market conditions
- rely on a comparative benchmark
- if there is no comparative benchmark, rely on adjusted or alternative benchmarks that are established on generally accepted assessment methods
- apply a presumption that a competitive, transparent and non-discriminatory tender procedure corresponds with normal market conditions
- check whether a benefit may be passed on from a company not active in the EU to a company engaged in an economic activity in the EU, and whether this could be relevant in the context of an FSR investigation

C.2 The Financial Contribution Must Be Provided to an Entity Engaging in Economic Activity in the Internal Market

The benefit must be conferred to 'an undertaking engaging in an economic activity in the internal market'. Those undertakings may be private or public, as specified in Article 1(2) FSR, irrespective of their place of establishment. This approach echoes the broad concept of an 'undertaking' in EU competition law, understood to cover any entity engaged in an economic activity, regardless of its legal status and how it is financed.[228]

Article 1(2) FSR specifies that '[a]mong others, an undertaking acquiring control of or merging with an undertaking established in the Union or an undertaking participating in a public procurement procedure in the Union is considered to be engaging in an economic activity in the internal market'.

The requirement of an economic activity in the internal market might affect the question of when a supplier could become a notifying party under the FSR's public procurement tool. This would not be an issue if the supplier is located in the EU or has sales into the EU. However, there might be situations where the supplier is located in a third country and sells in the third country to a customer that in turn participates in an EU tender. According to Articles 28(1)(b) and 29(5) FSR, if the supplier is a 'main' supplier, it would in principle become a notifying party. However, there would be an argument that the subsidies which the main supplier has received are not subject to the FSR because the main supplier has no 'economic activity' in the EU.

Recital 16 clarifies that a financial contribution provided exclusively for non-economic activities does not constitute a foreign subsidy. Nevertheless, if there is evidence that a financial contribution for non-economic activities is used to cross-subsidise the

---

[228] Case C-222/04 *Ministero dell'Economia e delle Finanze v Cassa di Risparmio di Firenze SpA* EU:C:2006:8, paras 107 and 108; Case T-461/13 *Kingdom of Spain v European Commission* EU:T:2015:891, para 35.

economic activity of a company, it may amount to a foreign subsidy falling within the scope of the FSR.

> *When is a company engaging in economic activity in the internal market?*
>
> - broad concept
> - the company can be private or public
> - carrying out economic activities in the EU internal market might require, at least, sales into the EU
> - the place of establishment is irrelevant

D. Which is 'Limited to One or More Undertakings or Industries'

According to Article 3(2) FSR, the financial contribution conferring a benefit must be 'limited, in law or in fact, to one or more undertakings or industries'. Recital 14 clarifies that for a 'foreign subsidy' within the meaning of the FSR to exist, the benefit conferred must be specific, in law or in fact, and should be conferred on one or more companies or industries.

This selectivity or specificity condition is taken from EU State aid law and the EU and WTO subsidies regimes. Before discussing these conditions in more detail, it should be noted that under the FSR, selectivity or specificity are relevant only to determine whether a financial contribution constitutes a subsidy. Even generally applicable (non-specific or non-selective) measures count as financial contributions towards contribution thresholds, and must be reported unless specifically exempted from the reporting requirements.

In EU State aid law, only measures favouring 'certain undertakings or the production of certain goods', ie, measures that provide a selective advantage to certain companies, fall within the scope of Article 107(1) TFEU. In other words, aid measures that are generally available do not constitute State aid. For instance, the Commission found in *Tax Support Measure* that a tax incentive available to Latvian taxpayers with outstanding tax debts, which was aimed at waiving the late payment interest rate and 90% of the audit penalty otherwise due, did not constitute State aid because it applied equally to all taxpayers without providing any form of selective advantage.[229]

The measure can be selective because it applies only to certain companies or certain sectors of the economy in a given Member State (material selectivity) or it favours companies in a specific area or region (regional selectivity). Furthermore, a financial contribution conferring a benefit can be *de jure* or *de facto* specific. *De jure* specificity means that the law governing the measure formally and expressly limits the

---

229 *Tax Support Measure (TSM)* (Case OMP/SA.33183) (Latvia) [2013] OJ C1/1, paras 16–24.

availability of the measure to certain beneficiaries. *De facto* specificity exists where the measure is generally applicable on its face, but its structure and operation result in significantly favouring a particular company or group of companies.[230]

As explained by the CJEU, the assessment of the selectivity of a measure under EU State aid law requires a determination of whether the measure favours 'certain undertakings or the production of certain goods' as compared to other companies which, based on the objective pursued by that regime, are in a comparable factual and legal situation and who accordingly suffer different treatment that is, in essence, discriminatory.[231]

The assessment of *de jure* selective measures under EU State aid law is often relatively straightforward (for example, in case of a capital injection for a single company). The assessment is usually less clear when the measures at stake are structured in general and non-selective terms,[232] as is the case for most tax measures. In this regard, there is some guidance under EU State aid law on how the Commission determines whether the measure is *de facto* selective, which implies an increased burden of proof for the Commission.

To determine *de facto* selectivity, the Commission typically applies a three-step test in tax cases. This test is aimed at assessing whether the measure at issue introduces, between operators that are, in the light of the objective pursued by the general tax system concerned, in a comparable factual and legal situation, a distinction that is not justified by the nature and general structure of that system.[233] First, the Commission identifies the reference system – in other words, the 'normal' tax system applicable in the Member State concerned. Second, the Commission assesses whether the tax measure at issue derogates from that reference system, in so far as it differentiates between operators who, in the light of the objective pursued by that system, are in a comparable factual and legal situation. Third, if that is the case, the Commission verifies whether that differentiation results from the nature or general structure of the system of which those measures form part.[234]

For example, in *World Duty Free Group*, the CJEU assessed a deduction from the taxable base for corporation tax in the form of an amortisation of the goodwill resulting from the acquisition by companies, resident for tax purposes in Spain, of at least 5% shareholdings in companies resident for tax purposes outside that Member State. The tax measure was generally accessible for essentially all companies. However, the CJEU found it conferred a selective advantage, because the measure at issue 'may be regarded as selective if it benefits undertakings carrying out cross-border transactions, in particular investment transactions, and is to the disadvantage of other undertakings which, while

---

230 See, eg, Joined Cases C-106/09 P and C-107/09 P *European Commission v Gibraltar* EU:C:2011:732, paras 101 and following.

231 See, eg, *Mediaset SpA* (n 222), para 36; *European Commission v Gibraltar* (n 230), paras 75 and 101; Case C-518/13 *R (on the application of Eventech Ltd) v Parking Adjudicator* EU:C:2015:9, paras 53–55; Case C-15/14 P *European Commission v MOL Magyar Olaj- és Gázipari Nyrt* EU:C:2015:362, para 59; Case C-20/15 P *European Commission v World Duty Free Group SA* EU:C:2016:981, para 54.

232 Commission Notice on the notion of State aid [2016] OJ C262/1 (n 42), para 127.

233 *European Commission v World Duty Free Group SA* (n 231), para 60.

234 *Fiat Chrysler Finance Europe* (n137), para 68.

in a comparable factual and legal situation, in the light of the objective pursued by the tax system concerned, carry out other transactions of the same kind within the national territory'.[235]

Likewise, under the Basic Anti-Subsidy Regulation, financial assistance provided by a government to its citizens and undertakings is not considered a subsidy as long as that assistance does not favour one company, industry or group of industries over others. In *Steel Wires (India, Korea)*,[236] the Commission explained the concept of specificity[237] in the following terms:

> 'The basic principle of specificity is that a subsidy that distorts the allocation of resources within an economy by favouring certain enterprises over others should be subject to countervailing measures if it causes injury [...]. If specificity under the [SCM Agreement] is to make any sense, it must cover situations where governments make subsidies subject to conditions which they know in advance will severely restrict the number of firms eligible to apply; such subsidies are designed to favour certain enterprises over others.'

In the EU and WTO subsidies regimes, *de jure* specificity arises where the terms of access to the subsidy by the granting authority, or the legislation pursuant to which the granting authority operates, explicitly favour an enterprise, industry or group of enterprises (for example, Company X or the steel industry). For that reason, the Commission has found that there was no *de jure* specificity where reductions in the price of electricity were available to any company with a relatively high consumption,[238] or where a subsidy was granted to encourage the use of renewable energy.[239]

As a result, *de facto* specificity arises where the subsidy, in the manner in which it is used, favours certain companies or industries by imposing conditions on access to the scheme which have the effect that only those specific companies or sectors may qualify. Article 4(1)(c) Basic Anti-Subsidy Regulation identifies the following relevant factors: 'use of a subsidy programme by a limited number of certain enterprises; predominant use by certain enterprises; the granting of disproportionately large amounts of subsidy

---

235 *European Commission v World Duty Free Group SA* (n 231), para 119.

236 Regulation 1599/1999 [1999] OJ L189/1 (n 215) recitals 67–68.

237 Although the concept of specificity is central under the Basic Anti-Subsidy Regulation and the SCM Agreement, two important distinctions must be drawn. First, the element of specificity does not form part of the definition of a 'subsidy' in Basic Anti-Subsidy Regulation (n 32), art 3 and SCM Agreement (n 2), art 1. However, similar to the FSR, the specificity of a subsidy is a requirement for the adoption of countervailing action against subsidised imports under the Basic Anti-Subsidy Regulation and Part V of the SCM Agreement, as well as a requirement for the challenge of an actionable subsidy in WTO dispute settlement. Second, prohibited subsidies, namely subsidies that are contingent, in law or in fact, upon either export performance or the use of domestic over imported products are deemed to be specific (see, Regulation (EU) 2016/1036 of the European Parliament and of the Council of 8 June 2016 on protection against dumped imports from countries not members of the European Union (Basic Anti-Dumping Regulation) [2016] OJ L176/21, art 4(4); SCM Agreement art 2.3.

238 Commission Regulation (EC) 618/1999 of 23 March 1999 imposing a provisional countervailing duty on imports of stainless steel wire having a diameter of 1mm or more originating in India and the Republic of Korea [1999] OJ L79/25, recital 203.

239 Commission Decision of 20 December 2012 terminating the anti-subsidy proceeding concerning imports of bioethanol originating in the United States of America and terminating the registration of such imports imposed by Regulation (EU) No 771/2012 [2012] OJ L352/70, recital 133.

to certain enterprises; the manner in which discretion has been exercised by the granting authority in the decision to grant a subsidy. In this regard, information on the frequency with which applications for a subsidy are refused or approved and the reasons for such decisions shall, in particular, be considered'.

The Commission tends to broadly apply the concept of *de facto* specificity. Schemes which are available to a large portion of the industry nevertheless have been found to be specific. For example, in *DRAMs (dynamic random access memories) (Korea)*,[240] the Commission concluded that a programme through which the Korean Development Bank engaged in the subscription, acceptance and investment or guarantee of debentures issued to finance certain projects or bonds issued by public organisations, was *de facto* specific because: (i) the programme was used by a limited number of companies, (ii) there was a predominant use by certain companies, and (iii) disproportionately large amounts of the subsidy were granted to certain companies. In the same investigation,[241] the Commission concluded that a subsidy scheme was *de facto* specific because, despite more than 200 companies fulfilling the eligibility criteria, the programme in question was in practice only used by six companies, four of which belonged to the same group of companies.

When considering tax or duty arrangements, the Commission has found specificity where:[242]

- tax benefits are available to certain industries or businesses or to certain enterprises;[243]
- duty exemptions are available to companies within a designated geographical region;[244]
- import duty exemptions are in fact disproportionately used by certain industry sectors;[245]
- tax credits are available only to companies investing in a certain type of investment, for example, stocks issued by certain (other) companies;[246] and
- certain companies are granted a duty exemption for 10 years, although the duty exemption scheme is, by law, only available for 5 years.[247]

So far, no guidance has been provided by the Commission on how it will assess *de facto* selectivity under the FSR.

---

240 Regulation 1480/2003 [2003] OJ L212/1 (n 160), recital 65.

241 ibid, recital 65.

242 See, Van Bael & Bellis (n 110) 641–642.

243 Regulation 1599/1999 [1999] OJ L189/1 (n 215), recital 86.

244 Commission Regulation (EU) 115/2012 of 9 February 2012 imposing a provisional countervailing duty on imports of certain stainless steel fasteners and parts thereof originating in India [2012] OJ L38/6, recital 113.

245 Commission Decision 284/2000/ECSC [2000] OJ L31/44 (n 140), recital 116; Commission Regulation (EC) 1741/2000 of 3 August 2000 imposing a provisional countervailing duty on imports of polyethylene terephthalate (PET) originating in India, Malaysia, Taiwan and Thailand [2000] OJ L199/6, recital 163.

246 ibid, recital 83; ibid, recital 149.

247 Council Regulation (EC) 1354/2008 of 18 December 2008 amending Regulation (EC) 1628/2004 imposing a definitive countervailing duty on imports of certain graphite electrode systems originating in India and Regulation (EC) 1629/2004 imposing a definitive anti-dumping duty on imports of certain graphite electrode systems originating in India [2008] OJ L350/24, recital 74.

Relevant factors for determining whether a financial contribution is specific

- legislation governing the measure formally and expressly limits the availability of the measure to certain companies or industries (*de jure* specificity)
- the structure and operation of the measure disproportionately favours certain companies or industries (*de facto* specificity)
- a measure limits benefits to companies in certain geographic regions

3. The Notion of a Foreign Subsidy Distorting the Internal Market

A. *General Principles*

A.1 Framework for the Distortion Analysis

Once the existence of a foreign subsidy has been established, the Commission must assess on a case-by-case basis whether that subsidy distorts the internal market.[248]

Under EU State aid law, the 'distortion of competition' requirement is easily met. Once an aid is found, it is deemed to distort or threaten to distort competition.[249] As explained in the Commission Notice on the notion of State aid, it is typically sufficient that the aid gives the beneficiary an advantage by relieving it of expenses it would otherwise have had to bear in the course of its day-to-day business operations.[250]

This approach is not transferable to the FSR. EU State aid is per definition related to an EU activity, because it is granted by an EU Member State to EU recipients active in the single market. In contrast, the FSR captures subsidies that might be completely unrelated to activities in the EU. There is therefore no justification for a truncated, State aid law-type distortion analysis. It follows that the assessment of the distortion condition under the FSR requires the Commission to engage in an in-depth and detailed assessment, and to find a distortion only when supported by a consistent and persuasive body of evidence showing its effects on competition in the EU.

Article 4(1) FSR confirms that establishing a 'distortion' requires a more demanding investigation than under EU State aid law. It clarifies that a distortion may be established only if there is evidence that 'a foreign subsidy is liable to improve the competitive

248 At the same time, the question of distortion of the internal market is immaterial to the FSR notification obligations.

249 Commission Notice on the notion of State aid [2016] OJ C262/1 (n 42), point 187.

250 ibid, point 189.

position of an undertaking active in the internal market' and that the 'foreign subsidy actually or potentially negatively affects competition in the internal market'. Thus, Article 4 FSR establishes a two-step distortion test, requiring evidence of: (i) the recipient's improved competitive position, *and* (ii) harm to competition. That test requires the Commission to demonstrate the effects of a subsidy before it may conclude that there is a distortion of competition in the internal market.

Like any other effects-based test, Article 4 requires the Commission to engage in an analysis of a counterfactual scenario, comparing the actual state of the market (in which the subsidy has been received) with an assessment of how the market likely would have developed absent the subsidy. Counterfactual analysis does not require establishing the effects of a subsidy with mathematical precision. Nevertheless, the Commission must at least outline a realistic scenario of competition in the market absent the subsidy, based on a 'sufficiently cogent and consistent body of evidence.'[251]

Thus, in an effects-based analysis, the Commission is to: (i) identify the main characteristics of the subsidies and the market(s) they might affect, (ii) develop a theory of harm explaining the likely impact of the subsidies, and (iii) provide evidence showing market impact, or likely market impact, consistent with the theory of harm (which would include a counterfactual analysis).[252]

A.2 Relevant Factors in the Distortion Analysis

The FSR provides some guidance for how to conduct the distortion analysis. For certain types of subsidies, distortion is presumed, shifting the burden to the recipient to establish the absence of harmful effects. The FSR also provides a non-exhaustive (although vague) list of indicative factors that are relevant for the distortion assessment. Finally, the FSR provides for *de minimis* thresholds under which a foreign subsidy is not considered to have a harmful impact on the internal market, irrespective of its nature.

A.2.1 Foreign Subsidies that Are Likely to Distort the Internal Market

Article 5 lists subsidies that, by their nature, are likely to cause a distortion in the internal market. In particular, Article 5 lists:

- a foreign subsidy granted to an ailing undertaking, meaning an undertaking which will likely go out of business in the short or medium term in the absence of any subsidy, unless there is a restructuring plan that is capable of leading to the long-term viability of that undertaking and includes a significant own contribution by the undertaking;

---

251 See, eg, Case C-382/12 P *MasterCard Inc v European Commission* EU:C:2014:2201, paras 108 and 111; Case C-376/20 P *European Commission v EFTA Surveillance Authority* EU:C:2023:561, paras 84–87 and 130. Although these judgments concerned EU competition and merger control law, the insight that establishing harmful effects requires an analysis of market absent the conduct or transaction under investigation would have general applicability.

252 See also N Robbins and F Couto, 'Familiar Tools in Foreign Settings: Practical Considerations for Complying with the New Foreign Subsidies Regulation' (Spring 2023) 2(1) *Antitrust Chronicle* 22.

- a foreign subsidy in the form of an unlimited guarantee for debts or liabilities of the undertaking, without any limitation as to the amount or the duration of such a guarantee;
- an export financing measure that is not in line with the OECD Arrangement (OECD Arrangement) on Officially Supported Export Credits;
- a foreign subsidy directly facilitating a concentration; and
- a foreign subsidy enabling an undertaking to submit an unduly advantageous tender, on the basis of which the undertaking could be awarded a public procurement contract.

The FSR does not provide much explanation for this selection of Article 5 subsidies. Presumably, the subsidies listed in Article 5 were chosen because the legislator assumed that they most likely might lead to the exclusion of potentially more efficient unsubsidised competitors that are unable to compete on an equal footing.

The list seeks to offer some degree of predictability to companies when determining whether a financial contribution is likely to raise material concerns under the FSR. Importantly, the list also helps notifying parties to focus early in the preparatory process on developing arguments to overcome the presumption that those subsidies are, in fact, distortive.

For some of the subsidies listed in Article 5, the FSR does provide a reasonable degree of legal certainty. For example, for aid granted to ailing companies, the Commission has issued detailed guidelines on State aid for rescuing and restructuring non-financial companies in difficulty (Guidelines on rescue and restructuring aid),[253] which provide the conditions under which aid measures may be considered compatible with the internal market on the basis of Article 107(3)(c) TFEU. The Guidelines on rescue and restructuring aid were adopted under the assumption that '[r]escue and restructuring aid are among the most distortive types of State aid',[254] but sometimes they might be necessary to correct disparities caused by market failures or to ensure economic and social cohesion.[255]

As explained in the Guidelines, restructuring aid cannot be limited to financial aid designed to make up for past losses without tackling the reasons for those losses. On the contrary, the aid must restore the beneficiary's long-term viability on the basis of an appropriate restructuring plan[256] and entail a significant contribution to the restructuring costs from the own resources of the aid beneficiary.[257]

The FSR's reference to subsidies for ailing companies is based on the approach under EU State aid law. In this sense, it is not surprising that the conditions under the FSR Implementing Regulation to assess whether a foreign subsidy was granted to an 'ailing undertaking' mirror those listed in the Guidelines on rescue and restructuring aid to

---

253 Commission Communication Guidelines on State aid for Rescuing and Restructuring Non-Financial Undertakings in Difficulty [2014] OJ C249/1.
254 ibid, para 6.
255 ibid, para 36.
256 ibid, paras 45–52.
257 ibid, paras 62–64.

identify an 'undertaking in difficulty'.[258] As a result, it is reasonable to assume that a foreign subsidy granted to an ailing company that appears to meet the conditions in the Guidelines on rescue and restructuring aid should be – in principle – considered as not being distortive.

Reasonable legal certainty also exists for identifying export financing measures not in line with the OECD Arrangement on Officially Supported Export Credits, a non-binding agreement among the participating jurisdictions[259] which aims to provide a framework for the orderly use of officially supported export credits .[260] In essence, the OECD Arrangement provides for a series of detailed limitations on the financing terms and conditions to be applied to export credits (eg, repayment terms, minimum premium rate, minimum interest rates), as well as the use of tied aid. These limitations are relevant to assess, in practice, whether a foreign subsidy in the form of an export financing measure is likely to distort the internal market. The Commission has clarified that, for the purpose of Article 5, the export financing measure at issue is to be assessed against the OECD Arrangement regardless of whether the grantor country is a member of the OECD.[261]

For other subsidies listed in Article 5, however, the practical guidance is limited. For example, as discussed in greater detail below, the FSR does not explain how to identify a subsidy that 'directly facilitates' a transaction or 'enables the recipient to submit an unduly advantageous tender'. A narrow interpretation of these terms would suggest that only direct cash infusions or grants with the explicit purpose of supporting the recipient in a transaction or procurement bid should be considered Article 5 subsidies. But there is nothing in the FSR that would prevent the Commission from taking a more expansive view. This uncertainty is particularly problematic because subsidies deemed to fall under Article 5 require detailed information in the notification forms (Forms FS-CO and FS-PP). Disagreements with the Commission about characterising certain subsidies as 'directly facilitating' a transaction or 'enabling an unduly advantageous tender' could result in material delays in the pre-notification process.

A recipient can rebut the presumption of distortion by demonstrating that the foreign subsidy at issue did not improve the competitive position of that beneficiary in the EU and, thus, does not actually or potentially negatively affect competition in the internal market. For example, a notifying party might be able to demonstrate that a subsidiary receiving a subsidy to prevent it from going out of business has only local operations limited to a third country and no connection with the notifying party's activities in the EU. Similarly, it might be relevant that export financing measures were clearly limited to exports into third countries and had no connection with the recipient's EU activities. Evidence supporting this claim might not conclusively overcome the presumption, but

---

258 See, in this regard, FSR Implementing Regulation 2023/1441 [2023] OJ L177/1 (n 30), Annex I paras 5.1.1–5.1.1.5. and ibid, Annex II paras 3.1.1–3.1.1.4.2., as well as the Commission Communication Guidelines on Rescuing and Restructuring Aid (n 253), para 20. See Chapter II 4.B below.

259 Australia, Canada, the EU, Japan, Korea, New Zealand, Norway, Switzerland, Turkey, the United Kingdom, and the United States.

260 OECD Arrangement on Officially Supported Export Credits, para 1 <https://www.oecd.org/officialdocuments/publicdisplaydocumentpdf/?cote=TAD/PG(2023)7&docLanguage=en> (accessed 18 December 2023).

261 See FSR M&A FAQs, question 21 (n 31).

it might make it more difficult for the Commission to maintain that it can rely on the presumption and is not required to engage in a fuller analysis of all relevant evidence to establish distortive effects.

Generally, the FSR's indicative factors for assessing the potential harmfulness of a foreign subsidy, discussed below, would also be relevant when the recipient of an Article 5 subsidy seeks to rebut the presumption of distortion.

A.2.2 Indicative Factors for Assessing the Potential Harmfulness of a Foreign Subsidy

Article 4(1) FSR provides a non-exhaustive list of indicators on the basis of which the Commission must assess the harmfulness of a particular subsidy and, as discussed above, establish that the subsidy has harmful effects on competition in the internal market. These indicators are:

- the amount of the foreign subsidy in absolute terms or in relation to the size of the market or to the value of the investment;
- the nature of the foreign subsidy;
- the situation of the company, including its size and the markets or sectors concerned;
- the level and evolution of economic activity of the company in the internal market; and
- the purpose and conditions attached to the foreign subsidy as well as its use on the internal market.

Recital 19 FSR indicates how these indicators might be relevant:

- the size of the subsidy matters because large subsidies can be particularly distortive to competition in the internal market. In the context of a concentration, a foreign subsidy that covers a substantial part of the purchase price of the target company is likely to be distortive. Moreover, distortions are likely to exist where the foreign subsidy covers a substantial part of the estimated value of a contract to be awarded in a public procurement procedure;
- a foreign subsidy granted for operating costs is considered more likely to distort competition in the internal market than if it is granted for investments costs;
- a foreign subsidy granted to small and medium-sized enterprises (SMEs) will be considered less likely to cause distortions than a foreign subsidy granted to large undertakings;
- a foreign subsidy granted in markets characterised by overcapacity or leading to overcapacity (in which unsustainable assets are sustained or investment in capacity expansions that would otherwise not have been built are encouraged) are likely to cause distortions;
- foreign subsidies can be especially problematic if they are granted to companies that operate in markets in which there are low levels of competition, because those subsidies can tilt the level playing field by further exacerbating a malfunctioning market with high entry barriers or can further consolidate market concentration; and

- a foreign subsidy granted to an undertaking which has a low degree of activity in the internal market (eg, in terms of turnover) is less likely to cause distortion than a subsidy granted to a company that has a more significant level of activity in the internal market.

Further guidance on how the Commission might evaluate these indicators can be found in the Commission's White Paper. The White Paper is not binding and is merely a preparatory document (not a guidance paper or notice issued for the purpose of interpreting the FSR). Nevertheless, it might capture the Commission's intended approach when evaluating subsidies. The White paper refers to a 'collection of indicators related to the subsidised acquisition and the relevant market situation'.[262] These indicators, which differ from the general set included in Article 4 FSR, include:[263]

- the *relative size of the subsidy*: the higher the amount of a subsidy in relative terms, the more likely it is to have a negative impact on competition in the internal market;
- the *situation of the beneficiary*: (i) the larger the EU target or the acquirer, the more likely that the subsidised acquisition is distortive, and, similarly, (ii) the more production capacity of the EU target or the acquirer is unutilised, the more likely a subsidised acquisition creates a distortion;
- the *situation on the market(s) concerned*: relevant considerations include the fact that subsidised acquisitions where the EU target is active in markets with structural excess capacity are more likely to cause a distortion. Similarly, subsidised acquisitions where the EU target is active in markets with a high degree of concentration or in fast-growing high-tech markets might more likely cause a distortion. The existence of competing offers can be used to assess whether a subsidy is distortive, but in itself not determinative;
- the *level of activity in the internal market of the parties concerned*: subsidised acquisitions where the parties, notably the target company, have limited activities in the internal market in comparison with their global activities are less likely to distort the internal market; and
- *privileged access by the beneficiary to its domestic market* (through measures equivalent to special or exclusive rights) leading to an artificial competitive advantage that could be leveraged in the EU internal market and thereby exacerbates the distortive effect of the foreign subsidy.

Nevertheless, despite these explanations, the indicators relevant for establishing a distortion remain vague, resulting in uncertainty about how the Commission will assess this condition in practice. In any event, it will be important that the Commission, in a distortion assessment, establishes how, in a concrete case, the foreign subsidy improved the competitive position of the recipient *and* distorted competition in the internal market, compared to a no-subsidy scenario.

---

262 White Paper COM (2020) 253 final (n 9) 26.
263 ibid 26–27.

Recital 73 FSR invites the Commission to publish and regularly update guidelines regarding the criteria for determining the existence of a distortion of competition in the internal market caused by a foreign subsidy.

Finally, the Article 4 criteria are relevant for all foreign subsidies, in particular those that are to be reported in a summary manner in the notification forms (Forms FS-CO and FS-PP). But, they can also provide guidance for evaluating the effects of Article 5 subsidies and for identifying arguments to overcome the presumption of a distortion.

A.2.3 Foreign Subsidies that are Unlikely to Distort Competition in the Internal Market

Article 4 FSR, which includes a reference to the Commission's 2013 Regulation defining *de minimis* State aid,[264] identifies situations in which a foreign subsidy is unlikely to distort competition in the internal market:[265]

- if the total amount of the foreign subsidy is below € 4 million over a consecutive period of three fiscal years;
- if the total amount of the foreign subsidy does not exceed the *de minimis* amount of €200,000 per subsidy granted per third country to a single recipient over any period of three fiscal years;[266] or
- if a foreign subsidy is aimed at making up for the damage caused by natural disasters or exceptional occurrences.

A.2.4 Foreign Subsidies that Cannot Be Remedied under the FSR

Subsidies that cannot be remedied under the FSR, such as those falling within the scope of the SCM Agreement, are only relevant for determining whether the relevant notification thresholds are met, but should be excluded from the distortion analysis. This is the case because a distortion analysis cannot be separated from any remedies that the Commission may impose at the end of an in-depth investigation.[267]

In principle, the same limitation should apply to subsidies that are equivalent to aid that is considered compatible with EU State aid law. Those subsidies should be considered as not

---

264 Commission Regulation (EU) 1407/2013 of 18 December 2013 on the application of Articles 107 and 108 of the Treaty on the Functioning of the European Union to de minimis aid (De Minimis Aid Regulation) [2013] OJ L352/1. This Regulation has been replaced by Commission Regulation (EU) 2023/2831 of 13 December 2023 on the application of Articles 107 and 108 of the Treaty on the Functioning of the European Union to de minimis aid [2023] OJ L2023/2831.

265 See Chapter III 3.B.1 , for a discussion of how these concepts are reflected in the notification forms.

266 Regulation 1407/2013 [2013] OJ L352/1 (n 264), art 3(2). The de minimis threshold is reduced to €100,000 for subsidies granted for road freight transport and does not apply when used for the acquisition of road freight transport vehicles. However, the 2023 Regulation on de minimis aid has raised the de minimis threshold to €300,000 and eliminated the lower threshold for freight transport: Commission Regulation (EU) 2023/2831 of 13 December 2023 on the application of Articles 107 and 108 of the Treaty on the Functioning of the European Union to de minimis aid, [2023] OJ L2023/2831. Article 4(3) FSR explicitly refers to the 2013 Regulation (and the thresholds set forth therein). The Commission will likely need to clarify, in further guidance or FAQs, whether the higher de minimis threshold in the 2023 Regulation is automatically incorporated in the FSR. In practice, the Commission's interest will be to seek to ensure alignment between EU State aid rules and the FSR.

267 See also FSR Public Procurement FAQs, 'Implementation issues', question 11 (n 31).

distortive under the FSR and should not be remedied by the Commission under this instrument. This result would be required by the obligation not to discriminate under WTO rules. It also would be consistent with recital 9 FSR, which provides that the FSR 'should be applied and interpreted in light of the relevant Union legislation, including that relating to State aid'.

The compatibility assessment under the State aid regime therefore is likely to have an impact on the distortion analysis under the FSR. Nevertheless, in certain situations a determination of whether a foreign subsidy is equivalent to an EU State aid compatible measure might require a complex exercise, and the Commission might have to carry out an in-depth assessment of the foreign subsidy.

However, the Commission is yet to clarify at what point in its assessment following a notification it will no longer take into account subsidies that cannot be remedied under the FSR. In any event, notifying subsidies that cannot be remedied under the FSR essentially enables an information collection exercise by the Commission, and the EU might wish to use this information to countervail subsidies under EU trade defence instruments.

Which foreign subsidies distort the internal market?

- certain foreign subsidies are presumed to distort competition in the internal market (Article 5 subsidies)
- indicative factors include the amount, nature, purpose and conditions of the foreign subsidy and the situation, the level and evolution of the economic activity of the company (Article 4 subsidies, but also relevant to overcome the distortion presumption in Article 5 FSR)
- reporting requirements in the notification forms (Forms FS-CO and FS-PP) vary depending on whether there is an Article 4 subsidy or an Article 5 subsidy
- foreign subsidies below certain monetary thresholds are unlikely to distort competition in the internal market

B. Distortion Analysis under the M&A Tool

The general principles governing the distortion analysis outlined above apply to all three tools of the FSR. But the FSR limits the Commission's distortion analysis in the context of the M&A tool: distortion must be merger-specific, and the theory of harm must focus on the market for corporate control or on product markets in which the company will be active post-transaction.[268]

---

268 In addition to limitations on the substantive test, the M&A tool also limits the Commission's review powers by specifying that the Commission is able to look only at 'foreign subsidies granted in the three years prior to the conclusion of the agreement, the announcement of the public bid, or the acquisition of a controlling interest.'

B.1 *Distortion Must be Merger-Specific*

Article 19 FSR clarifies that the Commission's assessment, using the M&A tool, is 'limited to the concentration concerned'. The language of Article 19 raises the question of how the Commission will interpret the bounds of 'limited to the concentration' when assessing the distortive effects of subsidies notified under the M&A tool. It is clear from this language that there must be a connection between the distortive subsidy and the concentration (ie, the effects must be *merger-specific*). Consequently, the Commission cannot assess a distortive subsidy that is reported in Form FS-CO but does not affect and is unaffected by the concentration at issue. That said, nothing would prevent the Commission from opening a separate, ex officio investigation into the effects of those subsidies (see Chapter VI).

B.2 *Distortion in the Market for Corporate Control*

The primary intent of the FSR's M&A tool is to address subsidies that have a distortive effect on competition in the market for corporate control. Recital 4 FSR notes that distortive effects in the concentration context could particularly arise 'where such concentrations are fully or partially financed through foreign subsidies'.[269] This wording implies that the market distortions of primary concern are those resulting from the fact that the transaction is completed due to resources – in whole or in part – coming from foreign subsidies. Thus, the distortion would consist in the fact that a company benefitting from foreign subsidies manages to win the competition to become the buyer, the partner to a merger, or the chosen parent of a new JV, to the detriment of other potential deal partners.

The intention to focus on competition on the deal-making market is also evident from the legislative history. The Commission's White Paper proposed a tool to fight distortions 'facilitating the acquisition of EU targets'.[270] In particular, the objective of the M&A tool was to 'ensure that foreign subsidies do not give an unfair advantage to their recipients *when acquiring* (stakes in) other undertakings'.[271] These considerations in the White Paper were also largely reiterated in the FSR Impact Assessment.[272] Consequently, the legislative history and the purpose of the FSR indicate that the assessment of distortive subsidies should be limited to those that facilitate a concentration and thus distort competition on the deal-making market.

Importantly, the FSR requires evidence of an improved *competitive* position and of harmful effects on competition in the internal market. This strongly suggests that concerns regarding the market for corporate control would apply only if there has been some form of competition for the target between the actual buyer and at least another potential buyer. This would not require that the seller have held an auction for the target, but at least that there is evidence that it considered alternative buyers

---

269 FSR Regulation 2022/2560 [2022] OJ L330/1 (n 1), recital 4.

270 White Paper COM (2020) 253 final (n 9) 22.

271 ibid (emphasis added).

272 FSR Impact Assessment SWD (2021) 99 final (n 14).

and their potential offers. If, on the other hand, the transaction is the result of purely bilateral, non-competitive negotiations (for example, resulting from the buyer reaching out to the seller or the seller reaching out only to one potential buyer), there would be no competition in the market for corporate control that a subsidy could distort. A theory of harm focusing on the effects on the market for corporate control would therefore not be applicable.

However, it cannot be excluded that the Commission will adopt a different view and also consider whether the foreign subsidies resulted in a distortion because the transaction would not have taken place absent the subsidy. The counterfactual analysis would, under that understanding, not focus on whether there likely would have been another buyer, but whether the subsidy allowed the buyer to overbid and the transaction likely would not have taken place absent the subsidies.[273] It remains nevertheless difficult to see how such an assessment of the effects on the market for corporate control could be reconciled with the FSR's requirement that, for remedies to be imposed, subsidies must distort 'competition'.

B.3 Distortion in Product Markets

In addition, the Commission likely will interpret its review powers as extending to the distortive effects of a subsidy on the downstream product markets on which the entity will be active post-transaction, provided that these effects are the result of (or perhaps even exacerbated by) the concentration (in other words, are still merger-specific). In defining the scope of the Commission's review under Article 19, the FSR does not expressly indicate that the Commission should specifically assess whether a subsidy *facilitates* the concentration at issue, but merely requires the Commission's review to be limited to the *context* of that concentration.

It is notable that Form FS-CO requires the parties to provide an equal amount of information about foreign contributions received by the *target* of an acquisition as for the notifying parties. However, it is unclear how even substantial subsidies received by the target could distort competition on the market for corporate control (where it is presumably the acquirer with the deepest pocket that has the commercial advantage). Likewise, Form FS-CO requires transaction parties to list the activities of the target in downstream product markets. The acquirer is only required to list its activities to the extent that they overlap with those of the target. It is not immediately clear why the EU legislator considers that that information is relevant to assessing potential distortions in the market for corporate control alone (where presumably only the activities of the acquirer would be relevant).

In light of the requirements in Form FS-CO, the Commission might consider that the effects of subsidies granted to either or both transaction parties could become particularly distortive in the context of the concentration. For instance, if the concentration were to combine two parties that each received subsidies conferring a competitive advantage in a particular downstream market, it could be argued that this advantage

---

273 See, eg, J Azevedo, 'Managing Foreign Subsidies in the EU' (2023) 2(1) *Antitrust Chronicle* 28.

would be further enhanced if they were to be combined. Arguably, such a theory of harm could still fall within the Commission's limitation to assess only 'the concentration concerned'.

C. Distortion Analysis under the Public Procurement Tool

The FSR limits the distortion analysis under the public procurement tool to the procurement project in which the recipient of the foreign subsidies participates. This follows from Article 27 FSR, which provides that the analysis of whether there is a distortion in the internal market 'shall be limited to the public procurement procedure in question'. Any impact of foreign subsidies on the recipient's other activities in the EU is therefore outside the scope of the distortion analysis (although those subsidies would still be reportable). Therefore, the Commission's distortion analysis in the context of the public procurement tool is even more narrowly focused than under the M&A tool.

It is not entirely clear what theory of harm the Commission will use to establish that foreign subsidies are distortive in the procurement context. Article 27 provides that: 'Foreign subsidies that cause or risk causing a distortion in a public procurement procedure shall be understood as foreign subsidies that enable an economic operator to submit a tender that is unduly advantageous in relation to the works, supplies or services concerned'. This language might be understood as replacing the distortion test in Article 4 – which requires evidence that the subsidies likely have improved the competitive position of the recipient *and* negatively affect competition – with a test focusing only on whether the foreign subsidies have enabled the recipient to submit an unduly advantageous tender.

Accordingly, the Commission would only have to establish that the price of the bid submitted by the recipient of the foreign subsidies was lower than the price it would have submitted absent those subsidies. This would still require the Commission to establish a (clear) connection between the foreign subsidies and the price of goods, works, or services offered by the recipient of those subsidies in the public procurement project. The Commission would, however, not be required to establish that the foreign subsidies put the recipient in a position to win the government contract (ie, that competition for the government contract was distorted).

Eliminating the Article 4 test – and the requirement of evidence of a harmful effect on competition – from the distortion analysis in the procurement context would produce curious results. If that were the case, the FSR would be concerned about the 'harm' that the contracting authority/entity might pay too little for the services, products or works it has procured because of foreign subsidies. The impact of the subsidies on the potential outcome of the competitive procurement process would not matter. It would thus be more coherent with the FSR's overall goals if the Commission's distortion analysis also assessed whether the foreign subsidies put the recipient in a position to win the government contract, which it could not have done absent the subsidies.

4. The 'Balancing Test'

If the Commission finds that a foreign subsidy has distortive effects (and, presumably, that these effects are substantial), it is expected to balance the negative and positive effects of the foreign subsidy at issue when deciding whether to intervene, impose redressive measures, or accept commitments. The balancing test can also help the Commission to determine the appropriate type and level of the commitments, or to decide that it should not intervene.

According to Article 6 FSR, the Commission is expected to balance the negative effects of a foreign subsidy in terms of distortion of competition in the internal market, as identified in Articles 4 and 5, and the positive effects on the development of the relevant subsidised economic activity in the EU, as well as on the relevant policy objectives. These policy objectives include environmental protection, the protection of social standards as well as the promotion of research and development.[274] It is unclear how the Commission will take into account, if at all, the environmental benefits that might occur in third countries, although the FSR itself does not preclude such a more comprehensive assessment.

Notably, the FSR does not explicitly list the interest of consumers as a relevant policy objective to be considered in the balancing test, reflecting a general shortcoming of the FSR. The FSR would in principle not preclude including positive effects on consumers in the EU, for example, by considering that subsidies might intensify competition in the EU and therefore benefit consumers. The protection of effective competition is a policy objective of the EU, and therefore could be included in the balancing test. The lack of a specific reference to consumer interests could therefore be remedied through the manner in which the Commission will apply the balancing test.

The FSR's balancing test leaves a significant degree of discretion to the Commission because it requires consideration of parameters that are not comparable and cannot be quantified. Nevertheless, the Commission, when performing a balancing test in an investigation, is expected to at least outline as concretely as possible the distortive effects as well as the benefits, and to try to find objective parameters to compare the two. However, considering that the Commission is inclined to issue guidance only after several years of experience, the uncertainty about the mechanisms of the balancing test will last for the first period of implementation of the FSR.

A. The Balancing Test (the Union Interest Test) under the EU Trade Defence Regime

The FSR balancing test corresponds, to a certain extent, with the Union interest test used in anti-subsidy investigations under the Basic Anti-Subsidy Regulation.

Under Article 31 Basic Anti-Subsidy Regulation, the Commission may refrain from applying countervailing duties, even where subsidisation, injury and a causal link are

---

[274] FSR Regulation 2022/2560 [2022] OJ L330/1 (n 1), recital 21.

established, if it concludes that that remedial action is *not* in the Union interest.[275] When applying the Union interest test, the Commission carries out 'an appraisal of all the various interests taken as a whole, including the interests of the domestic industry and users and consumers'. In other words, it involves assessing whether the need to eliminate the trade distorting effects of injurious subsidisation through the imposition of countervailing duties outweighs any Union interest against that action.

There has been only one case where the Commission decided against the imposition of countervailing duties on the basis of the Union interest.[276] In that case, the Commission focused on the degree of subsidisation in the period covered by the investigation and the resulting injury to the EU industry. It did not examine, for example, the positive effects of the subsidised import flows on the EU downstream industries or EU consumers. The investigation revealed that, although the subsidy at issue had been granted by the foreign government for the most part of the period of investigation, it had been discontinued, thus 'removing the source of the injury'. In those circumstances, the Commission considered that 'the interests of the Community no longer require the collection of a countervailing duty, from the importers concerned, destined to offset the effects of a subsidy already formally discontinued by a foreign government'.[277]

To better understand how the Union interest test is applied, the practice of the Commission in anti-dumping proceedings in which the same Union interest test is used is also instructive. In anti-dumping proceedings, the imposition of anti-dumping measures has never been refused on the grounds of Union interest. This is because the Basic Anti-Subsidy and Anti-Dumping Regulations grant the Commission a wide margin of discretion as to the methods for analysing and weighing the various interests represented by cooperating interested parties.[278]

That being said, the assessment of the Union interest has had an impact on the form of the final measures imposed. In *GOES*,[279] the Commission imposed *ad valorem* duties capped by a minimum import price, a change from the initial *ad valorem* duties it had initially considered, because the investigation revealed that there was a shortage of certain types of the product concerned on the market which affected EU industrial users. The Union interest test also affected the duration of the measures in *Solar Modules and*

---

275 Case T-459/07 *Hangzhou Duralamp Electronics Co Ltd v Council of the European Union* EU:T:2013:369, para 182.

276 Commission Decision 85/233/EEC of 16 April 1985 terminating the anti-subsidy proceeding concerning imports of soya meal originating in Brazil [1985] OJ L106/19. See, however, a recent decision on the termination of an anti-subsidy investigation following the withdrawal of the complaint, Commission Implementing Decision (EU) 2023/617 of 17 March 2023 terminating the anti-subsidy proceeding concerning imports of fatty acid originating in Indonesia [2023] OJ L80/99, recitals 9–11. Where a complaint is withdrawn, the Commission enjoys a wide margin of discretion to continue or terminate an anti-subsidy investigation on the basis of Union interest. See Case T-469/07, *Philips Lighting Poland SA and Philips Lighting BV v Council of the European Union* EU:T:2013:370, para 87.

277 Commission Decision 85/233/EEC [1985] OJ L106/19 (n 276), recital 27.

278 Case T-1/07 *Apache Footwear Ltd and Apache II Footwear Ltd (Qingxin) v Council of the European Union* EU:T:2009:483, para 111.

279 Commission Implementing Regulation (EU) 2015/1953 of 29 October 2015 imposing a definitive anti-dumping duty on imports of certain grain-oriented flat-rolled products of silicon-electrical steel originating in the People's Republic of China, Japan, the Republic of Korea, the Russian Federation and the United States of America [2015] OJ L284/109, recitals 110–112, 147–149 and 169.

Cells.[280] In that case, the Commission decided to limit the extension of the applicable measures to 18 months, rather than the standard five years, after balancing the likely negative effects on the upstream and downstream industries as well as the consumers against the benefits for the Union industry.

The CJEU has emphasised, for anti-dumping investigations, the importance of balancing the various interests of all parties involved when assessing the Union interest. In *T.KUP SAS*,[281] the CJEU held that '[t]he examination of the Union interest in the adoption or maintenance of an anti-dumping measure [...] constitutes a very strict procedural operation which requires a balancing of the interests of all the parties and the assessment of complex economic situations implying a limited review by the EU judicature'.

When assessing the Union interest, the Commission examines successively, where appropriate, the interests of the following interested parties:

- *the interests of the Union industry.* The Commission will typically conclude that, having established that material injury has been caused to the Union industry by the dumped/subsidised imports, the imposition of anti-dumping or countervailing measures is in the interest of the Union industry. The imposition of duties is expected to restore fair competition on the EU market and enable the Union industry to recover. Conversely, the Commission will usually conclude that, in the absence of measures, a further deterioration of the Union industry would be likely;
- *the interests of EU industrial users.* In the vast majority of cases, the Commission found that, on balance, measures should be nevertheless imposed for various reasons, including because the impact of a price increase of the product concerned would be limited when compared to the total cost of production of users[282] or the impact on users would be limited due to the availability of other sources of supply or the possibility of users to pass on the duty to their customers; [283] and
- *the interests of importers, distributors, and traders.* However, in practice, the Commission has always found that the likely impact of the measures would not put the economic activity of these importers, distributors and traders at serious risk because they import the product concerned from various sources and dealt with a variety of other products.[284]

---

280 Commission Implementing Regulation (EU) 2017/367 of 1 March 2017 imposing a definitive anti-dumping duty on imports of crystalline silicon photovoltaic modules and key components (ie cells) originating in or consigned from the People's Republic of China following an expiry review pursuant to Article 11(2) of Regulation (EU) 2016/1036 of the European Parliament and of the Council and terminating the partial interim review investigation pursuant to Article 11(3) of Regulation (EU) 2016/1036 [2017] OJ L56/131, recitals 334–335.

281 Case C-349/16 *T KUP SAS v Belgische Staat* EU:C:2017:469, para 44.

282 See, eg, Commission Implementing Regulation (EU) 2017/1759 of 27 September 2017 imposing a definitive anti-dumping duty on imports of barium carbonate originating in the People's Republic of China following an expiry review pursuant to Article 11(2) of Regulation (EU) 2016/1036 of the European Parliament and of the Council [2017] OJ L250/34, recital 140.

283 Commission Implementing Regulation (EU) 2015/1081 of 3 July 2015 imposing a provisional anti-dumping duty on imports of certain aluminium foils originating in Russia [2015] OJ L175/14, recitals 153–158.

284 See, eg, Commission Implementing Regulation (EU) 2017/1444 of 9 August 2017 imposing a provisional anti-dumping duty on imports of certain corrosion resistant steels originating in the People's Republic of China [2017] OJ L207/1, recitals 149–150.

In practice, the Commission will likely consider only that the interests of the Union industry, and not those of other groups, may justify the non-imposition of remedies. The interests of consumers have been given little weight by the Commission, which often justifies the imposition of measures on the limited impact of the measures on the final product.[285]

Therefore, the Commission's consideration of consumer interests in future FSR investigations will reveal which of these two approaches will drive the FSR's balancing test. In addition, it remains uncertain whether the FSR balancing test will focus on the interests of the Union industry as in anti-dumping investigations, or consider more broadly EU policies such as sustainability goals.

B. The Compatibility Assessment under the State Aid Regime

Under EU State aid law, the relevant legal framework does not envisage a proper 'balancing test' as envisaged under the FSR and – partly – trade defence regimes. Nonetheless, once the Commission finds that a measure falls within the definition of State aid under Article 107(1) TFEU, it must assess the compatibility of the aid at issue with the internal market pursuant to Article 107(2) and (3) and Article 106(2) TFEU.

Article 107(3) TFEU provides a list of aid that may be considered compatible with the TFEU – namely:

- aid to promote the economic development of areas where the standard of living is abnormally low or where there is serious underemployment, and of the regions mentioned in Article 349 TFEU, in view of their structural, economic, and social situation;
- aid to promote the execution of an important project of common European interest or to remedy a serious disturbance in the economy of a Member State;
- aid to facilitate the development of certain economic activities or of certain economic areas, where that aid does not adversely affect trading conditions to an extent contrary to the common interest;
- aid to promote culture and heritage conservation where that aid does not affect trading conditions and competition in the Union to an extent that is contrary to the common interest; and
- other categories of aid as may be specified by a decision of the Council on a proposal from the Commission.

---

285 Council Implementing Regulation (EU) No 1194/2013 of 19 November 2013 imposing a definitive anti-dumping duty and collecting definitively the provisional duty imposed on imports of biodiesel originating in Argentina and Indonesia [2013] OJ L315/2, recital 196.

In EU State aid law, legislation – such as the Block Exemption Regulations for State aid[286] and sector-specific rules[287] – delineates specific categories of State aid as compatible with the TFEU if they fulfil certain conditions. Such a structured and regulated approach is not yet available for foreign subsidies.

For example, the recent Temporary Crisis and Transition Framework for State Aid measures to support the economy following the aggression against Ukraine by Russia[288] (Temporary Framework) envisages the possibility for the Member States to support the production of the specific equipment and components needed for the transition towards a net-zero economy, such as batteries, solar panels, wind turbines, etc, as well as their key components and raw materials.[289] At the same time, the Temporary Framework establishes a number of conditions that the aid scheme must meet to be considered compatible.[290]

How will the balancing test work?

- the Commission has significant discretion in applying the test
- the balancing test involves weighing the negative effects in terms of distortion of competition in the internal market (Articles 4 and 5 FSR) with the positive effects on EU policy objectives
- relevant policy objectives include environmental protection, protection of social standards, and promotion of research and development
- relevant policy objectives could also include increased competition, but it is unclear to what extent the interests of consumers will be considered

286 See, eg, Commission Regulation (EU) 2023/1315 of 23 June 2023 amending Regulation (EU) 651/2014 declaring certain categories of aid compatible with the internal market in application of Articles 107 and 108 of the Treaty and Regulation (EU) 2022/2473 declaring certain categories of aid to undertakings active in the production, processing and marketing of fishery and aquaculture products compatible with the internal market in application of Articles 107 and 108 of the Treaty [2023] OJ L167/1.

287 See, for instance, Commission Communication [2022] OJ C80/1 (n 87).

288 Commission Communication Temporary Crisis and Transition Framework for State Aid measures to support the economy following the aggression against Ukraine by Russia [2023] OJ C101/3.

289 ibid, point 85.

290 ibid, point 85.

Chapter III
The Concentrations (M&A) Tool

1. Introduction

The FSR's M&A tool is an ex-ante instrument to assess the impact of foreign subsidies on concentrations that involve merging parties, acquisition targets or JVs established in the EU. The rules specific to the FSR's M&A tool are covered by Articles 20–26 FSR. The rules on the substantive assessment and the investigatory process that are common to multiple instruments are covered elsewhere in the FSR. The FSR Implementing Regulation outlines the modalities of making an FSR notification and other aspects of the Commission's review process. Annex 1 provides a specific form that must be completed in a notification (Form FS-CO).

Like the FSR more broadly, the M&A control tool was designed to bridge a perceived enforcement gap in the Commission's ability to assess and control the influence of foreign subsidies on mergers affecting the internal market. Specifically, in its 2020 White Paper proposing the establishment of the FSR, the Commission noted that '[n]either EU antitrust rules nor EU merger control specifically take into account whether an economic operator may have benefited from foreign subsidies……and they do not allow the Commission (or Member States) to intervene and decide solely or even mainly on this basis.'[291]

Accordingly, the M&A tool allows the Commission to focus on the distortive effects of subsidies in the context of concentrations. It primarily aims to ensure that foreign subsidies do not confer an unfair advantage on entities seeking to acquire control of companies established in the EU, whether directly through subsidies linked to the acquisition, or indirectly by increasing the financial strength – and therefore acquisitive competitiveness – of the acquirer. In addition, the M&A tool allows the Commission to examine whether a transaction could have the effect of distorting competition on the product market(s) on which the entity will be active post-transaction.

Many companies that might be affected by the M&A tool will already be quite familiar with the longstanding European merger control regime, governed by the EU Merger Regulation (EUMR).[292] The M&A tool operates in parallel to the EU merger control mechanism, but mirrors that mechanism in many aspects. Several concepts and procedural mechanisms of the M&A tool are directly borrowed from that legislation. As the FSR is a new instrument, and there is no established body of practice or procedural guidance documents to aid in its interpretation, it can be expected that the Commission will leverage the existing merger

---

291 White Paper COM (2020) 253 final (n 9), s 3.1.

292 EUMR Regulation 139/2004 [2004] OJ L24/1 (n 35).

control precedent and guidance when applying parallel concepts under the FSR. Nevertheless, there are also significant differences between these two instruments. Similarities with, and differences from, the EUMR are raised where applicable throughout this chapter.

This chapter discusses:

- the FSR's mandatory notification thresholds and standstill requirements;
- the information that must be included in the notification form (FS-CO);
- the Commission's review process and timeline;
- the Commission's powers to ask the parties questions and to require the production of further documents and evidence;
- the scope of the Commission's substantive review of the transaction at issue; and
- the possible outcomes of the review process and the remedies that may be offered if a competitive concern is identified.

2. Mandatory Notification

The FSR establishes a mandatory notification regime for concentrations that meet the contribution and turnover thresholds set forth in the FSR. While the basic model of this ex ante notification mechanism parallels the EU merger control regime, unlike in merger control, the FSR's thresholds are based not only on turnover but also on the level of foreign 'financial contributions' received. However, while the FSR requires notification where a transaction meets these thresholds, it also gives the Commission the power to investigate transactions that fall below the thresholds. Where a notification is mandatory – or where the Commission has requested a notification – a mandatory standstill requirement applies, prohibiting the parties from closing the transaction until FSR approval is granted or the statutory timeframe for the Commission to assess the transaction has expired.

An M&A transaction will require notification under the FSR if it is a concentration in which:

- at least one of the merging entities, the acquired entity, or the JV is established in the EU and generates an aggregate turnover in the EU of at least *€500 million* and
- the following entities were granted combined aggregate financial contributions of more than *€50 million* from third countries in the three years preceding the conclusion of the agreement, the announcement of the public bid, or the acquisition of a controlling interest:
  - in the case of an acquisition, the acquirer or acquirers and the acquired entity
  - in the case of a merger, the merging entities
  - in the case of a JV, the entities creating a JV and the JV

The Commission may request that concentrations falling below these thresholds be notified on its own initiative

If a concentration meets the threshold or the Commission requests a notification, the concentration cannot be completed until:

- at least 25 working days after formal notification or
- at least 90 days after the initiation of an in-depth review by the Commission or
- after the Commission has issued a decision clearing the transaction (unconditionally or subject to remedies)

A. Transactions that Require Notification

A.1 Requirement for the Transaction to Be a 'Concentration'

The M&A applies only to 'concentrations'. Article 20 FSR defines the existence of a concentration in the same way as the EUMR. Namely, a concentration arises where there is a change in control on a lasting basis resulting from:

- a merger of previously independent companies or parts of companies;
- the acquisition, whether by purchase of securities or assets, by contract or by any other means, of direct or indirect control of the whole or parts of one or more other companies; or
- the creation of a JV performing on a lasting basis all the functions of an autonomous economic entity.

In sum, for a transaction to be considered a concentration, there must be an acquisition of control, regardless of how this change is brought about (eg, through the purchase of shares, a sale of assets, or other means). Consequently, purely internal restructurings or operations that confer a non-controlling interest to another party are not considered concentrations and are thus not subject to the FSR notification requirements. Nor does the creation of a non-full function JV trigger an FSR notification requirement.[293] However, these transactions might nonetheless trigger merger notification or other regulatory clearance requirements in the Member States, such as under a national FDI screening mechanism.

---

[293] The notion of a full function JV refers to an entity that performs on a lasting basis all the functions of an autonomous economic entity, ie, has an autonomous market presence. A JV will be considered non-full function if it lacks an autonomous market presence and only takes over one specific function within the parent companies' business activities.

Whether or not the types of transaction above lead to an acquisition of control in a specific instance will depend on whether they confer the possibility of exercising decisive influence over the target. Control may be exercised solely (by one company) or jointly (by several) and can consist of either positive control rights (eg, the ability to exercise a majority vote on strategic matters) or negative control rights (eg, the ability to block strategic decisions). This definition of control has been extensively elaborated in the context of the EUMR, and detailed guidance can be found in the Commission's Jurisdictional Notice.[294] The Commission has indicated that it will adopt the same approach to establishing the existence of a concentration (and of control) under the FSR.[295]

A.2 Turnover and Contribution Thresholds

Pursuant to Article 20(3) FSR, concentrations are subject to the FSR's mandatory notification and standstill requirements if they meet the following turnover and financial contribution thresholds:[296]

- *turnover threshold*: 'at least one of the merging undertakings, the acquired undertaking or the joint venture is established in the Union and generates an aggregate turnover in the Union of at least *€500 million*'; and
- *contribution threshold*: 'the following were granted combined aggregate financial contributions of more than *€50 million* from third countries in the three years preceding the conclusion of the agreement, the announcement of the public bid, or the acquisition of a controlling interest:
  - in the case of an acquisition, the acquirer or acquirers and the acquired undertaking;
  - in the case of a merger, the merging undertakings;
  - in the case of a joint venture, the undertakings creating a joint venture and the joint venture'.

A.2.1 The Turnover Threshold

The FSR's turnover threshold is set relatively high so as to capture only concentrations that concern the acquisition or creation of an entity with a sizeable EU presence. Transactions in which the merging parties (for mergers), the target (for acquisitions), or the JV are not established in the EU and/or fall below the €500 million threshold in aggregate EU turnover are excluded from the notification requirements.

There is no compelling logic behind the choice of a €500 million threshold. During the consultation phase of the legislative process, there was no consensus among stakeholders regarding what would constitute an appropriate threshold. Certain Member States criticised the creation of a high turnover threshold, noting that while this would limit

294 Commission Consolidated Jurisdictional Notice under Council Regulation (EC) 139/2004 on the control of concentrations between undertakings (Jurisdictional Notice) [2008] OJ C95/1, paras 11–35.

295 As confirmed by the Commission in its FSR M&A FAQs, question 6 (n 31).

296 The notification requirements apply to transactions for which the agreement was signed on or after 12 July 2023 (provided they were not already implemented by 12 October 2023).

the administrative burden on the Commission, it would fail to capture acquisitions of innovative start-ups.[297] The Commission's FSR Impact Assessment observed that setting a threshold inherently involved a trade-off between the administrative burden of a notification and the general effectiveness of the instrument.[298] The FSR Impact Assessment further observed that, under a higher threshold, only a small part of the transactions requiring an EUMR merger control notification would be notifiable under the FSR, reducing overlaps.

Ultimately, in its FSR Proposal, the Commission noted that it had set the turnover threshold relatively high, 'in order to capture only the potentially most distortive subsidies'. The Commission further observed that it could pursue cases below the threshold at its own initiative to ensure that no particularly problematic cases would slip through the cracks.[299] The purported aim of the turnover threshold is thus to identify transactions that have the potential to have a significant effect on the EU internal market.

There are several elements of the FSR's turnover threshold that have important consequences for notification obligations:

Established in the EU. The FSR's turnover thresholds are only met if the relevant entity is 'established in the Union'. Form FS-CO clarifies that this requirement 'must be understood in accordance with the case law of the Court of Justice and includes the incorporation of a subsidiary in the Union, as well as a permanent business establishment in the Union'.[300] This broad definition will therefore capture many entities that do business in the EU but might be headquartered elsewhere. For example, if the target of an acquisition is headquartered in Asia, and comprises six subsidiaries, one of which has a permanent business establishment in the EU, then the target is considered to be 'established in the Union'. This approach differs from the EUMR's turnover thresholds, which do not consider whether the parties involved are established in the EU. This difference appears logical as the FSR is concerned with the subsidised acquisition of EU-based assets, whereas the EUMR is concerned with competition on the downstream product markets (regardless of the location of the parties or target).

Turnover in the EU. The concept of EU turnover is broad, and includes not only revenue generated from EU assets (or by the part of the relevant entity that is 'established' in the EU), but also revenue generated from sales or services provided by the relevant entity to other entities or consumers located within the EU (even if these sales/services were provided from a part of the relevant entity established outside the EU).[301] To take the example of a target headquartered in Asia with six subsidiaries, one of which

---

297 European Commission, *Consultation Summary Report, of 17 June 2020* (23 September 2020) <https://ec.europa.eu/info/law/better-regulation/have-your-say/initiatives/12621-Trade-investment-addressing-distortions-caused-by-foreign-subsidies/public-consultation_en> accessed 18 December 2023.

298 FSR Impact Assessment (n 14) 45.

299 FSR Proposal COM (2021) 223 final (n 16) 8.

300 Form FS-CO, Section 4, fn 4, also referring to judgments in Case C-230/14 *Weltimmo sro v Nemzeti Adatvedelmi es Informacioszabadsag Hatosag* EU:C:2015:639, paras 29–30; Joined Cases C-39/13, C-40/13 and C-41/13 *Inspecteur van de Belastingdienst/Noord/kantoor Groningen v SCA Group Holding BV* EU:C:2014:1758, paras 24–27; and Case C-196/87 *Steymann v Staatssecretaris van Justitie* EU:C:1988:475, para 16.

301 FSR Regulation 2022/2560 [2022] OJ L330/1 (n 1), art 22(1).

is established in the EU, all EU turnover (sales into the EU) generated by *any* of the target's subsidiaries is counted toward the threshold, including turnover generated with sales into the EU by entities without an established EU presence.

Recognising the jurisdictional reach of the M&A tool is important because it is inconsistent with the general narrative that the FSR is designed to protect 'European companies' against subsidised acquisitions. As the above example illustrates, the FSR also captures foreign-to-foreign transactions (and therefore potentially 'protects' non-EU companies), as long as the EU permanent presence requirement is fulfilled.

Only turnover of the merging parties, target or JV is considered. The turnover of the acquirer or of the parents of a JV is *not* relevant to the calculation of turnover under the FSR thresholds. This has several important consequences.

First, the creation of an entirely *new* (greenfield) JV – which has no turnover of its own yet – cannot meet the FSR's turnover thresholds. Therefore, the establishment of a new JV (regardless of the identity or assets of the parents) will not trigger mandatory FSR notification obligations.[302] However, where the transaction concerns a change in control over an *existing* JV (eg, due to the entry of a new controlling shareholder), then the turnover of that JV will count toward the FSR turnover threshold. In all cases, however, the turnover of the JV's current parents is not included when determining whether the turnover threshold is met. This differs from the EUMR's approach, in which the turnover of the parents of a JV is always included in the turnover calculations, regardless of whether the JV is newly formed or exists already.

Second, certain deal structures can avoid notification obligations entirely – even if they still result in a concentration, because the FSR's focus is on the turnover of the *object* of the transaction. For example, a *merger* between two companies established in the EU that each generate €250 million in turnover will meet the FSR turnover threshold (as the turnover of each party is counted). However, if that same deal were to be structured as an *acquisition* rather than a merger of equals, only the target's turnover would then be relevant to the FSR notification thresholds, and the deal would not trigger a mandatory notification. Transaction parties might wish to consider the notification implications of structuring deals as acquisitions versus mergers if this helps avoid triggering the FSR notification threshold. By contrast, as the EUMR's turnover thresholds consider both the turnover of the acquirer and target, there is no jurisdictional difference for merger control purposes in whether a transaction is structured as an acquisition or a merger.

These differences between the FSR and EUMR's turnover thresholds are logical given the different aims of the two instruments. The turnover threshold under the FSR exists to identify sizeable acquisitions of entities with an EU presence (and therefore the turnover thresholds are focused on the size of the *object of the transaction*). By contrast, the EUMR's turnover thresholds seek to identify transactions that bring together parties with substantial resources and activities that might affect competition on the downstream markets (and therefore also take into account the overall size of the *resulting entity*).

---

302 The Commission confirmed this reading of the FSR's threshold requirements in its FSR M&A FAQs, question 2 (n 31).

Calculation of turnover. Despite the above-mentioned differences regarding which entities' turnover are relevant to meeting the FSR threshold, the provisions regarding the *methodology* of calculating turnover under Article 22 FSR mirror the provisions of Article 5 EUMR. This includes the corporate affiliates within a control group that must also be taken into account when calculating turnover of the relevant entities. Consequently, the provisions of the Jurisdictional Notice that concern turnover allocation and calculation methodology (eg, which parts of an entity's revenue should be calculated as turnover, how the turnover of joint ventures co-controlled by the entity should be attributed, how turnover should be allocated geographically and special consideration for certain types of turnover)[303] are relevant to interpreting the FSR.

Timing. The relevant time period for assessing the aggregate turnover is the turnover generated in the financial year preceding the notification.[304] This is also the case for calculating turnover under the EUMR. Therefore, the same turnover figures (using different thresholds) can be used as a basis for establishing whether a concentration meets either the FSR or the EUMR thresholds.

A.2.2 The Contribution Threshold

In contrast to the turnover threshold, the contribution threshold is set quite low. Given the broad notion of a 'financial contribution' (see Chapter II), the threshold of €50 million in contributions over three years is likely to be relatively easily met by many companies engaging in the types of large-scale transaction that are caught by the FSR's turnover threshold. Moreover, the contribution threshold does not require contributions to have any form of EU nexus. In other words, the contribution received by one of the 'undertakings concerned' does not need to relate to the EU operations of that entity, but could have been received by any other part of that entity operating globally. Moreover, all contributions received count toward the contribution threshold, regardless of whether these contributions ultimately need to be reported in the notification form.

The relevant period for calculating contributions is three years preceding the conclusion of the agreement, the announcement of the public bid or the acquisition of a controlling interest (and not three years before the time of the notification) (see Chapter II).

The 'undertakings involved' that are relevant for calculating contributions are different from the undertakings to consider for calculating turnover. The relevant parties of which aggregate contributions must be assessed are:

- in the case of an acquisition: the acquirer or acquirers and the acquired entity;
- in the case of a merger: the merging parties;
- in the case of a JV: the parties creating a JV and the JV.

Thus, while the turnover threshold does not consider the turnover of the acquirer or the JV parents, these are relevant to assessing whether the contribution threshold is met. If joint control is being acquired over a JV that was previously solely controlled

---

303 See, eg, Jurisdictional Notice [2008] OJ C 95/1 (n 294), paras 157–220.

304 FSR Regulation 2022/2560 [2022] OJ L330/1 (n 1), art 22(1).

by one company, all parents that will have joint control as a result of the transaction are considered as parties creating the JV (thus the contributions received by all future JV parents and the JV itself are relevant to reaching the contribution threshold). In this respect the 'undertakings involved' for assessing *contributions under the FSR* are the same as those relevant to calculating *turnover under the EUMR*. Importantly, the notion of 'undertaking' encompasses all entities (including parents and subsidiaries) in which a control relationship exists. As confirmed by Article 23 FSR, the relevant relationships that need to be taken into account for the purpose of defining the scope of an 'undertaking involved' are listed in Article 22(4) FSR.[305] As this article mirrors the provisions of Article 5(4) EUMR, precise guidance and examples on what entities are part of the control relationships listed can be found in the Jurisdictional Notice and applied by analogy.[306] For example, if one party to the concentration jointly controls one or more JVs (that are not the subject of the transaction at hand), any contributions received by those JVs should be taken into account if the JVs fall within the control relationships as established under Article 22(4)(b) FSR (whereas if they fall outside such relationships any contributions they receive can be disregarded).

The calculation of financial contributions in accordance with Article 23 FSR might nevertheless deviate from the turnover calculation in one important aspect: for turnover calculation, only entities that are part of the control group at the time of the notification can be relevant. Turnover of entities that have been divested or liquidated prior to notification is not attributable to the control group. For the calculation of financial contributions, however, the outcome might be different. This could be the case because the FSR considers relevant all contributions granted to the parties in the three years preceding the conclusion of the agreement, the announcement of the public bid, or the acquisition of a controlling interest. Moreover, the fact that the M&A tool takes into account financial contributions to all entities within a control group reflects the view that money is fungible, and contributions received by any entity within a control group could potentially benefit the control group's entity involved in a transaction.

Considering these two elements in combination appears to support the conclusion that financial contributions received in the three-year period by an entity that has been divested or liquidated prior to notification is attributable to the control group. These financial contributions would thus be relevant when determining whether the control group meets the contribution threshold. They may also be reportable, unless they are exempted from reporting requirements in accordance with the explanatory notes to Section 5, Table 1 of Form FS-CO, or the Commission grants a waiver. On the other hand, it could be argued that Article 23 FSR explicitly refers to the relevant entities within a control group listed in Article 22(4) FSR, and therefore that only the Article 22(4) entities that are relevant for turnover calculation purposes are potential recipients of financial contributions according to Article 23 FSR. This would exclude divested or liquidated entities from the group of potential recipients of financial contributions.

---

305 Although FSR Regulation 2022/2560 [2022] OJ L330/1 (n 1), art 22(4) applies to turnover, FSR art 23 indicates that the relationships listed are also relevant to determining which contributions should be aggregated for the purposes of the contribution threshold.

306 See Jurisdictional Notice [2008] OJ C 95/1 (n 294), paras 157–220.

The Commission is understood to have informally expressed the view that financial contributions received by entities that have been divested prior to notification are attributable to the control group and therefore within the scope of the FSR. It remains to be seen whether the Commission will maintain this view and, if so, will generally be receptive to waiver requests on the ground that information about previously divested or liquidated entities is not available when a party prepares a notification.

Practically speaking, a transaction party may determine that it will already meet the FSR notification requirements simply by assessing its own contributions, and regardless of the other parties involved. Alternatively, it may determine that it receives under €50 million in contributions, and that therefore the determination of whether a notification is required will depend on the contributions received by the other parties to the transaction. This suggested self-assessment process, including with regard to which entities should be considered to form part of the same control group (particularly in the case of state-owned enterprises), is discussed in detail in Chapter V.

Finally, the determination of the entities of which the contributions are relevant in the M&A tool described above (ie, based on the wide concept of an 'undertaking' in EU competition law) differs substantially from the entities of which the contributions are relevant under the public procurement tool (see Chapter IV). The public procurement tool does not rely on the concept of 'undertakings' but specifically lists the entities of which the contributions are relevant based on their affiliation with the tender participant (the economic operator).[307] As a result, if the same company participates in an EU acquisition and EU public procurement process through the same subsidiary, a much larger range of contributions (from all entities in the control group) will need to be taken into account to determine whether the M&A tool's threshold is met than to determine whether the public procurement tool's threshold is met.

B. Transactions That Fall Outside the Mandatory Notification Regime

The FSR's notification thresholds are not jurisdictional. In other words, the M&A tool does not limit the Commission's powers to review only those transactions that meet the notification thresholds. Rather, Article 21(5) FSR empowers the Commission to request prior notification of *any* concentration that does not meet the thresholds prior to its implementation, if it suspects that a company might have received foreign subsidies within the previous three years. In theory, this means that the Commission could require an FSR review of any concentration, regardless of the turnover of the parties or the amounts of the financial contributions involved. For example, the Commission could request the notification of a greenfield JV (which by definition would not meet the FSR's turnover thresholds). The Commission could not use the power under the M&A Tool to require notification of transactions that are not considered concentrations

[307] See Case C-416/21 *Landkreis Aichach-Friedberg v J Sch Omnibusunternehme* EU:C:2022:689, para 47.

(for example, the acquisition of minority interests without control rights or the creation of a non-full-function JV). The Commission could review these transactions, however, under the ex officio tool (see Chapter VI).

In practice, given the volume of concentrations that will need to be notified to the Commission and the relatively modest size of the case teams initially assigned to review these filings, it is unlikely that the Commission will routinely call in transactions. This being said, if a concentration not meeting the notification thresholds is heavily and directly subsidised, particularly by geopolitically targeted countries such as China, the Commission might well choose to request a notification.

Likewise, consistent with the language of recital 2 FSR, the Commission might pay greater attention to transactions involving the acquisition of what it considers to constitute 'strategic assets', including 'critical infrastructure' and 'innovative technologies'. Moreover, the EU merger control form (Form CO) requires parties to specify whether they have received foreign subsidies in the context of the transaction and whether they anticipate making an FSR notification. The Commission might choose to call in transactions where the parties have noted the presence of subsidies in Form CO but fall under the notification requirements. Finally, the Commission can also review any such a transaction post-completion at its own initiative under its ex officio tool (see Chapter VI).

The broad scope of the Commission's jurisdiction under the FSR is at least conceptually different from that under the EUMR. The EUMR does not allow the Commission to assert jurisdiction unless the turnover thresholds are met. Competence belongs to the Member States unless the transaction has an EU dimension justifying the Commission's involvement. By contrast, as the control of foreign subsides belongs entirely to the Commission, it has maximum flexibility in examining the role of distortive subsidies in mergers and in any other context. In practice, this conceptual difference becomes increasingly insignificant, as the referral practice under Article 22 EUMR expands.

C. Mandatory Notification and Standstill Regime

Concentrations that meet the FSR's thresholds must be notified 'following the conclusion of the agreement, the announcement of the public bid, or the acquisition of a controlling interest'.[308] The parties may also notify once they have demonstrated a 'good faith' intention to conclude an agreement[309] (for example, by signing a memorandum of understanding, letter of intent, or similar document). This is the same ex ante notification language as contained in the EUMR. Therefore, in practice, a FSR notification and an EU merger control filing might be submitted at the same stage in the deal timeline (assuming similar pre-notification discussions).

308 FSR Regulation 2022/2560 [2022] OJ L330/1 (n 1), art 21(1).
309 ibid, art 21(2).

Article 24 FSR also imposes a standstill requirement, obliging parties to wait to implement any notifiable transaction until it has been notified and the Commission has completed its review. Specifically, this means that a notifiable concentration cannot be implemented until:

- at least 25 working days after formal notification; or
- at least 90 days after the initiation of an in-depth review by the Commission; or
- after the Commission has issued a decision clearing the transaction (unconditionally or subject to remedies).

Notably, this differs from the EUMR in that the Commission is not obliged to issue a decision formally clearing a transaction and will not routinely do so after a 25-working day review (or earlier if a notification benefits from a simplified procedure). If the above-mentioned time periods elapse without a Commission decision being issued, the parties may proceed to implement the transaction.

The concept of 'implementation' of a concentration – like the notification and standstill requirements more broadly – is taken from the EUMR and can be assumed to have the same interpretation under the FSR. The EU Courts have considered that implementation includes any steps that contribute to a lasting change in control of an entity, even if those steps do not, in themselves, lead to a change in control.[310] However, implementation does not include unilateral actions taken in anticipation of the transaction (such as a target severing legal ties with its parent company or other preparatory steps).[311] Nevertheless, the line between what actions are considered merely preparatory and those that are considered as implementing steps is exceedingly blurred, particularly in the case of multi-step transactions.[312] Consequently, parties are advised to carefully consider whether initial phases of a transaction might be considered 'implementation' that would require ex ante notification under the FSR (and/or EUMR).

The Commission may fine transaction parties up to 10% of their annual turnover for 'gun jumping' – namely a failure to notify a concentration and/or to observe the standstill period.[313] Those fines can be imposed regardless of whether the transaction at issue ultimately proves to be unproblematic from a substantive point of view. It can be presumed that these fines are cumulative where the transaction parties fail to notify and consequently to observe the standstill period.[314] The Commission has become increasingly

---

310 See Case T-609/19 *Canon Inc v European Commission* EU:T:2022:299, paras 67–73; Case C-633/16 *Ernst & Young P/S v Konkurrenceradet* EU:C:2018:371, para 59.

311 ibid, para 64.

312 See the lengthy reasoning outlined by the General Court in *Canon* (n 310) (a two-step warehousing transaction); see also the reasoning finding no gun jumping in Commission decision of 17 December 2020, *Veolia/Suez* (Case COMP/M.9969) (a different type of multi-step transaction).

313 FSR Regulation 2022/2560 [2022] OJ L330/1 (n 1), art 26(3)(a)–(b).

314 The CJEU considered the same 'gun jumping' provisions contained in the EUMR and ruled that the Commission could impose sperate fines for violations of each provision, even though a violation of the notification requirement would inevitably also lead of a violation of the standstill provision. See Case C-10/18 P *Mowi ASA (formerly Marine Harvest ASA) v European Commission* EU:C:2020:149.

aggressive in enforcing procedural violations in recent years.[315] It will likely not take a lenient approach to any incidences of gun jumping under the FSR.

The FSR's suspensory obligation does not apply in two instances.

First, according to Article 24(2), the FSR does not prevent the implementation of a 'public bid or of a series of transactions in securities', provided that the transaction is then notified 'without delay' and the acquirer does not exercise its voting rights in the shares purchased (or does so only to maintain the full value of its investment). This provision is taken directly from an analogous provision of the EUMR.[316] Therefore, the Commission's guidance and court precedent relevant to the EUMR's provision should apply equally here.

Second, Article 24(3) FSR envisages that the transaction parties may request a derogation from the FSR's suspensory obligations. If the Commission grants this request, the parties may close the transaction while the review is still in progress. The decision to grant a derogation is entirely at the Commission's discretion, and the Commission can attach conditions to any derogation issued. This provision also has an analogue in the EUMR.[317] In practice, the Commission rarely grants those derogations in the merger control context.[318] It can be expected that the Commission will be similarly stringent in allowing parties to avoid the FSR's suspensory requirements. This would likely occur only in transactions that are both presumed to be substantively unproblematic and where the parties present a strong case that a delay would cause significant damage (eg, the bankruptcy of the target business).

3. The Scope of the Notification

The notification process is outlined in the FSR Implementing Regulation. Completion of a lengthy notification form will present a considerable compliance burden. Although the FSR notification process resembles that of the EUMR, the bulk of an FSR notification will consist of information that does not need to be provided in merger control clearance or during most other regulatory procedures that routinely arise in the course of deal-making. In particular, the parties will need to provide extensive details on foreign contributions received. Parties will also need to provide any other information deemed necessary to evaluate any distortive effects of those contributions on the internal market.

---

315 In 2023 the Commission imposed its highest gun jumping fine to-date of €432 million against Illumina for closing its acquisition of Grail in violation of the EUMR's standstill provisions *Illumina/Grail* (Case COMP/M.10483). Other recent gun jumping fines include €28 million in *Canon/Toshiba Medical Systems* (Case COMP/M.8179) [2019] OJ C362/8, €124.5 million in *Altice/PT Portugal* (Case COMP/M.7993) in 2019, and €20 million in *Marine Harvest/Marpol* (Case COMP/M.7184) [2014] OJ C455/5.

316 EUMR Regulation 139/2004 [2004] OJ L24/1 (n 35), art 7(2).

317 ibid, art 7(3).

318 As of May 2023, the Commission granted derogations in only 1.6% of all notified merger cases (periodically updated statistics are available on the Commission's website at <https://competition-policy.ec.europa.eu/mergers/statistics_en>) accessed 18 December 2023.

Form FS-CO requires the notifying parties to submit substantial information on financial contributions received

Form FS-CO contributions fall into three categories, requiring different degrees of disclosure for each:

- *likely distortive subsidies*: contributions that fall within the problematic categories listed in Article 5(3) FSR must be declared individually and require extensive documentation
- *reportable contributions*: other contributions must be listed in a table in Form FS-CO in aggregated form only if they amount to more than €45 million
- *non-reportable contributions*: certain contributions, including most transactions at market rates, do not need to be reported in Form FS-CO regardless of their amount

The Commission may agree to extend waivers for certain information that is not available or not relevant to the case. However, as waivers can only be requested during the pre-notification process and the Commission has not issued guidance on what circumstances are likely to qualify for a waiver, notifying parties should not rely on the possibility of obtaining a waiver during their FSR preparations

A. Overview of the Submission and Structure of Form FS-CO

The FSR only sets out the criteria to identify what transactions are notifiable under the FSR's merger tool. The modalities of notification are outlined in the FSR Implementing Regulation, which also includes Form FS-CO.

A.1 Submission of Form FS-CO

Article 21(3) FSR specifies that in a merger or an acquisition of joint control, the notification must be submitted jointly by the parties acquiring control. In all other cases the notification is to be made by the party acquiring control of another entity. The 'notifying party/parties' are therefore the same as under the EUMR.[319]

Like the EUMR, a complete FSR notification must contain information about all parties involved in the concentration. As a consequence, this section refers to information that must be provided by the 'parties' (even though, as a legal matter, it is incumbent on the notifying party/parties to ensure that this information is submitted as part of the notification and that it is accurate).

319 See EUMR Regulation 139/2004 [2004] OJ L24/1 (n 35), art 4(2).

The formal review period (and all resulting deadlines) only start once the Commission accepts a Form FS-CO that it deems to be complete. Within the bounds laid out under the FSR, the FSR Implementing Regulation, and Form FS-CO, the Commission has wide latitude to determine the level of detail required for a notification to be complete and may request additional information for assessing the concentration. This, again, resembles the practice under the EUMR.

The Commission likewise has wide powers under Article 4(4) FSR Implementing Regulation to dispense the parties from providing any information required in the notification form upon written request. The Commission will consider waivers if the parties give 'adequate reasons' why the information is either:

- not reasonably available (and, where possible supply estimates of the missing data or information); or
- not necessary for the Commission's examination of the case.

It remains unclear how generous the Commission will be in granting waivers – particularly as the parties and the case team might differ on the necessity of certain information for assessing the transaction. These waiver requests must be made during the 'pre-notification' phase, before a formal notification is submitted. Unfortunately, at present the Commission has not issued guidance to provide additional clarification on when it will be particularly amenable to granting waivers, nor can parties inquire about the availability of a waiver in the abstract (ie, before the pre-notification phase of a particular transaction). Parties should therefore not assume that a waiver will be available to avoid gathering and producing the information requested in Form FS-CO.

A.2 Structure of Form FS-CO

Form FS-CO consists of nine sections:

- *Sections 1-3* – request the parties to provide general information concerning the description of the concentration, the identity of the parties and details of the concentration (including ownership and control). These sections closely resemble the information collected in the context of merger control proceedings, and should not present a significant compliance burden for transaction parties.
- *Section 4* – seeks to verify that the FSR notification thresholds are met. Consequently, this section requires the notifying party to:
  - indicate the EU turnover of the relevant parties under Article 20(3)(a) FSR (each merging undertaking, the target for an acquisition, or the JV, as the case may be);
  - declare that the total amount of financial contributions granted to the relevant parties (as specified in Article 20(3)(b) FSR) in the previous three years exceeds €50 million. Importantly, the parties are not required to specify the total amount of all contributions – merely to confirm that these exceed the threshold for notification. As discussed in Chapter V, this means that – although all contributions (including those considered

'non-reportable' in the notification form) count toward the threshold, parties do not need to specifically identify or itemise all financial contributions unless they need to be reported in other sections of the notification.

- *Section 5* – requires the parties to provide specific information on presumptively distortive foreign contributions. It requires the parties to provide extensive information and documents about certain contributions most likely to be considered distortive subsidies. They must provide information about certain other contributions in an aggregated table format. This will likely be the most time-consuming section of Form FS-CO for parties to complete.
- *Sections 6 and 7* – request information relevant for the Commission's substantive assessment of the concentration. In particular, Section 7 requests information relevant to the 'balancing test', in which the Commission weights the distortive effects of any subsidies received against any positive effects of the subsidised activity on the internal market. This test is discussed in more detail in Chapter II. Section 7 gives the parties the option to list and substantiate any possible positive effects of the subsidies on their activities. The parties can also explain any broader positive effects in relation to the relevant policy objectives (particularly those of the EU) and specify when and where those effects have or are expected to take place.
- *Section 8* – requires the parties to supply an extensive range of supporting documentation related to certain contributions provided in Section 5 of the form that fall into the category of subsidies that are likely to distort competition on the internal market. As in an EU merger filing, this section also requests the parties to provide internal documents prepared for management concerning the concentration as well as the parties' annual reports.
- *Section 9* – is a declaration that the information provided is, to the best of the notifying party's knowledge, true, correct and complete, including in terms of documents attached, estimates and opinions expressed.

B. Information on Foreign Financial Contributions

The Commission does not request details on all foreign financial contributions, but instead divides contributions into three categories: (i) contributions likely to constitute distortive subsidies, (ii) contributions that constitute subsidies, but are not presumed to be problematic, and (iii) contributions that are presumptively unproblematic and are not reportable. Each category carries different reporting obligations, as outlined below. How to gather and provide the advice required to complete this section of Form FS-CO is addressed in Chapter V.

For all three categories of contributions, only financial contributions granted to the parties within the three years preceding the conclusion of the agreement, the announcement of the public bid, or the acquisition of a controlling interest are taken into account. Moreover, no individual contribution needs to be reported if it is under a *de minimis* threshold of €1 million, regardless of the type of contribution concerned.[320]

Finally, the Commission maintains the power to request additional information on any financial contribution.[321]

B.1 Contributions Likely to Be Considered Distortive Subsidies (Likely Distortive Subsidies)

As discussed in Chapter II, Article 5(3)(a–d) FSR includes a list of types of foreign subsides 'most likely to distort the internal market'. Section 5.1 of Form FS-CO asks a series of questions to determine whether the contributions received fall into these presumptively distortive categories. These subsidies are:[322]

- a foreign subsidy granted to an ailing firm (ie, one that 'will likely go out of business in the short or medium term' absent the subsidy), unless the firm is subject to a restructuring plan leading to its long-term viability and in which the firm must make a significant own contribution;
- a foreign subsidy in the form of an unlimited (as to amount or duration) guarantee for debts or liabilities;
- an export financing measure that is not in line with the OECD Arrangement; and
- a foreign subsidy directly facilitating a concentration.

Section 5.2 of Form FS-CO requires the parties to respond to specific and detailed questions for each individual contribution (above the *de minimis* threshold) that falls into the above definitions. The details to be provided concern the nature and characteristics of the contribution, including: (i) the form of the contribution, (ii) the identity of the granting entity (and, particularly, whether it is a public authority, publicly owned entity or private entity entrusted with public functions or otherwise directed by public entities), (iii) the amount of the contribution, (iv) the purpose and economic rationale for granting the contribution to the parties, (v) the description of the conditions attached to the financial contribution and its use, and (vi) the description of the main elements and characteristics of the contribution (eg, interest rate, duration, etc).

Form FS-CO also requires the parties to provide information concerning whether the contribution can be understood to confer a benefit, and whether that benefit is selective (*de jure* or *de facto*). As outlined in Chapter II, these factors determine whether a contribution is a 'subsidy'.

Furthermore, Section 8 of Form FS-CO requires the parties to submit copies of all the supporting documents relating to all likely distortive subsides declared in Section 5. The parties must also provide all analyses, reports, studies, surveys, presentations and

---

320 To determine whether the €1 million threshold is reached, contributions granted to different parties are not aggregated (thus contributions by the same country to two different parties need not be reported if each is below €1 million even if cumulatively they amount to more than €1 million).

321 Form FS-CO 24, para 8.

322 See Chapter II 3.A.2.

any comparable documents that were prepared for or received by any member of the management board, board of directors or supervisory board of any party regarding the purpose, use and economic rationale of these likely distortive subsidies. Form FS-CO also requires parties to submit any such documents that were prepared by or for, or received by, the entity granting the foreign financial contribution to the extent they are in the possession of the parties.[323]

B.2 Other Reportable Contributions (Reportable Contributions)

Section 5.3 of Form FS-CO requires that any contributions that do not fall into the category of likely distortive subsidies to be declared in Table 1 (unless exempted according to the explanations accompanying Table 1). Table 1 is provided at the end of Form FS-CO, and each party must complete it separately.

The table does not require the contributions to be listed individually. Rather, contributions must be grouped by third-country grantor and type of contribution (eg, direct grant, loan, capital injection etc). The estimated value of Table 1 contributions can be aggregated per country within wide ranges. Both countries and, if possible, types of contribution should be ranked by their total amount from the highest to the lowest.

Importantly, Form FS-CO specifies that no listing in the table is required where the aggregate contributions granted to a party by a single third country amount to less than €45 million.

If any listed contributions have a link with the concentration, a short description of that link must be indicated in the table. It is not clear how close a connection the Commission would consider to be a 'link' to a concentration. Absent additional guidance from the Commission on this topic, parties may ultimately wish to consider on a case-by-case basis whether it is advisable to list both direct and indirect links. Moreover, in some cases the determination of whether a particular contribution needs to be included in the table or can be excluded from reporting altogether will not be immediately clear. For example, certain tax arrangements may need to be considered carefully before they can be accurately categorised.

Finally, although Form FS-CO allows reportable contributions to be declared in aggregated form – which allows for contribution amounts to be approximated and explained in general fashion – this does not mean that the Commission will take no interest in this section of that form. The Commission might still be interested in checking that contributions reported in Table 1 do not present a distortion risk. It can be expected that the Commission will scan the aggregated tables and ask the parties to provide additional details and documentation regarding certain contributions listed. It is also possible that the Commission might ask questions regarding contributions that were not listed in Table 1 because the parties considered that they were exempted. As a consequence, transaction parties should strive for accuracy even when completing the aggregated table. They should be in a position to substantiate the figures provided and methodology used if asked to do so.

---

323 Form FS-CO, Sections 8.1 and 8.2(a).

B.3 Presumptively Unproblematic Contributions (Non-Reportable Contributions)

In drafting the FSR Implementing Regulation and Form FS-CO, the Commission acknowledged that certain types of financial contribution were unlikely to amount to subsidies that could cause a distortive effect on the internal market. Generally speaking, these are items that fall under the FSR's broad definition of 'financial contributions' but do not amount to subsidies because they are not selective and/or are based on market-rate conditions. Financial contributions falling into the following categories do not need to be reported at all in Form FS-CO, regardless of their amount:

deferrals of payment of taxes and/or of social security contributions, tax amnesties and tax holidays as well as normal depreciation and loss-carry forward rules that are of general application. However, any tax benefits of general application that are not explicitly listed as exempted in the FS-CO form must be reported. Moreover, if any of these listed measures are limited, for example, to certain sectors, regions or (types of) companies, they must also be reported.

- application of tax reliefs for avoidance of double taxation in line with the provisions of bilateral or multilateral agreements for avoidance of double taxation. However, unilateral tax relief applied under national tax legislation must be reported.
- supply/purchase of goods/services (except financial services) at market terms in the ordinary course of business: for example, the supply/purchase/lease of goods, services or real estate carried out following a competitive, transparent and non-discriminatory tender procedure.
- financial contributions granted to other investment funds managed by the same investment company but with different investors (or granted to portfolio companies controlled by these other funds) in the case of concentrations by an investment fund or by a legal entity controlled by or via an investment fund, provided that the following conditions are cumulatively met:
  - the fund which controls the acquiring entity must be subject to Directive 2011/61/EU of 8 June 2011 on Alternative Investment Fund Managers[324] or to an equivalent third-country legislation in terms of prudential, organisational and conduct rules, including requirements aimed to protect investors; and
  - the economic and commercial transactions between the fund which controls the acquiring entity and other investment funds (and the companies controlled by these funds) managed by the same investment company are non-existent or limited.[325]

---

324 Directive 2011/61/EU of the European Parliament and of the Council of 8 June 2011 on Alternative Investment Fund Managers and amending Directives 2003/41/EC and 2009/65/EC and Regulations (EC) 1060/2009 and (EU) 1095/2010 [2011] OJ L/1741.

325 In this regard, the notifying party/parties must provide the Commission with evidence of any economic and commercial transactions that have taken place in the three years prior to the conclusion of the agreement, the announcement of the public bid, or the acquisition of a controlling interest. Economic and commercial transactions include, but are not limited to, the sale of assets, including ownership in companies, loans, credit lines, or guarantees.

The list of exemptions is exhaustive. Non-selective tax benefits not specifically mentioned in the list do not benefit from the exemption and therefore would have to be reported in Table 1.

C. Information on Market Distortion and the Balancing Test

Section 6 of Form FS-CO requests information that the Commission needs for assessing the impact of the financial contributions (declared in Section 5) on the internal market. As indicated in Chapter II, the Commission's examination will focus on whether the contributions cause a distortion of the internal market, primarily (although not exclusively) with regard to the impact of the contributions on the market for corporate control. Form FS-CO therefore requires the parties to submit information concerning:

- *whether the concentration at issue arose in the context of a structured bidding process*: if so, the parties must provide information concerning the bidding process and a description of the participants. Form FS-CO clarifies that the information should be provided to the extent it is known to the notifying party/parties;[326]
- *the activities of the target and related activities of the other party/parties*: the parties must specify the various activities and business lines of the target, indicating the types of product and/or service offered and the target customers. The notifying party (or parties in the case of parents of a JV) should then indicate whether it is (or they are) also active in the same or related activities or business lines;[327]
- *turnover in the business lines of the target and, potentially, of the other party/parties*: the turnover for each business line or activity of the target – as well as of the notifying party/parties if it is active in the same or related activities – must be specified at both global and EU levels, as well as the percentage of the firm's global activities that the EU-specific turnover figure represents;[328]
- *impact of likely distortive subsidies on competition in the internal market*: the parties should provide information on whether and how each likely distortive subsidy reported in Section 5.2 of Form FS-CO might grant them a competitive advantage in the internal market;[329] and
- *other regulatory processes*: the parties must indicate whether the concentration meets the merger control thresholds at EU or Member State level or if it triggers any other regulatory filings within the EU (eg, FDI screenings) and the status of those processes;[330] and

---

326 Form FS-CO, Section 6.1.
327 ibid, Section 6.2.
328 ibid, Section 6.3.
329 ibid, Section 6.4.
330 ibid, Sections 6.5–6.6.

- *competitors*: the parties must provide the five largest competitors of the target active in the EU as well as the contact details of any/all competitors provided to competition authorities in the context of any EU or Member State level merger control filings.[331]

The information requirements of Section 6 are unusual in that they echo, but do not replicate the requirements of the EUMR's Form-CO. The parties are required to specify the downstream market activities of the target (or JV) and indicate where the parents engage in overlapping activities. However, unlike under the merger control regime, the parties are not required to specify the overall size of these downstream markets, nor their own market shares.

As discussed in greater detail in Chapter II, the types of information requested leave some doubt as to whether the Commission intends to restrict its analysis to competition on the market on which the transaction itself takes place (as indicated by the requirement to submit information about the structure of any bidding processes) or whether it intends also to examine the effect of any subsidies on the downstream product markets (as suggested by the questions on the parties' activities and contact details of competitors). The implication of this data and the open-ended requirement to describe the potential distortive impact of any likely distortive subsidies on the parties' 'competitive position' (without limitation to the market for transactions) appears to imply that at least some competitive assessment of the downstream markets might be carried out.

Notably, the requirement to explain the competitive impact on the internal market is limited to the effects of the likely distortive subsidies (and does not cover all reportable contributions). This said, the parties are required to specify whether any reportable contributions have a link with the concentration, and the Commission maintains the power to request additional information about any contributions. Therefore, to avoid delays in pre-notification, it is advisable for notifying parties to be prepared to provide an assessment of any competitive impact of reportable contributions linked to the concentration, or to confirm that they do not anticipate that any reportable contributions would have any competitive impact.

4. Review Process and Timeline

A. The FSR Review Timeline

The FSR review process consists of two formal phases that occur once an FSR notification has been filed: a mandatory first phase preliminary review, and a second phase in-depth review for cases that are more complex and/or raise substantive concerns. These phases have statutory timelines prescribed under Article 24 FSR. In addition, the Commission encourages transaction parties to engage in informal 'pre-notification' discussions with the FSR case team before a formal notification is submitted.

---

331 ibid, Sections 6.7–6.8.

The general timeline for an FSR review is as follows:

- a pre-notification phase of indeterminate length
- a preliminary review phase lasting up to 25 working days from the time of notification
- (potentially) an in-depth investigation that should be concluded within 90 working days

These phases are discussed in greater detail below. In keeping with the Commission's standard practices, the relevant time period begins on the working day after the receipt of a complete notification or following the adoption of the Commission decision opening an in-depth investigation.[332]

B. The Review Process, Stage-By-Stage

B.1 Pre-Notification

Pre-notification is a period during which the notifying parties and the Commission engage in informal discussions on the contents and timing of the notification. It is not a formal stage of the investigation and no rules concerning pre-notification are specified in the FSR.[333] Form FS-CO states that notifying parties are 'encouraged to engage in pre-notification discussions in sufficient time prior to notification, preferably on the basis of a draft notification'.[334] While not mandatory, engaging in pre-notification discussions is practically important to ensuring the smooth outcome of an FSR filing, as is also the case in the EUMR process. Pre-notification begins when the parties request a case team assignment by sending a completed Case Team Allocation Request form (CTAR) to the Commission.[335]

Pre-notification discussions benefit the transaction parties in several ways.

First, as noted in the preamble to the FSR, if there are any doubts as to whether the transaction meets the FSR thresholds and needs to be notified at all, these can be resolved informally with the Commission case team before any formal submission is made.

Second, the Commission case team has the power to decide whether a notification is complete. If a notification is determined to be incomplete after it is formally filed, the Commission can 'bounce' the notification – effectively preventing the preliminary

---

332 FSR Regulation 2022/2560 [2022] OJ L330/1 (n 1), art 24(1); FSR Implementing Regulation 2023/1441 [2023] OJ L177/1 (n 30), art 21(2).

333 The preamble to the FSR notes that in the context of the M&A tool, transaction parties should also be able to engage in pre-notification discussions with the Commission to determine whether the notification thresholds are met. FSR Regulation 2022/2560 [2022] OJ L330/1 (n 1), recital 38.

334 Form FS-CO (Introduction), para 8.

335 The CTAR is available to download on the Commission's website, at <https://competition-policy.ec.europa.eu/index_en> accessed 18 December 2023.

review phase clock from running until a complete notification is made.[336] It is therefore to the parties' advantage to avoid these delays by ensuring that the notification meets the Commission's expectations before filing. Indeed, attempting to notify a transaction without going through the pre-notification process or obtaining the Commission's green light would be exceedingly unwise, particularly as there is no precedent for how the Commission would view or react to such a filing.

Third, the pre-notification process can significantly reduce the amount of information that needs to be provided in the notification. The Commission has the power to grant waivers for certain categories of information.[337] These waivers are requested during the pre-notification phase.[338] Moreover, even outside the formal waiver process, it is likely that Commission case teams will exercise a wide measure of discretion when judging a notification to be complete. For instance, the case team might need to assess whether certain contributions fall within the categories for which reporting is required under Form FS-CO, whether the level of detail provided about specific contributions is sufficient, or how to interpret the reporting thresholds in individual cases. Engaging in a dialogue with the Commission on these issues allows the transaction parties to present reasoned arguments and may encourage the case team to adopt a position that supports their view.

Finally, pre-notification contacts provide a first opportunity for constructive contact between the parties and the Commission case team that will be handing the FSR review. This allows the parties to present their FSR case in the best light. There might be situations in which the notification itself presents complex reporting problems. If the case team is convinced early on that there is no substantive FSR concern, they might be more willing to engage with the parties to find reasonable solutions to move a notification forward. Moreover, establishing a good working rapport with the case team at the outset can only benefit the smooth outcome of the FSR review process. Transaction parties have found this to be the case in the context of the Commission's merger review process, and it would seem logical that the same human factors should also apply in the case of the FSR review.

Given the informal nature of the pre-notification process, there is no standard timeline as to how long those interactions might last. The Commission has indicated that in the first months following the application of the notification regime, pre-notification periods have ranged between a week between the CTAR submission and notification to over two months. The variation appears to depend on the level of preparation of the parties prior to requesting a case team allocation. The Commission has indicated that it intends to handle straightforward FSR cases quickly and lightly, though it will take time to assess carefully cases that are presented as more complex. For instance, the Commission has indicated it might have more questions and take a closer look at transactions in which a government owned or linked entity is the acquirer.[339] As the FSR review process becomes more established, some general expectations on what timing to expect in more

---

336 FSR Implementing Regulation 2023/1441 [2023] OJ L177/1 (n 30), art 6(2).

337 Form FS-CO (Introduction), para 8-11.

338 ibid, para 9. See Chapter III 3.A.1.

339 Remarks made by Commission officials at the 137th GCLC Lunch Talk, 'FSR merger tool – first experiences' (8 December 2023).

or less complex notifications might emerge. However, even in the EU's well-established merger control process, the length of pre-notification discussions often remains difficult to gauge at the outset.

Pre-notification ends when the parties formally file their FSR notification, ideally after receiving an indication from the Commission case team that the notification appears complete. As in EU merger control, there is no formal decision or opinion issued by the Commission at the end of the pre-notification process.

B.2 Preliminary Review Phase

The first phase of the Commission's review begins when the Commission receives a notification it considers complete. If the Commission receives a notification that it deems to be incomplete, the review clock will only begin once the notifying parties supply a complete version of the notification.[340]

Unlike notifications under the EUMR, FSR notifications are not published in the *Official Journal*. It will therefore be difficult for third parties to submit their observations on a notified transaction, unless the Commission reaches out to them in the form of a third-party RFI.

During the preliminary review phase, the Commission aims to determine whether it has sufficient indications that the parties have received foreign subsidies that distort the internal market, and that further examination during an in-depth investigation is warranted. The parties can also expect the Commission to review the notification form and any accompanying documentation. The case team may ask clarifying questions and request additional documentation by issuing RFIs.[341] Unlike questions that may be asked during pre-notification, these formal RFIs will likely have a tight response deadline in light of the short review period.

The Commission may stop the review clock during the 25-working day period if the parties fail to provide complete information in response to a Commission RFI sent under Article 13 FSR, or where the parties have refused to submit to an inspection as ordered under Article 14 FSR.[342] However, the FSR indicates that those suspensions of the review time limits should only occur on an exceptional basis.[343] The FSR also requires the RFI to indicate whether failure to provide complete information of the specified time limit will suspend the review timeline.[344]

Notably, the Commission's power to 'stop the clock' during the preliminary review phase contrasts with its policy of not stopping the clock at all during Phase 1 of a merger control review. The ability to suspend the preliminary review process under the FSR

---

340 FSR Implementing Regulation 2023/1441 [2023] OJ L177/1 (n 30), art 6(1)–(2).

341 FSR Regulation 2022/2560 [2022] OJ L330/1 (n 1), art 13.

342 ibid, art 24(5). The Commission may also suspend the review period if information is not provided or is not provided in full in response to an RFI directed toward a third party under ibid, art 13, if the failure is due to circumstances for which one of the parties involved is responsible. FSR Implementing Regulation 2023/1441 [2023] OJ L177/1 (n 30), art 23(1)(b).

343 FSR Regulation 2022/2560 [2022] OJ L330/1 (n 1), art 24(5).

344 ibid, art 25(5).

might indicate that the Commission recognises that it might be practically very difficult for transaction parties to provide further information about specific contributions within the tight 25-working day timeframe of a preliminary review and has chosen to build in a safety valve.

The 25-working day review period (not counting any time during which the clock is stopped) defines the deadline by which the Commission must choose whether or not to initiate an in-depth investigation. If the Commission does not choose to open such an investigation, it should inform the parties.[345]

Unlike in Phase 1 of the Commission's merger control review process, the Commission does not issue a formal decision 'clearing' the deal under the FSR after a preliminary review. Therefore, if the Commission does not issue a decision opening an in-depth review during this timeframe, the FSR's suspensory obligations on the parties are automatically lifted, and they may proceed to close the transaction (subject to any other necessary regulatory clearances) even without any response from the Commission. This might facilitate the review process in unproblematic transactions, as the Commission will not be required to gather sufficient detailed information that can serve as a basis for a formal decision and should not be concerned about the precedential value of a decision to 'clear' a transaction.

It is notable that the Commission will neither publish that a notification has been submitted, nor a preliminary review clearance decision. Reviews of transactions under the FSR will therefore completely stay under the radar and the public will not be aware if or when specific transactions are being reviewed under the FSR. The only way for third parties to submit comments (if not contacted by the Commission) would be to scan public sources for transactions that might require an FSR notification and contact the Commission with substantiated concerns, with the hope that the Commission might contact them if and when the transaction is reviewed.

This also means that, unlike under the EUMR, the Commission will not issue a conditional clearance decision in the preliminary review phase, and therefore cannot accept commitments to resolve any problems until an in-depth investigation is opened. The 25-working day preliminary review period can therefore more properly be considered a period during which the Commission may choose to take action.

B.3 In-Depth Investigation

The Commission may open an in-depth investigation within the 25-working day preliminary review period if it has 'sufficient indications that an undertaking has been granted a foreign subsidy that distorts the internal market'.[346] The Commission will open an in-depth investigation by issuing a formal decision. It will also inform the Member States and publish a notice in the *Official Journal* inviting comments.[347]

---

345 ibid, art 10(4).

346 ibid, art 10(3).

347 ibid.

The Commission decision opening the in-depth review should summarise 'the relevant issues of fact and law' and include a 'preliminary assessment of the existence of a foreign subsidy and of the actual or potential distortion in the internal market'. This decision to open an in-depth investigation would be equivalent to a so-called Article 6(1)(c) decision under the EUMR, although the latter is not published.

Considering the practice under the EUMR, the transaction parties will typically submit a paper or other comments responding to the views expressed in the Commission's decision. Third parties might also wish to submit their views on the transaction. The Commission can fix a deadline for the receipt of those comments, which should normally not exceed one month from the issuance of the decision.[348] In practice, the parties' reply to the decision has no formal effect, but – as in the merger control process – doing so might be useful to help address the case team's concerns or shape the team's views during the in-depth investigation.

The issuance of the decision starts the 90-working day review period. This review timeline may be extended in several ways. First, the review period is automatically extended by an additional 15 working days if the transaction parties offer commitments to remedy the competitive distortion identified by the Commission.[349] Second, the review period may also be extended once at the request of the transaction parties, if such a request is made within 15 working days from the start of the in-depth investigation.[350] Third, the parties and the Commission may also jointly agree to extend the review period at any point during the in-depth investigation process.[351] However, any extensions granted at the request of the parties or by agreement with the Commission must not exceed 20 working days.[352]

Fourth, as during the preliminary review phase, the review period may also be suspended entirely in exceptional circumstances where the parties fail to provide information requested in accordance with Article 13 FSR or to submit to an investigation pursuant to Article 14 FSR.[353] The EUMR provides for similar mechanisms to 'stop the clock' or extend the deadlines during a Phase 2 merger control review. As a result, in practice, merger reviews rarely last only the statutory 90 working days, and generally take far longer as parties need extra time to provide the additional information and analyses the Commission might require in completing its investigation. It can be expected that an in-depth FSR review might also extend well beyond the 90-working day period for similar reasons.

During the in-depth review, the Commission will conduct a close examination of the subsidies identified in its decision, seeking to confirm whether these in fact distort the internal market (see Chapter II). In addition to issuing further RFIs, the Commission can conduct interviews[354] and/or inspections[355] to gather more information. Although the

---

348 FSR Implementing Regulation 2023/1441 [2023] OJ L177/1 (n 30), art 8(1).
349 FSR Regulation 2022/2560 [2022] OJ L330/1 (n 1), art 24(1)(b).
350 ibid, art 24(4).
351 ibid.
352 ibid.
353 ibid, art 24(5).
354 ibid, art 13(7).
355 ibid, art 14.

Commission has the power to conduct inspections or interviews during the preliminary review phase of an investigation, it is likely that the Commission would only exercise these powers in the context of an in-depth review.

Article 42(1) FSR – like the EUMR – provides that the Commission should issue a formal charge sheet outlining the grounds on which it intends to take a decision before issuing a negative decision. The Commission's ultimate decision must be based only on the grounds presented to the parties and on which they have had an opportunity to comment.[356] Once this charge sheet is issued, the parties have a right to gain access to the case file (including any supporting documents on which the decision will be based) and to submit a written response.[357]

In the merger control context, such a response rarely, if ever, sways the Commission from its intended decision. While this is likely to be the case in the FSR context as well, the arguments which the parties raise in such a reply might prove useful should they later seek an annulment of a prohibition decision from the General Court. Moreover, during this period the parties might also seek to advance political or policy-based arguments to sway the Commission into adopting a more favourable decision. That influence might also be exercised separately from the review process itself, potentially with the support of public relations firms, or Member State governments, though it might not necessarily impact the outcome of the Commission's review. Unlike the EUMR, the FSR does not provide for the possibility of an oral hearing (which in any event is not often used in the merger control context).

The FSR Implementing Regulation fixes the deadline for the transaction parties to submit proposed commitments at working day 65.[358] If the in-depth review period is extended, this deadline is automatically extended as well. The FSR Implementing Regulation allows the Commission to consider commitments offered after this deadline in exceptional cases. However, any extension of this deadline must take into account the need to comply with the advisory procedure under Article 48(2) FSR that precedes the issuance of a formal decision.[359] As a consequence, transaction parties should not expect that the Commission will accept commitments submitted at the eleventh hour.

Pursuant to Article 25(3) FSR, the Commission is obliged to issue a formal decision at the conclusion of the in-depth investigation, either prohibiting or clearing (unconditionally or subject to commitments) the transaction. However, the FSR authorises the parties to implement the transaction after the 90-working day in-depth investigation period (or the period as extended) has ended if the Commission fails to issue a decision within that deadline.[360] In practice, as noted, it is highly unlikely that the Commission would fail to issue a formal decision within the timeframe originally allotted by the FSR.

---

356 ibid, art 42(3).

357 ibid, art 42(4). See Chapter III 4.B.3.

358 FSR Implementing Regulation 2023/1441 [2023] OJ L177/1 (n 30), art 13(1).

359 FSR Regulation 2022/2560 [2022] OJ L330/1 (n 1), art 11(3); FSR Implementing Regulation 2023/1441 [2023] OJ L177/1 (n 30), art 13(3). See Chapter VI 5.

360 FSR Regulation 2022/2560 [2022] OJ L330/1 (n 1), art 25(4).

C. Alignment with Timing of Merger Control Review

Many – though not all – transactions that are notifiable under the FSR will also be notifiable under the EUMR.[361] The Commission has constructed the two reviews as parallel processes and has aligned the FSR timeline with that already established under the EUMR. As a result, both reviews anticipate an initial 25-working day review for uncomplicated transactions and the possibility of a 90-working day in-depth investigation for ones that present substantive concerns. It can also be expected that the FSR and merger control case teams will communicate with one another during the course of their respective reviews.

Although these timelines appear aligned on paper, the two review processes may not synchronise so neatly in practice. First, any alignment is contingent on both the FSR and EUMR notifications being ready to be filed at the same time. While Form FS-CO consists of only one form for all notifications (which might require more or less information depending on the parties involved) the merger process could require either a full notification (Form-CO) or a simplified filing (Short Form-CO) depending on the competitive relationships of the parties involved.

Moreover, while many large transaction parties might be able to reasonably anticipate the length of time needed to complete a merger filing, none will have practical experience completing Form FS-CO or of the timelines involved to gather the requisite information. It might therefore be quite difficult to align the preparatory process for the two notifications. In addition, given the variable length of pre-notification discussions, one Commission case team might indicate that one notification is complete and has the 'green light' to be filed well before the other, particularly where the transaction presents more substantively complex issues under one instrument versus the other.

Furthermore, even if both the formal FSR and EUMR filings are made on the same date, there is no guarantee that the review processes will continue to proceed simultaneously. As noted above, the Commission has the power to stop the clock in the initial phase of an FSR review, but this is never done in an EUMR review. Depending on the substantive concerns identified in each review process, one notification might require remedies to be cleared and the other not. Alternatively, even if both require remedies, only the EUMR allows these remedies to be offered in Phase 1 (prolonging that review phase), whereas the FSR requires the opening of an in-depth investigation for remedies to be offered. Likewise, one case team might clear the transaction unconditionally at the preliminary review phase, while the other might decide to open an in-depth investigation. Finally, once an in-depth review is opened under either mechanism, the process is unlikely to last only the prescribed 90 working days.

---

361 Moreover, some transactions that do not meet the FSR notification thresholds might be called in for a review based on information supplied in the merger control notification form (Form CO).

Consequently, while transaction parties might wish to align the timing of their FSR and EUMR notifications to the extent possible, they should bear in mind that in practice the processes might diverge leading, to clearance being achieved at different times.

5. Scope of the Commission's Powers

The FSR confers extensive investigative and punitive powers on the Commission in the context of its M&A review.

The Commission's powers include:

- issuing RFIs and conducting interviews to obtain information needed to assess the transaction[362]
- carrying out inspections within and/or outside the EU[363]
- imposing interim measures to ensure that competition is not distorted pending a final decision[364]
- issuing decisions prohibiting problematic transactions or accepting commitments in order to remove competition concerns as a condition of clearance[365]
- imposing fines for failing to observe the FSR's notification and/or standstill rules or for providing incomplete or misleading information in the context of the Commission's review[366]

The FSR confers most of the abovementioned powers to the Commission in the general provisions – notably Articles 12–17 – that apply to all three FSR tools (ex officio, M&A and public procurement). These are discussed in more extensive detail in Chapter VII, but their specific relationship to the review of concentrations is detailed briefly below. Many of these powers closely mimic those granted to the Commission under the EUMR in the merger control context, while others further extend the Commission's powers.

A. *RFIs, Interviews and Inspections*

The FSR grants the Commission broad powers to request additional documentation and evidence needed to complete its review of a transaction. The Commission's powers to issue RFIs, to interview parties and to conduct inspections inside and

362 FSR Regulation 2022/2560 [2022] OJ L330/1 (n 1), art 13. See Chapter VII 3.A.
363 ibid, arts 14 and 15. See Chapter VII 3.B.
364 ibid, art 12. See Chapter VII 2.C.
365 ibid, art 25. See Chapter VI 5.
366 ibid, art 17. See Chapter VII 4.A.

outside the EU are paralleled in the EUMR, and therefore should be familiar to transaction parties with experience notifying concentrations under the EU merger control regime. The Commission may also issue RFIs to other persons, companies or States that are not parties to the transaction. The Commission also enjoys this power under the EUMR, and often sends questionnaires to third parties (although not to States).

As under the EUMR, it can be expected that written RFIs will be the most frequently used tool for the case team to gather information during its review. Similarly, the FSR does not limit the type or quantity of information that may be requested through an RFI, empowering the Commission to collect 'all necessary information' under Article 13. There is also no appeal mechanism if parties consider the case team's information requests overburdensome, excessive or otherwise unreasonable. This is an aspect of the EUMR that transaction parties frequently criticise, and it appears that the same expansive power to compel documents and data is repeated in the FSR.

As in EU merger control, an FSR case team might issue informal RFIs during the course of the pre-notification process to clarify the information provided in the draft notification. Once the formal review process starts, the RFIs will be issued under the express authority of Article 13 FSR. This requires the Commission to indicate a fixed compliance deadline, to inform the parties that incorrect, incomplete, or misleading information may lead to the imposition of penalties, and that in absence of a response the Commission may make a decision based on the facts available to it.[367] The RFI must also indicate whether the review period will be suspended in the event of non-compliance.[368] If the addressee of an RFI fails to respond within the prescribed deadline, the Commission may issue a decision imposing a fine. Unlike the EUMR, the FSR does not provide for both a 'simple request' and a 'formal request' RFI mechanism (under the EUMR, only the latter empowers the Commission to stop the review clock or issue periodic penalty payments until a response is provided).[369]

While the FSR also envisages the possibility to use interviews and inspections during the M&A review process, it is unlikely that these will be frequently used in practice, particularly with respect to third-country inspections. The EUMR grants the Commission the same powers in its merger control review, but these are rarely used – in part due to the tight timeframes involved. If these powers are used in the context of the M&A tool, it will likely be to substantiate Commission suspicions that the parties provided incomplete, incorrect, or misleading information in the notification form or in context of an investigation (and thus to justify punitive measures against the parties concerned), rather than as part of the usual information-gathering process.

---

367 ibid, art 13(4).

368 ibid, art 25(5).

369 EUMR Regulation 139/2004 [2004] OJ L24/1 (n 35), art (11)1 and 3.

B. Interim Measures and Final Decisions

Interim Measures. The FSR empowers the Commission to issue a decision ordering interim measures to protect competition temporarily for a specific period of time or pending the issuance of a final decision on a transaction.[370] As discussed in Chapter VII, as a general matter, interim measures may only be ordered if there are sufficient indications that a relevant transaction party has received a subsidy that distorts the internal market and there is a risk of 'serious and irreparable damage' to the same.[371]

Given the mandatory standstill requirements of the M&A tool, any distortive subsidies received by a transaction party are likely only to have an effect on the market if the transaction is implemented. Consequently, the FSR indicates that, in the context of the M&A tool, the Commission may order interim measures where:

- a concentration has been implemented in breach of the standstill requirement under Article 21 FSR; or
- a concentration has been implemented in breach of a conditional clearance decision imposing commitments under Article 25(3)(a) FSR.[372]

The FSR does not explicitly limit the type of interim measure the Commission may impose. Instead, it specifies that interim measures might include, offering 'fair, reasonable, and non-discriminatory' (FRAND) access to infrastructure (such as R&D, production, capabilities or essential facilities); offering licensing to assets acquired with the help of the subsidies on FRAND terms; or refraining from certain investments.[373] These types of interim measure are available under all three FSR tools. It is unclear, however, how these measures could be imposed in the M&A context, as the concerns they would seek to address are not transaction specific.

Final Decisions. The Commission has the power to clear a transaction, to clear a transaction conditionally, or to prohibit it entirely.[374] The FSR also grants the Commission powers to ensure that conditional clearances or prohibition decisions are enforced even if the transaction has already been implemented.

Specifically, the Commission may order the dissolution of the concentration at issue or the disposal of all the acquired shares or assets to restore the competitive situation that prevailed before the transaction.[375] The Commission may also mandate 'any other appropriate measure' to ensure that the transaction parties unwind the concentration or take any other restorative measures the Commission had ordered.[376] The FSR allows the Commission to take those actions if:

- a notifiable concentration (regardless of whether it was actually notified) has already been implemented and foreign subsidies involved in the

---

370 FSR Regulation 2022/2560 [2022] OJ L330/1 (n 1), art 12.
371 ibid, art 12(1)(a) and (b).
372 ibid, art 25(7).
373 ibid, art 12(2).
374 ibid, art 25(3). See Chapter VI 5.A.
375 ibid, art 25(6)(a).
376 ibid, art 25(6)(b).

transaction distort the internal market (ie, meet the criteria for a prohibition decision);[377] or

- a concentration is implemented in breach of the Commission's decision under Article 25(3) FSR approving the transaction conditionally (where absent the commitments the decision would have been prohibited).[378]

As discussed below, the Commission may also impose fines where parties implement a transaction without waiting for clearance or in contravention of a Commission decision. These measures are similar to those applicable to notifiable concentrations under the EU's merger control process, though the EUMR does not list specific actions that constitute appropriate interim measures.[379]

C. *Fines and Periodic Penalty Payments*

As discussed in Chapter VII, the FSR empowers the Commission to impose fines or periodic penalties to ensure compliance. Fines are one-off punitive measures whereas periodic penalty payments continue until the recipient adopts the particular conduct the Commission requires.

As discussed below, in the case of the M&A tool, the Commission may impose fines or periodic penalty payments for failure to observe the notification and/or standstill requirements (so-called 'gun jumping'), for failure to abide by the Commission's decisions, and for the supplying of incomplete, incorrect or misleading information in the context of the notification, RFI responses or inspections. These fines and their amounts are consistent with the fines prescribed under the EUMR.

Although the FSR sets a maximum fine that may be imposed for each type of conduct, it indicates that the specific amount of the fine should take into account the 'nature, gravity and duration of the infringement' in light of the 'principles of proportionality and appropriateness'.[380] Under the EUMR, the fines imposed almost never reach the maximum allowed under the legislation. It is likely that this might also be the case when the FSR fining rules are applied in the review of concentrations.

Failure to observe the notification and/or standstill requirements. Under Article 26(3) FSR, the Commission may fine a company up to 10% of its aggregate annual turnover for:

- failing to notify a notifiable concentration pursuant to Article 21 FSR prior to implementation (except where the Commission has expressly authorised it to do so);[381]

---

377 ibid, art 25(6).
378 ibid.
379 EUMR Regulation 139/2004 [2004] OJ L24/1 (n 35), art 8(5).
380 FSR Regulation 2022/2560 [2022] OJ L330/1 (n 1), art 17(6).
381 ibid, art 26(3)(a).

- implementing a notified concentration before the expiry of the applicable standstill periods under Article 24 FSR;[382]
- implementing a notified concentration after the Commission has issued a prohibition decision under Article 25(3)(c) FSR;[383]
- circumventing or attempting to circumvent the FSR's notification requirements through the arrangement of financial operations or contracts.[384]

Failure to respect the Commission's decisions imposing conditions, interim measures. Article 17(5) FSR empowers the Commission to fine a company up to 10% of aggregate annual turnover or to impose periodic penalty payments of up to 5% of their average aggregate daily turnover for failing to comply with:

- the commitments agreed as a condition of the Commission's decision to clear the transaction; or
- a Commission decision imposing interim or redressive measures.[385]

During the notification process, RFIs or inspections. Under Article 26(2) FSR, the Commission may fine a party up to 1% of annual turnover for intentionally or negligently supplying incorrect or misleading information in the notifications or any supplemental information submitted.

Under Article 17 FSR, the Commission may also impose fines of up to 1% of annual turnover or periodic payments up 5% average aggregate daily turnover under Article 17 FSR, where a company intentionally or negligently:

- submits incomplete, incorrect or misleading information in response to an RFI or does not comply with the deadline stated in the RFI; or
- refuses to submit/allow access, impedes access, or produces incomplete records or otherwise misleads the Commission in the context of inspections.

In theory, the FSR allows the Commission to impose fines on third parties for failing to respond to an RFI. Although the Commission also has this power under the EUMR, the Commission has only once fined a third party for non-compliance with an RFI (where that party's input is crucial to the Commission's assessment of the case).[386] It seems less likely that the Commission would use fines to enforce third party compliance with RFIs. This is because, under certain circumstances, the FSR allows the Commission to take a decision based on incomplete information – a power it does not have under the EUMR.

Specifically, in the event that the transaction parties or the country providing the subsidy at issue provide incorrect, incomplete, or misleading information in response to a Commission RFI, refuse to submit to an inspection, or otherwise impede the Commission's investigation, the FSR empowers the Commission to make a determination based

382 ibid, art 26(3)(b). See Chapter VII 4.B.

383 ibid, art 26(3)(c).

384 ibid, art 26(3)(d), referring to ibid, art 39.

385 ibid, art 17(5).

386 Commission Decision of 12 July 2000, *Mitsubishi Heavy Industries* (Case COMP/M.1634) [2000] OJ L4/31.

on 'facts available'.[387] In particular, where a State-controlled entity fails to provide the necessary information requested by the Commission to determine the existence of a subsidy, the FSR specifically allows the Commission to presume that the subsidy has been granted (see Chapter VII).[388] These presumptions, in addition to the possibility of fines, disincentivise non-compliance with the Commission's investigation.

6. Substantive Review

Article 25 FSR permits the Commission to take action to block concentrations where it concludes that 'a foreign subsidy distorts the internal market pursuant to Articles 4 to 6'.[389] Article 4 FSR states that a subsidy is considered distortive where it 'is liable to improve the competitive position of an undertaking in the internal market and where, in doing so, that foreign subsidy actually or potentially negatively affects competition in the internal market'. Finally, Article 6 FSR prescribes a balancing test to weigh the distorted effects against other positive effects of the subsidy.

For a more detailed discussion on how these tests could be applied under the FSR, both in general and specifically in the context of an FSR merger review, see Chapter II.

7. Outcomes of the Review Process

A. *Potential Outcomes*

Preliminary review. Following a preliminary review, the Commission can either:

- issue a decision opening an in-depth investigation; or
- allow the review period to expire without opening an investigation, allowing the parties to implement their transaction.

Pursuant to Article 25(3) FSR, after conducting an in-depth investigation of a concentration, the Commission must issue a formal decision either:

- clearing (raising no objection to) the transaction;[390]
- conditionally clearing the transaction subject to commitments offered by the parties;[391] or
- prohibiting the transaction.[392]

---

387 FSR Regulation 2022/2560 [2022] OJ L330/1 (n 1), art 16(1).
388 ibid, art 16(3).
389 ibid, art 25(3)(c).
390 ibid, arts 25(3)(b) and 11(4).
391 ibid, arts 25(3)(a) and 11(3).
392 ibid, art 25(3)(c).

As discussed in Chapter II, a prohibition decision is issued where the Commission finds that a foreign subsidy distorts the internal market and is on balance harmful.[393] Where the Commission finds that a concentration has already been implemented and has led to distortions in the EU market, it may adopt any measures needed to restore the competitive situation prevailing prior to the implementation of the concentration[394] as well as 'gun jumping' fines.[395]

As discussed below, if the Commission has identified a foreign subsidy that distorts the internal market and is on balance harmful, it also has the power to conditionally clear the transaction, subject to commitments offered by the parties to resolve these concerns.

B. Remedies

The FSR enables the Commission to accept commitments offered by transaction parties as a condition of clearance following an in-depth investigation (commitments cannot be offered during the preliminary review phase). These commitments form part of the Commission's clearance decision under Article 11(3) FSR and become binding on the parties. The Commission can monitor compliance with the commitments, and, if needed, issue further decisions imposing fines or periodic penalty payments to ensure compliance,[396] and can revoke its decision authorising the transaction entirely in the event of non-compliance.[397] Notably – and unlike the EUMR – the Commission can also revoke its approval decision if the agreed commitments prove to be 'ineffective'.[398]

Once the Commission has determined that a foreign subsidy distorts the internal market and that the distortion, on balance, is not outweighed by the beneficial effects of that subsidy, the Commission must consider whether the commitments offered by the party are sufficient to remove the distortive effect of the subsidy. The FSR requires that any commitments 'fully and effectively remedy the distortion in the internal market'.[399] In other words, the commitments must entirely remove the competitive distortion, not merely mitigate it. The FSR explicitly instructs the Commission that it should not take into account any of the positive effects of the subsidy identified in the 'balancing test' when determining the suitability of the proposed commitments.[400] The EUMR takes the same approach toward commitments in the merger control context, prohibiting the Commission from accepting commitments that do not fully resolve the competitive concerns identified.[401]

---

393 ibid, art.

394 ibid, art 25(6).

395 ibid, art 26(3). See Chapter III 2.C.

396 ibid, art 17(5).

397 ibid, art 18(1).

398 ibid, art 18(1)(c).

399 ibid, art 7(2).

400 ibid, art 6(2).

401 EUMR Regulation 139/2004 [2004] OJ L24/1 (n 35), art 6(2). Commission Notice on remedies acceptable under the Council Regulation (EC) 139/2004 and under Commission Regulation (EC) 802/2004 (Remedies Notice) [2008] OJ C267/1, para 9.

Article 7 FSR provides a non-exclusive list of potential remedies that can be offered under any of the FSR's three instruments. These include some remedies that are also typically seen in the merger control context including:

- divestment of certain assets;
- offering FRAND access to infrastructure (eg infrastructure, R&D or other essential facilities) that were acquired or supported by foreign subsides;
- licensing under FRAND terms of assets acquired or developed with the help of foreign subsidies (ie certain types of 'behavioural remedies' in the EUMR context);
- publicising R&D results; and
- refraining from certain investments.

The first item in this list – divestment remedies – are referred to as 'structural remedies' in the EUMR context, whereas the other types of commitment are considered 'behavioural remedies'. The Remedies Notice sets out extensive guidance on these types of remedy in the EU merger control context.[402] In merger control, the Commission strongly favours structural remedies over behavioural ones, as structural remedies are seen to be a permanent solution, whereas behavioural remedies require the Commission to engage in ongoing compliance monitoring and are often considered less effective.[403]

The Commission has yet to adopt a similar instrument setting out how the Commission should evaluate the sufficiency of remedies offered to address FSR concerns. It is likely that the Commission will only issue a comparable notice after it has gained sufficient experience evaluating the outcome of particular types of commitment in the FSR context. Although the concerns that these remedies would need to address to resolve an FSR concern are substantively different from those under the EUMR, it is nevertheless possible that the Commission will look to the general considerations outlined in the Remedies Notice when evaluating whether to accept these types of commitment.

Article 7 FSR also includes potential remedies that are inspired by EU State aid law and are not contemplated in the EU merger control context, namely:

- repaying the foreign subsidy;
- requiring a company to adapt their governance structure; and
- reducing capacity or market presence.

There is therefore less guidance that can be derived from the EUMR on how these remedies might be applied in the context of transactions.

As discussed in Chapter II, the FSR M&A tool's primary concern is the distortive effect of a subsidy on competition on the market for corporate control (rather than on the downstream product markets concerned in the transaction). While the potential remedies proposed in Article 7 FSR appear well-suited to address general competitive distortions

---

402 ibid, paras 22–76.

403 ibid, paras 15–17.

caused by foreign subsidies (eg, those identified under the FSR ex officio tool), it remains unclear whether most are suitable for redressing competition on the market for corporate control. Both the structural and behavioural remedies common to the FSR and EUMR appear better suited to address competition on specific product markets, rather than on a market for corporate control (in which a transaction party simply having more funds allows it to outbid its rivals when competing for targets).

While repaying the foreign subsidy would appear to be the surest way to remove the distortive impact of the subsidy in question on the market for transactions, it is unlikely that parties will be able to offer such a remedy in practice and under what conditions the Commission would consider such a remedy credible. If the subsidy is not primarily aimed at facilitating the concentration at issue, and touches on wider aspects of a party's commercial operations, it may not be feasible for parties to offer this commitment to enable the transaction to close.

In sum, it remains uncertain what commitments the Commission might deem to resolve FSR concerns under the M&A tool. While the Commission's past track record in accepting commitments under the EUMR might provide some general guidance, the substantive context in which these remedies are offered differs significantly between the two instruments.

8. Other EU Regulatory Processes

The FSR introduces another regulatory obligation into a European M&A process that is already subject to multiple different clearance processes. A transaction involving an EU target might trigger a number of different regulatory filings: FSR, EUMR, and FDI.[404]

The FSR's M&A tool is drawn from the EUMR in terms of process and many of the underlying conceptual frameworks. It is also the Commission-level structure that many large companies will already be familiar with from previous M&A activities in the EU. Consequently, the parallels and differences between the FSR and EUMR have been outlined in the course of this chapter. In theory, it is possible for the timeline of an FSR and EUMR review by the Commission to align very closely, particularly in unproblematic cases.

However, while the Commission has sole authority to review transactions under the FSR, the same deal may not necessarily meet the EU notification thresholds for a merger notification. If the deal does not meet the EU merger notification thresholds, it may still be subject to the merger control regimes of the various Member States and could therefore undergo several national merger review processes in parallel with the FSR investigation. While national merger reviews generally follow the EUMR in terms of substance and,

404 Other regulatory filings may be required depending on the jurisdiction (ie, Member States may each have a different set of applicable regulatory frameworks and some administrative processes may be required at regional or municipal level), structure of the business (eg, publicly held companies) and industry (eg special sectoral rules may apply to M&A in healthcare, media, defence, and other sectors). These processes may be managed by different regulatory bodies at various administrative levels. See also Chapter V 4.D.

to a lesser extent, structure, these processes do not follow a synchronous timeline and can proceed at different speeds.

Likewise, almost all Member States require that certain types of transaction undergo FDI screening. FDI review has come increasingly into focus in the EU in recent years, with most Member States introducing new, or expanding existing, FDI legislation conferring review powers and requiring ex ante notification of M&A activity in certain cases. As FDI is primarily aimed at ensuring that countries are able to protect their national security interests, most EU Member States have their own, specific FDI regime, with minimal harmonisation and coordination at EU level. The industries considered sensitive as well as the conditions that will require a filing therefore differ from Member State to Member State. Depending on the nature of the transaction, one or more FDI filings may be required in the EU.

There is no coordination between the process or timeline of any FSR or EUMR filing and national FDI filings, although the Member States are required to inform the Commission about starting FDI reviews. This being said, national FDI rules and the FSR regime share some common concerns. There might be considerable overlap between what sector or assets a Member State's FDI rules have deemed sensitive to the national interest and those that might be of greatest interest to the Commission (particularly in light of the wording of recital 2 FSR, noting the particular importance of the FSR regime to transactions affecting strategic assets such as critical infrastructure or innovative technologies). The Commission might be more interested to call in transactions that trigger FDI reviews. Likewise, FDI notifications often contain questions probing whether the parties are receiving subsidies from foreign countries.

Chapter IV
The Public Procurement Tool

1. Introduction

The FSR's public procurement tool enables the Commission to examine whether economic operators participating in public procurement projects[405] in the EU have a competitive advantage as a result of foreign subsidies they have received. Articles 27–33 FSR set out specific rules on the public procurement tool, which are complemented by the general provisions in Articles 1–18 and 34–54 FSR. The FSR Implementing Regulation outlines the modalities for making an FSR notification or declaration in the context of public procurement projects and other aspects of the Commission's review process. Annex 2 to the FSR Implementing Regulation provides the form that must be used for notifications and declarations (Form FS-PP).

Like the FSR more broadly, the public procurement tool was designed to bridge a perceived regulatory gap in the Commission's ability to assess and control the influence of foreign subsidies on public procurement projects and to effectively deal with distortions in the internal market caused by foreign subsidies. The public procurement tool allows the Commission to focus specifically on the distortive effect caused by foreign subsidies in the context of public procurement. It aims to ensure a level playing field throughout the internal market and to ensure that foreign subsidies do not provide an economic advantage to an economic operator, enabling it to submit an unduly advantageous bid for a public works, supplies, or services contract. EU procurement directives allow a contracting authority or entity to assess whether a bid is abnormally low because of EU State aid (under strict conditions, as explained by the CJEU).[406] But under these directives the effects of foreign subsidies cannot be taken into account to the same extent.

Levelling the playing field in procurement projects, as envisaged by the FSR, might negatively impact competitive intensity. Prices paid by contracting authorities or entities, and therefore costs to taxpayers, likely will increase in certain procurement projects. Some bidders likely will refrain from participating in procurement projects because they are not willing, or not allowed, to disclose subsidies received in their home country. Other bidders might decide not to rely on specific suppliers or subcontractors offering the best price because of concerns that choosing that subcontractor/supplier would complicate the FSR review and/or even endanger participation in the tender.

---

405 On terminology and the reference to procurement "projects", see above, footnote 4.

406 See Chapter II 3.C.

The public procurement tool shares certain features with the FSR's M&A tool. For example, it also relies on a combination of value and contribution thresholds to trigger notification obligations, preliminary and in-depth review periods, and suspension periods pending Commission review. Both tools incorporate forms and concepts generally applicable under the FSR (such as the definition of the terms 'financial contributions' and 'subsidies'). The notification forms under the two tools are similarly structured.

However, there are also important differences between the M&A tool and the public procurement tool. Those differences notably relate to the purpose of the value and contribution thresholds, the authority receiving notifications, the definition of entities considered to be the relevant recipients of foreign subsidies, the content of notifications, the exemptions from financial contributions reporting requirements, and the structure and length of the preliminary review period. Moreover, as explained in Chapter II, the substantive test to determine whether foreign subsidies result in a distortion of competition likely will rely on different parameters. Where relevant, this chapter highlights the similarities and differences between the M&A and public procurement tools.

The features that are unique to the public procurement tool can be explained by the close relationship between the FSR notification mechanism and the national procurement procedures. In essence, the legislator has attempted to align the two procedures as closely as possible, and to reduce the (inevitable) risk that FSR reviews will interfere with national public procurement procedures and the award of government contracts. This explains, for example, the use of shorter and less flexible preliminary review periods and the requirement to submit two notifications in multi-stage procurement projects.[407] The Commission has also taken the position that it needs more detailed information upfront in public procurement notifications (and therefore provides for less generous exemptions from reporting requirements) because of the tighter review deadlines. Another example is the option for notifying parties to incorporate in the Form FS-PP information about the public procurement project contained in the European Single Procurement Document (ESPD).

It remains an open question whether all the specific features of the public procurement tool are, in fact, necessary in the – legitimate – interest of minimising the risk that FSR notifications will interfere with national public procurement procedures. For example, it is not clear why the rationale for the more generous exemption thresholds for financial contributions that are not presumptively distortive does not apply under the FSR's public procurement tool. If it can be assumed that financial contributions below €45 million per country over three years are highly unlikely to result in distortion of competition in the internal market (as is the case under the FSR's M&A tool), this should in principle also be true if the recipient bids for a public procurement project.

The different reporting requirements in the two notification forms seriously complicate the information-gathering process for companies preparing for both M&A and public procurement notifications: public procurement notifications capture fewer entities as relevant

---

407 In a two-stage procurement procedure, a contracting authority or entity first invites market participants to express an interest in participating in the procurement project. Those who have submitted a request to participate are then selected to submit their bids in the second stage.

recipients of financial contributions, but those entities must comply with more detailed reporting requirements in respect of the financial contributions they have received.

In addition, the FSR public procurement tool (including Form FS-PP) has replaced certain concepts used in Form FS-CO with concepts taken from public procurement law which lack a clear definition. One example is the notion of a 'subsidiary without commercial independence', which the FSR uses to distinguish subsidiaries of the main bidder that are relevant recipients of foreign subsidies from those that are not. In public procurement case law, the ECJ has used this concept to identify scenarios in which to entities belonging to the same control group may be allowed to independently compete in a procurement project, without, however, providing a clear definition of the 'commercial independence' concept.[408] This reference to vaguely defined concepts in public procurement law adds further uncertainty about how the Form FS-PP must be completed.

Reflecting the close relationship between the FSR and EU procurement law, the FSR also provides that the Commission as well as the contracting authorities or entities involved must respect all principles governing public procurement projects, including the principles of proportionality, non-discrimination, equal treatment, transparency, and competition during the review. The review process under the FSR may not result in contracting authorities or entities treating economic operators in a manner contrary to these principles.[409]

This chapter will discuss the following aspects to the public procurement tool:

- public procurement projects requiring a notification or a declaration;
- the scope of notifications and declarations (Form FS-PP);
- the Commission's review process and timeline;
- the scope of the Commission's powers;
- the scope of the Commission's substantive review; and
- possible outcomes of the review process.

---

408 See, e.g., Case C-538/07 *Assitur Srl v Camera di Commercio, Industria, Artigianato e Agricoltura di Milano*, EU:C:2009:317.

409 FSR Regulation 2022/2560 [2022] OJ L330/1 (n 1), art 32(7).

2. Public Procurement Projects Requiring a Notification or a Declaration

A. Public Procurement Projects Falling under the Mandatory Notification and Declaration Regime

A.1 Public Procurement Projects Falling within the Scope of the FSR

The public procurement tool applies only to public procurement projects governed by the EU public procurement Directives listed in Article 2 FSR, namely:[410]

- any type of award procedure covered by Directive 2014/24/EU or Directive 2014/25/EU (relating to public works, supply and services contracts in all sectors, including special sectors such as water, energy, transport and postal services);[411]
- a procedure for the award of a works or service concession covered by Directive 2014/23/EU (relating to concession contracts);[412] and
- procedures for the award of contracts referred to in Article 10(4), point (a), Directive 2014/23/EU, Article 9(1), point (a), Directive 2014/24/EU or Article 20(1), point (a), Directive 2014/25/EU.[413]

The public procurement tool also applies to framework agreements. If a framework agreement meets the relevant thresholds, notifications are required. However, in order to preserve the benefit of concluding a framework agreement (that is, the flexibility offered to purchasers after the conclusion of the framework agreement), the notification obligations under the public procurement tool do not apply in respect of individual contracts based on the framework agreement.[414]

---

410 Directive 2014/25/EU of the European Parliament and of the Council of 26 February 2014 on procurement by entities operating in the water, energy, transport and postal services sectors and repealing Directive 2004/17/EC [2014] OJ L94/243.

411 Directive 2014/24/EU of the European Parliament and of the Council of 26 February 2014 on public procurement and repealing Directive 2004/18/EC [2014] OJ L94/65; Directive 2014/25/EU [2014] OJ L94/243 (n 410).

412 Directive 2014/23/EU of the European Parliament and of the Council of 26 February 2014 on the award of concession contracts [2014] OJ L94/1.

413 These provisions concern concessions, public contracts and design contests, respectively, which the contracting authority or entity is obliged to award or organise in accordance with procedures established by a legal instrument creating international law obligations, such as an international agreement concluded in conformity with the Treaties, between a Member State and one or more third countries or subdivisions thereof and covering works, supplies or services intended for the joint implementation or exploitation of a project by their signatories.

414 FSR Regulation 2022/2560 [2022] OJ L330/1 (n 1), recital 42.

Certain public procurement projects are excluded from the scope of the public procurement tool. Those include public procurement projects for awarding contracts: (i) falling under Directive 2009/81/EC (relating to public works, supply and services contracts in the fields of defence and security),[415] and (ii) covered by Article 32(2), point (c), Directive 2014/24/EU[416] and Article 50, point (d), Directive 2014/25/EU.[417] However, these procurement projects are covered by the general provisions in Articles 1–18 and 34–54 of the FSR, and therefore may be the subject of an ex officio review.[418]

Public procurement projects of the EU institutions that are covered by the Financial Regulation[419] are, for now, not within the scope of the FSR. However, the rules of the Financial Regulation are being revised, and the current proposal for a revised regulation includes the same rules as those under the FSR.[420] At the time of writing, it is envisaged that the revised Financial Regulation will be adopted by mid-2024. It therefore can be expected that the rules of the FSR and the rules governing public procurement projects of EU institutions will become aligned with respect to foreign subsidy control.

A.2 Requirement for Meeting the Estimated Value and Contribution Thresholds

Like the M&A tool, the public procurement tool defines a value threshold and a contribution threshold. Similar to the M&A tool (see Chapter III), the estimated value threshold is set relatively high whilst the contribution threshold is very low. However, the function of these two thresholds is different under these two tools. Under the M&A tool, notification is required only if both thresholds are met. Under the public procurement tool, the value threshold (based on the estimated value of the public procurement project) alone determines whether a bidder (the 'economic operator' and potentially other notifying parties) must submit a completed Form FS-PP to the Commission. If a procurement project meets the value threshold, the contribution threshold determines whether the bidder must submit a (fuller) notification or a (less detailed) declaration.

---

415 Directive 2009/81/EC of the European Parliament and of the Council of 13 July 2009 on the coordination of procedures for the award of certain works contracts, supply contracts and service contracts by contracting authorities or entities in the fields of defence and security and amending Directives 2004/17/EC and 2004/18/EC [2009] OJ L216/76.

416 This concerns the negotiated procedure without prior publication used for public works contracts, public supply contracts, and public service contracts in so far as is strictly necessary where, for reasons of extreme urgency brought about by events unforeseeable by the contracting authority or entity, the time limits for the open or restricted procedures or competitive procedures with negotiation cannot be respected.

417 This concerns the negotiated procedure without a prior call for competition used in the case in so far as is strictly necessary where, for reasons of extreme urgency brought about by events unforeseeable by the contracting authority or entity, the time limits laid down for open procedures, restricted procedures and negotiated procedures with prior call for competition cannot be respected.

418 FSR Regulation 2022/2560 [2022] OJ L330/1 (n 1), art 28(3) and (4).

419 Regulation (EU, Euratom) 2018/1046 of the European Parliament and of the Council of 18 July 2018 on the financial rules applicable to the general budget of the Union [2018] OJ L193/1.

420 European Commission, Proposal for a Regulation of the European Parliament and of the Council on the financial rules applicable to the general budget of the Union (recast) COM (2022) 223 final.

A.2.1 The Estimated Value Threshold

Pursuant to Article 28(1)(a) and (2) FSR, public procurement projects are subject to mandatory notification and declaration obligations if they meet the following estimated value threshold:

- public contracts not divided into lots: the estimated value threshold is based on the estimated value of a public procurement or a framework agreement (excluding VAT), calculated in accordance with the provisions laid down in Article 8 Directive 2014/23/EU, Article 5 Directive 2014/24/EU and Article 16 Directive 2014/25/EU, or a specific procurement under the dynamic purchasing system. This estimated value must be equal to or greater than €250 million;[421]
- public contracts divided into lots: the estimated value threshold is twofold: (i) the estimated value of the public procurement (excluding VAT) must exceed the estimated value of equal to or greater than €250 million, and (ii) the value of the lot or the aggregate value of all lots to which the bidder applies must be equal to or greater than €125 million.[422]

The estimated value threshold is set relatively high to capture only economically significant cases while minimising the administrative burden and not hindering the participation of SMEs in public procurement.

The determination of the estimated value threshold falls under the purview of the contracting authority or entity, as is standard in public procurement projects. Only the estimated value published by the contracting authority or entity (and not the value of the winning bid) determines whether a project meets the value threshold. As a result, when the project value is set at or above €250 million, the project will be subject to the notification obligation under the public procurement tool even if all bids are below the estimated value and do not reach the procurement tool's value threshold.

In general, contracting authorities or entities have wide latitude in designing their projects, even if this means that their projects fall below the value threshold. However, when determining the estimated value of a public procurement project as well as the relevant time period for assessing this estimated value, the contracting authority or entity must respect the applicable provisions in the EU public procurement Directives, in particular those in Article 8 Directive 2014/23/EU, Article 5 Directive 2014/24/EU and Article 16 Directive 2014/25/EU.[423] Taking into account that Article 28(1)(a) FSR must be applied 'in accordance with' the EU public procurement Directives, a contracting authority or entity is precluded from calculating the estimated value of a project, or without objective justification subdividing a project into separate projects, with the specific intention of excluding a project from the scope of the FSR (and regardless of the anti-circumvention provision in Article 39 FSR).

---

421 FSR Regulation 2022/2560 [2022] OJ L330/1 (n 1), art 28(1)(a).

422 ibid, art 28(2).

423 ibid, art 28(1)(a).

In addition, Article 18.1, second sentence, Directive 2014/24/EU indicates that the design of a procurement project (even if the result is that the project does not meet the value threshold of that Directive) could be challenged if there is evidence of an intention to unduly favour or disadvantage certain economic operators.[424]

At least for government contracts for work, the EU Courts have identified a number of criteria that can be used for determining whether a procurement authority has 'artificially split' a project. These include whether separate projects fulfil the same economic and technical function, their proximity in time and geographic coverage, and the identity of the contracting authority or entity.[425] The EU Courts, however, have not provided similar guidance, in respect of a contract for services, on the criteria that can be applied to determine whether a government contract has been 'artificially split'. Presumably, a substantive connection between the services procured in separate procurement projects, a temporal proximity, and the identity of the procurement authority could be relevant factors.

Contracting authorities or entities can decide, whilst respecting the prohibition against artificially splitting procurement projects, to divide a project into separate lots.[426] In fact, the EU procurement Directives encourage splitting projects into smaller lots to increase competition and create more opportunities for SMEs to participate in public procurement projects.[427]

Even if a project is divided into lots, the €250 million value threshold for the entire project applies. If the aggregate value of all lots meets the value threshold, a bidder is subject to the mandatory notification regime if: (i) it bids for a lot valued at €125 million or more, or (ii) it bids for smaller lots with an aggregated value of €125 million or more. As a result, if a project meeting the value threshold is divided into lots below €125 million, notification obligations may apply asymmetrically to various bidders. A public contract with a value below €250 million divided into lots is excluded from the notification and declaration obligations irrespective of the value of each lot.

A public procurement procedure not meeting this estimated value threshold is not subject to the notification and declaration obligations. While this is not entirely clear from the wording of Article 29(4) FSR, the Commission has confirmed this limitation of the reach of the mandatory notification regime.[428] However, even if a public procurement project does not meet the value threshold (or the value of a lot is below €125 million), the Commission can still require a notification on its own initiative.

---

424 See also Case C-598/19 *Conacee v Feacem* EU:C:2021:349, Opinion of the Advocate General, para 79 (suggesting that the concept of 'artificial narrowing' has a broader scope than the intention to unduly favour/disadvantage certain economic operators).

425 Case T-384/10 *Spain v European Commission* EU:T:2013:277; see also Case C-16/98 *Commission of the European Communities v French Republic* EU:C:2000:541.

426 See also FSR Regulation 2022/2560 [2022] OJ L330/1 (n 1), recital 46 (referring to the prohibition against 'artificial splitting' of projects).

427 See, eg, Directive 2014/24/EU [2014] OJ L94/65 (n 411), art 46. Recital 78 of the same Directive explains: 'Public procurement should be adapted to the needs of SMEs, [...]. To that end and to enhance competition, contracting authorities should in particular be encouraged to divide large contracts into lots.'

428 FSR Public Procurement FAQs, question 11 (n 31), question 11.

A.2.2 The Contribution Threshold

Pursuant to Article 28(1)(b) and (2) FSR, the following contribution threshold applies in the context of public procurement projects:

- the aggregate financial contributions granted in the three years prior to notification or, if applicable, the updated notification to the economic operator, including its subsidiary companies without commercial autonomy, its holding companies, and, where applicable, its main subcontractors and suppliers involved in the same tender in the public procurement procedure, must be *equal to or greater than €4 million per third country*.[429]

In contrast to the estimated value threshold, which determines whether a notification obligation exists, the contribution threshold determines whether a notifying party must submit a notification or a declaration. If the notifying party (or any of the notifying parties if there are several) meets the contribution threshold in any third country, the party/parties must submit a notification. If the notifying party does not meet the contribution threshold (or, if there are several, none of the notifying parties meets the contribution threshold), the party/parties must submit a declaration.

The contribution threshold is very low. Given the wide scope of the notion of a 'financial contribution' (see Chapter II), the contribution threshold is likely to be relatively easily met by many economic operators participating in high-value public procurement projects that meet the value threshold, unless they (and their relevant corporate affiliates) have no or only insignificant operations outside the EU.[430] Ultimately, bidders that are active only in the EU or bidders that are part of a larger control group, but where the corporate structure makes it possible to disregard financial contributions received by corporate affiliates that are active outside the EU, likely would remain below the contribution threshold. This means that they would be able to submit a declaration instead of a notification.

A.2.2.1 *Entities Relevant for Determining whether the Contribution Threshold Is Met*

Chapter 4 FSR (on the public procurement tool) uses its own, distinct definitions of the entities of which the financial contributions must be taken into account for applying the notification obligation. Unlike the M&A tool, which considers relevant financial contributions received within the entire control group, the public procurement tool considers relevant financial contributions only if they have been received by:

- the economic operator participating in a tender;
- the economic operator's subsidiaries without commercial autonomy;
- the economic operator's direct and indirect parents (holding companies); and

---

429 FSR Regulation 2022/2560 [2022] OJ L330/1 (n 1), art 28(1)(b).

430 If they have no or only insignificant operations in third countries, there are less likely to receive financial contributions from those countries.

- the economic operator's main subcontractors and main suppliers in the public procurement project.[431]

It is not entirely clear why the public procurement tool draws the circle of entities that are considered relevant recipients of financial contributions more narrowly than the M&A tool. The logic for the M&A tool's decision to consider financial contributions received by all entities within a control group as relevant must be that money is fungible – regardless of which entity receives a subsidy, the benefits can in principle always be moved around within a control group. The same logic would in principle also appear to apply in a procurement context. However, in the context of the public procurement tool, the legislator has decided that this logic should not be determinative.

A.2.2.2 *The Economic Operator and Certain Corporate Affiliates*

The starting point to determine which entities are considered relevant recipients of financial contributions is always the economic operator, ie, the entity or person that submits a bid in a public procurement project in a Member State. The EU procurement Directives indicate that the term 'economic operator' should be broadly interpreted, to include 'any natural or legal person or public entity or group of such persons and/or entities, including any temporary association of undertakings'.[432] In the case of a bidder consortium, each consortium member is considered an economic operator under the FSR, and each consortium member must notify.

An economic operator must then determine whether its direct and indirect parents have received financial contributions. The FSR refers to 'holding companies', without further defining this term. It is understood that this term comprises any parent, meaning any entity that has direct or indirect control rights in the economic operator.

Finally, the economic operator must determine whether its subsidiaries without commercial autonomy have received financial contributions. This includes both direct and indirect subsidiaries of the economic operator. The FSR provides no explanation for why subsidiaries with commercial autonomy are not included in the circle of relevant recipients of financial contributions. Nor does it provide any guidance on how to distinguish between subsidiaries that have commercial autonomy and those that do not.

The choice of using 'commercial autonomy' instead of – more objective and predictable – control rights as the parameter to identify which subsidiaries fall in the circle of relevant recipients of financial contributions is the result of the attempted alignment of the FSR with EU public procurement law. Under the EU procurement Directives, entities belonging to the same control group are in principle not precluded from independently participating (ie, from competing) in the same procurement project, provided that they enjoy 'a certain autonomy in the conduct of their commercial policy

---

431 FSR Regulation 2022/2560 [2022] OJ L330/1 (n 1), art 28(1)(b).

432 See, eg, Directive 2014/24/EU [2014] OJ L94/65 (n 411), art 2(10). See also ibid, recital 14: 'Thus, firms, branches, subsidiaries, partnerships, cooperative societies, limited companies, universities, public or private, and other forms of entities than natural persons should all fall within the notion of economic operator, whether or not they are "legal persons" in all circumstances.'

and their economic activities' with respect to the public procurement project.[433] This should support the EU policy goal of ensuring the widest possible participation of bidders in a public procurement project.[434] Thus, when two entities belonging to the same control group are permitted to independently participate in the same project meeting the value threshold as a matter of EU public procurement law, each of them would be considered an economic operator and required to independently submit its own FSR notification.

Unfortunately, EU public procurement law has not developed a set of criteria applicable to the autonomy determination. The CJEU has held that when a contracting authority or entity is aware of evidence questioning the autonomous and independent character of the tenders submitted by certain bidders, it must verify whether the two bidders are in fact autonomous and independent.[435] The existence of control rights is not in itself determinative, but no further guidance has been offered in the case law. In *Assitur*, the CJEU suggested that entities belonging to the same control group may be governed by specific contractual provisions ensuring their independence when participating in the same procurement project.[436] But those contractual provisions likely are not very common.

This legal uncertainty is problematic in a notification context, where the notifying entity must, by way of self-assessment, determine which entities it must include when calculating thresholds and reporting financial contributions in Form FS-PP. In practice, it might be prudent to include all subsidiaries of an economic operator (ie, consider only control rights), unless there is evidence that a subsidiary has previously independently participated in a public procurement process in which other members of the same control group have also participated.

In this context, particular questions arise if the economic operator holds an interest in a JV. For JVs, there can be many grades of commercial independence and autonomy. It might not be practical to reliably determine on a case-by-case basis whether the economic operator should include financial contributions received by the JV. Again, it might be prudent to assume that a JV in which the economic operator holds control rights over the JV's commercial policy should be considered a subsidiary without commercial independence. On the other hand, JVs in which the economic operator only holds a minority interest and no control rights beyond rights protecting its investment arguably would fall into the category of subsidiaries with commercial autonomy.

The public procurement tool's choice of entities that are considered relevant recipients of financial contributions risks giving rise to arbitrary and random results. For example, if the economic operator is controlled only by entities that do not have their own commercial operations and are commercially active only through other subsidiaries, it would be less likely to meet the contribution threshold and would have fewer financial contributions to report than an economic operator with parents that are themselves commercial operators

---

433 Case C-538/07 *Assitur Srl v Camera di Commercio, Industria, Artigianato e Agricoltura di Milano* EU:C:2009:317, paras 26 and 28; Case C-531/16 *Šiaulių regiono atliekų tvarkymo centras and 'Ecoservice projektai' UAB* EU:C:2018:324, para 21.

434 ibid.

435 *Šiaulių regiono atliekų tvarkymo centras* (n 433), para 40.

436 *Assitur* (n 433), para 31.

and active outside the EU. This applies irrespective of whether the economic operator could potentially benefit from intra-group transfers through which it could become the indirect beneficiary of foreign subsidies received by a corporate affiliate.

A.2.2.3 *Main Subcontractors and Main Suppliers*

The economic operator's subcontractors and sub-suppliers are considered 'main' subcontractors/suppliers (and therefore included in the group of notifying parties) if: (i) they provide key elements for the performance of the government contract, or (ii) the value of their contribution exceeds 20% of the value of the submitted tender.[437] The status of a main subcontractor or supplier must be determined at the time the notification is effective (that is, when the Commission has received the complete notification).[438] Subsequent changes do not trigger new notification requirements.

Unlike in the case of the economic operator, only the entity acting as the main subcontractor or main supplier is considered relevant. Any corporate affiliates of the subcontractor/supplier are excluded. Thus, any financial contribution received by the subcontractor's or supplier's parents or other corporate affiliates are not relevant for calculating the thresholds and for meeting reporting obligations. However, the Commission might be able to use the anti-circumvention provision to pierce through corporate arrangements where there is clear evidence that a front company has been set up for the sole purpose of shielding foreign subsidies received by the entity that acts *de facto* as the main supplier.[439]

Determining whether a supplier or sub-contractor meets the 20% value threshold will frequently be a relatively straightforward exercise. This is not the case when determining whether a supplier or subcontractor provides a 'key input'. The FSR explains that the key supplier status can be determined in light of the selection criteria of the public procurement project – if the economic operator relies on the supplier's input to fulfil one or more selection criteria, the supplier would be considered to provide a key input. The FSR lists specific know-how, technology, staff, and patents as examples. Moreover, the input must have specific relevance for a particular public procurement project.[440] The specificity requirement indicates that if, for example, the economic operator has entered into a technology license agreement or relies on third-party knowhow for all its operations (and not specific to the public procurement project), the licensor is not considered a provider of a key input.

Only the entity that has the contractual relationship with the economic operator/customer is considered the main subcontractor or supplier. Even if a corporate affiliate will partially

---

437 FSR Regulation 2022/2560 [2022] OJ L330/1 (n 1), art 29(5).

438 FSR Implementing Regulation 2023/1441 [2023] OJ L177/1 (n 30), art 7(1). However, where the Commission finds that the information, including documents, contained in the received notification is incomplete, it must inform the notifying parties or their authorised external representatives in writing without delay, and the notification shall only become effective on the date on which the complete information is received by the Commission. See FSR Implementing Regulation 2023/1441 [2023] OJ L177/1 (n 30), art 7(1) *juncto*; FSR Regulation 2022/2560 [2022] OJ L330/1 (n 1), art 29(4).

439 FSR Regulation 2022/2560 [2022] OJ L330/1 (n 1), art 39. See Chapter VII 6.

440 ibid, recital 54.

or entirely perform the contract and supply the contracted goods or services, only the entity that is party to the contract with the economic operator is considered the main subcontractor or supplier. Similarly, a main supplier might purchase goods from third parties and re-sell them to the economic operator. The design choices of the public procurement tool indicate that only financial contributions received by the main supplier would be relevant. If the main supplier purchases goods that are subsidised by third countries, those subsidies would be out of scope (see Chapter II).

Article 28(1)(b) FSR appears to apply to sub-contractors or suppliers irrespective of whether they have any form of EU nexus and they might never have exported goods or services to the EU – if they meet the criteria of a main supplier or contractor because of their relationship with the economic operator, they will be considered notifying parties and become subject to FSR notification obligations. As discussed above (Chapter II), there could be a question of whether a supplier or subcontractor without any EU nexus (apart from having a customer that participates in a procurement project in the EU) can be considered to be 'engaging in an activity in the internal market' and thus be subject to the FSR.

But an economic operator planning to participate in a procurement project in the EU might have little incentive to rely on the argument that a main supplier or subcontractor without an EU nexus cannot be considered a notifying party. If the Commission disagrees, the economic operator risks being excluded from the procurement project. Thus, submitting a notification or declaration with the main supplier or subcontractor as a notifying party should normally be the preferred option. Nevertheless, ensuring that such a supplier, which might never have heard of the FSR, understands its reporting obligations under the FSR and is willing to comply might create significant challenges for the economic operator.

A.2.2.4 *Calculation of Aggregate Foreign Financial Contributions*

The amount of individual financial contributions is irrelevant when determining whether the contribution threshold is met. All financial contributions must be taken into account.

A notification is required when a notifying party individually reaches the contribution threshold of €4 million over three years per third country. If there are several notifying parties, the financial contributions they received are not aggregated to determine whether the contribution threshold is met. In other words, if none of the notifying parties individually meets the €4 million threshold, there is no obligation to submit a notification. A declaration will still be required.

Conversely, if any one of several notifying parties has received financial contributions of €4 million over three years in any third country, all notifying parties must submit a notification, including those that have not received notifiable financial contributions.

Timing. An economic operator (and any other notifying party) must take into account all aggregate financial contributions granted to it in the three years prior to its notification.[441] The effective date of a notification is the date on which it is received by the Commission.[442]

---

441 ibid, art 28(1)(b).

442 FSR Implementing Regulation 2023/1441 [2023] OJ L177/1 (n 30), art 7(1).

In multi-stage procedures, it is possible that the conditions for triggering the notification obligation are met at the time of the submission of the request to participate but not at the time of the submission of the tender (because early contributions predate the beginning of the three-year period at the time of the second notification). The Commission is understood to assume that if there was an obligation to submit a notification at the time of the request to participate, there is also an obligation to submit an updated notification even if at that time the value threshold is no longer met. It would nevertheless be advisable to indicate in the second, updated notification that the value threshold is no longer met.

A.3 Notice of Applicability of the Mandatory Notification and Declaration Regime

When contracting authorities or entities publish a contract notice for a new public works, supplies or services contract, the notice must state that economic operators participating in the public procurement procedure are subject to the FSR. In the case of a procedure without a prior publication, the contracting authorities or entities must include such a notice in the procurement documents.[443]

However, there are no legal consequences if a contracting authority or entity fails to provide that statement in the contract notice or the procurement documents. Even in the absence of such a notice, the FSR's notification and declaration obligations apply.[444]

A.4 Exception to the FSR's Mandatory Notification Regime

A contracting authority or entity may use a negotiated procedure without a prior call for competition if works, supplies, or services can be supplied only by one particular economic operator. This could be the case because the aim of the procurement is the creation or acquisition of a unique work of art or artistic performance, competition is absent for technical reasons, or for the protection of exclusive rights, including intellectual property rights.[445]

If the procurement authority or entity uses a negotiated procedure in a project that meets the FSR's value threshold, and the economic operator meets the contribution threshold, the economic operator must inform the Commission of all financial contributions received. This information, however, will not be considered a notification and will not be subject to the review process under Chapter 4 FSR.

---

443 FSR Regulation 2022/2560 [2022] OJ L330/1 (n 1), art 28(6).

444 ibid.

445 Directive 2014/24/EU [2014] OJ L94/65 (n 411), art 32(2)(b); Directive 2014/25/EU [2014] OJ L94/243 (n 410), art 50(c); Directive 2014/23/EU [2014] OJ L94/1 (n 412), art 31(4).

B. Public Procurement Projects Falling outside the Mandatory Notification and Declaration Regime

Article 29(8) FSR authorises the Commission to request an economic operator in any public procurement project below the value threshold to submit a notification of financial contributions granted by third countries. The Commission may exercise this power if it suspects that the economic operator concerned might have benefitted from financial contributions in the three years prior to the submission of its request to participate or tender in the public procurement procedure.[446]

Information leading the Commission to suspect foreign subsidies and to require a notification could come from any legal or natural person. Complaints by competitors in a public procurement project will most likely be the principal source of information. In principle, contracting authorities or entities could also inform the Commission of suspected financial contributions benefiting one of the bidders in any project remaining below the FSR's value threshold. It remains uncertain, however, whether contracting authorities or entities will have a strong incentive to inform the Commission in these situations, as they might be concerned about possible delays caused by the FSR review and/or about the potential outcome of the review process which could eliminate the most favourable bid.

In principle, this means that the Commission could initiate a review under Chapter 4 FSR of any public procurement project in the EU, regardless of the project's estimated value or the level of suspected financial contributions involved. In practice, given the expected number of public procurement projects that will require FSR notifications, and the – for now – modest size of the team assigned to review public procurement filings, it appears unlikely that the Commission will frequently rely on the power to proactively bring public procurement projects within the scope of application of Chapter 4 FSR.

The Commission must request a notification before the award of a public contract. Once the contract has been awarded, the Commission may only use the ex officio tool to review subsidies in relation to public procurement projects. Ex officio reviews, however, cannot result in the cancellation of an already awarded government contract.

C. Standstill Period

If a public procurement project meets the value threshold, a notification or declaration becomes mandatory. In this case, Article 32 FSR imposes a mandatory (targeted) standstill period on contracting authorities or entities during the Commission's preliminary review and in-depth investigation. As a general principle, a contracting authority or entity receiving a notification or declaration from an economic operator may continue

446 FSR Regulation 2022/2560 [2022] OJ L330/1 (n 1), art 29(8).

with all procedural steps in its public procurement procedure. It can evaluate bids or ask bidders for clarifications. It may not, however, award the public contract pending the Commission's review of a notification or declaration by any of the bidders.[447] Exceptions apply in limited circumstances, as described below.

The moment at which the standstill period ends depends on the outcome of the Commission's review. As a general rule, the contracting authority or entity can always award the contract after the Commission has concluded its review of all notifications or declarations it has received in connection with the project. This would be the case, for example, if the Commission does not adopt a decision at the end of the 20-day preliminary review period with respect to any notification or declaration it has received, and thus the Commission's review has ended for all bidders. Similarly, a contract may be awarded if the Commission, at the end of an in-depth investigation (of any bidder's notification), either adopts a 'no objection decision', a decision with commitments, or fails to adopt a decision within the time limits set forth by the FSR.[448]

By way of exception to this general rule, the contracting authority or entity may award the contract to the economic operator with the most economically advantageous tender, provided that the economic operator has submitted only a declaration and the Commission has not initiated an in-depth investigation. In these circumstances, the contract can be awarded while the preliminary review of other bids is pending and before the Commission has adopted a final decision in the review of other bidders' notifications.[449]

If the Commission adopts a prohibition decision with respect to the economic operator that has submitted the most economically advantageous tender, the contracting authority or entity may award the contract to the economic operator with the next best bid, provided that the Commission has not adopted a prohibition decision concerning this economic operator.[450]

D. Non-Compliance with Notification or Declaration Obligations

An economic operator that fails to comply with the obligation to submit a notification or declaration when submitting a bid or request to participate in a tender risks seeing its bid or request to participate being declared irregular and rejected from the public procurement project.

If a contracting authority or entity determines that an economic operator that has submitted a bid or a request to participate has failed to comply with its FSR's notification or declaration obligations, it may request the economic operator to make the mandatory

447 ibid, art 32(1).
448 ibid, art 32(2).
449 ibid, art 32(3).
450 ibid, art 32(4).

FSR submission within 10 working days. This request is mandatory if the contracting authority or entity wants to take a subsequent decision declaring the request to participate or tender irregular.

If the economic operator concerned fails to comply with this request, the contracting authority or entity must declare irregular the bid or request to participate and reject it. The contracting authority or entity must inform the Commission accordingly.[451]

A similar mechanism to cure deficiencies exists where the economic operator has submitted a notification or declaration which the Commission deems incomplete (a decision that the contracting authority or entity cannot take because it essentially acts as a mailbox without the power to review a notification or declaration). In this case, the Commission must grant the economic operator a period of 10 working days to cure the incompleteness of the notification or declaration. If the economic operator fails to comply, the Commission will adopt a decision declaring the bid or request to participate irregular and request the contracting authority or entity to adopt a rejection decision. This particular mechanism, and the short period to cure deficiencies in a notification or declaration, highlights the importance of engaging with the Commission in pre-notification discussions in a timely manner.

3. The Scope of Notifications and Declarations

The FSR's mandatory notification and declaration process requires completing Form FS-PP. Details of this process are set forth in the FSR Implementing Regulation. Frequently, completing Form FS-PP will present a considerable compliance burden on economic operators. They will need to, among others, provide extensive details on financial contributions received and might need to provide information deemed necessary to evaluate any distortive effects of those contributions on the internal market. They might also have to ensure that additional notifying parties, such as main subcontractors and supplier or consortia members, comply with their reporting obligations.

A. *Submission of a Mandatory Notification or Declaration*

The requirement to submit a notification or declaration depends on the type of public procurement procedure chosen by the contracting authority or entity:

- open (one stage) procedure:[452] the economic operator must submit a notification or declaration when it submits its bid;

---

[451] ibid, art 29(3).

[452] An open procedure is a 'single-stage' public procurement procedure. See, Directive 2014/24/EU [2014] OJ L94/65 (n 411), art 27; Directive 2014/25/EU [2014] OJ L94/243 (n 410), art 45.

- multi-stage procedure:[453] the economic operator must submit a notification or declaration twice. First, together with its request to participate and, second, as an updated notification or updated declaration together with its bid that must reflect any changes since the initial submission.[454]

In both scenarios, the economic operator must submit its notification or declaration to the contracting authority or entity, which must forward it without delay to the Commission.[455] In general, notifications and declarations must be transmitted to the Commission through digital means.[456]

Form FS-PP may be submitted in one of the official EU languages. Supporting documents that are not in one of the official EU languages must be translated. As this could become very burdensome, it would be advisable to discuss with the Commission during pre-notification discussions whether translations of only the relevant parts of documents would be acceptable, which is a common practice under the EUMR.

As discussed above, there can be more than one notifying party. For example, if the economic operator uses main subcontractors and/or main suppliers, they will also have to prepare a notification or declaration. In addition, in bidding consortia, each consortium member will be considered a notifying party. Nevertheless, the main contractor must ensure the submission of a complete notification or declaration on behalf of all notifying parties. The FSR clarifies, however, that in these situations the main contractor is liable only for the correctness of its own data, and not of the data submitted by other notifying parties.[457]

Submission of a Mandatory Notification or Declaration:

- Notification and declaration requirements depend on the public procurement procedure chosen by the contracting authority or entity
- Reporting requirements in Form FS-PP differ for notifications and declarations
- Main contractor responsible for submission of notification or declaration if there is more than one notifying party, but is liable only for correctness of its own data

453 A multi-stage procedure means a restricted procedure, a competitive procedure with negotiation/negotiated procedure with prior call for competition, a negotiated procedure without prior publication/negotiated procedure without prior call for competition, a competitive dialogue or an innovation partnership in accordance with, respectively, Directive 2014/24/EU [2014] OJ L94/65 (n 411), arts 28 to 32 and Directive 2014/25/EU [2014] OJ L94/243 (n 410), arts 46 to 50, or a similar procedure in accordance with Directive 2014/23/EU [2014] OJ L94/1 (n 412). See also FSR Regulation 2022/2560 [2022] OJ L330/1 (n 1), art 2(6).

454 FSR Regulation 2022/2560 [2022] OJ L330/1 (n 1), art 29(1).

455 ibid, art 29(2).

456 FSR Implementing Regulation 2023/1441 [2023] OJ L177/1 (n 30), art 26(1).

457 FSR Regulation 2022/2560 [2022] OJ L330/1 (n 1), art 29(6).

B. Form FS-PP

Annex 2 to the FSR Implementing Regulation includes Form FS-PP, which specifies the information that economic operators must provide when submitting a notification or declaration. The same form must be used for both notifications and declarations. However, the number of sections that must be completed depends on whether Form FS-PP serves as a notification or a declaration:

- notification: all sections (including Table 1, but excluding Table 2) must be completed, with the exception of Section 7.
- declaration: only Sections 1, 2, 7 (including Table 2, but excluding Table 1) and 8 must be completed. The remaining sections must be left blank, which means that even if a notifying party has received (small) presumptively distortive subsidies listed in Article 5 FSR, these would have to be reported in Section 7 and not (in more detail) in Section 3.

Form FS-PP consists of the following eight sections:

- *Section 1:* Description of the public procurement project
  For Sections 1 and 2, Form FS-PP envisages populating both sections by reference to the EU's digital procurement platform, the Tenders Electronic Daily (TED),[458] and the ESPD, an electronic document typically used when a party submits a request to participate or a tender in public procurement projects.[459]

  Notifying parties that do not use the ESPD in the public procurement project must manually complete both sections, providing information that corresponds to the ESPD, Annex 2, Parts I and II. This could apply, for example, to a supplier of the economic operator that would be considered a 'main supplier' under the FSR because it contributes 20% or more of the total contract value, but does not have to complete an ESPD because its input is not relied on to meet the public procurement project's selection criteria.
- *Section 2:* Information about the notifying parties
  See the above description in connection with Section 1.
- *Section 3 (and Table 1):* Foreign financial contributions
  Section 3 requires the notifying parties to provide specific information on certain types of financial contribution. This will likely be the most time-consuming section of Form FS-PP for notifying parties to complete.

---

458 See Tenders Electronic Daily <https://ted.europa.eu/TED/main/HomePage.do> accessed 18 December 2023.

459 See ESPD <https://ec.europa.eu/isa2/solutions/european-single-procurement-document-espd_en/#:~:text=The%20ESPD%20is%20a%20tool,EU%20above%20the%20EU%20threshold> accessed 18 December 2023. When notifying parties use the ESPD in a public procurement procedure and consequently submit the information required to complete Section 2 of Form FS-PP via the ESPD, this part of Form FS-PP will be directly imported from the ESPD into Form FS-PP using a digital service to be provided by the Commission. In the absence of such a service, the contracting authority or entity must forward to the Commission this notification along with the completed Part II of Annex 2 to the ESPD.

Section 3 of Form FS-PP largely corresponds to Section 5 of Form FS-CO, dividing reportable financial contributions into three groups. For presumptively distortive contributions listed in Article 5 FSR, the notifying party must provide detailed information and supporting documents. All other financial contributions must be reported in Table 1 in summary form and with aggregated estimates.[460] Financial contributions that are exempted from reporting obligations can be excluded (see also Chapter III). For all three categories of contributions, only contributions granted to the parties in the three years preceding the date of the notification are taken into account.

As in Form FS-CO, only financial contributions of at least €1 million granted to the notifying parties in the three years prior to the notification must be reported in Section 3. The €1 million threshold applies per individual financial contribution provided by a single third country to a notifying party. Financial contributions received by different notifying parties in the same country, or by the same notifying party in different countries, do not have to be aggregated.

Table 1 in Form-FS-PP, in which financial contributions that are not presumed to be distortive must be reported, also largely corresponds to Table 1 in Form FS-CO. The table does not require the contributions to be listed individually. Rather, contributions must be grouped by third country and type of contribution (for example, direct grant, loan, capital injection etc). Countries and, if possible, types of contribution should be ranked by their total amount from the highest to the lowest. Each notifying party must complete Table 1 separately.

Both tables exempt financial contributions in the form of certain, specified non-selective tax benefits and buy/sell relationship at market terms (except financial transactions) from reporting requirements, as explained in Section B of the explanatory notes accompanying the table.

Importantly, Table 1 of Form FS-PP uses a much lower exemption threshold than Form FS-CO according to which certain financial contributions received per third country must not be reported. Point 3 of the instructions accompanying Table 1 provides that contributions received from certain third countries may be excluded from Table 1 only if the aggregate contributions from a particular third country over the past three years have been below €4 million.

Unlike the calculation in the case of other thresholds, for this calculation the contributions received by all notifying parties in a given country over three years must be aggregated.[461] Unfortunately, the FSR Implementing Regulation does not explain why the threshold below which financial contributions are considered unlikely to risk distorting competition is more than eleven times higher in Form FS-CO than in Form FS-PP.

---

460 Estimates can be provided in ranges in the following increments: €4–50 million, €> 50–100 million, €> 100–500 million, €> 500–1,000 million, more than €1,000 million.

461 This contrasts with the calculation for determining whether the €4 million notification threshold in FSR art 28(1)(b) is met, which must be assessed separately per individual contribution received by each notifying party. See Chapter IV 2.A.2.2.

Finally, as in the case of Form FS-CO, despite the opportunity to aggregate information and exclude certain financial contributions from reporting altogether, the notifying parties should strive for accuracy even when completing Table 1. The Commission has discretion to request further information about all financial contributions, and might still be interested to examine that contributions reported in Table 1 do not present a distortion risk. The Commission might also ask questions regarding contributions that were not listed in Table 1 because the parties considered that they were exempted. Notifying parties should therefore ensure that they are in a position to (expeditiously) substantiate, if asked, the figures provided and the methodology used.

- *Section 4*: Explanations for why a bid is not unduly advantageous
  This explanation may consist of all elements that the notifying parties can use to demonstrate that their bid is not unduly advantageous, and does not directly or indirectly benefit from financial contributions. Providing full explanations in Section 4 will be particularly important if the parties have reported significant subsidies, especially in Sections 3.1 and 3.2.

  The explanatory elements include the economics of the manufacturing process, the services provided or the construction method. They may also cover the technical solutions chosen or any exceptionally favourable conditions available to the notifying party for the supply of the products or services or for the execution of the work. Section 4 also mentions the originality of the work, supplies or services proposed by the notifying party, compliance with applicable obligations in the fields of environmental, social and labour law, and compliance with obligations regarding subcontracting as potential explanations.

  Although not mentioned in Section 4, evidence that a bid is not unduly advantageous may also include references to previous bids in other public procurement projects comprising essentially the same type of products, works, or services. If those previous bids were similar, but not successful, this could be credible evidence that the bid cannot be considered advantageous.

- *Sections 5*: Possible positive effects
  Section 5 gives the parties the option to list and substantiate any possible positive effects of the relevant financial contributions on the development of the relevant subsidised economic activity. The notifying parties can also explain any broader positive effects in relation to the relevant policy objectives (particularly those of the EU) and specify when and where those effects have or are expected to take place.[462]

- *Section 6*: Supporting documentation
  This section requires the notifying parties to supply an extensive range of supporting documentation related to certain financial contributions provided in Sections 3.1 and 3.2 of Form FS-PP, together with a summary table. This section also requests the notifying parties to provide internal documents prepared for management concerning the financial contributions and the public procurement procedure as well as the parties' annual reports.

---

462 See Chapter VII B.

- *Section 7:* Declarations
  Only parties submitting a declaration must complete this section (after leaving empty Sections 3 to 6). As discussed above, if there are several notifying parties, they can submit a declaration only if none of them has received notifiable financial contributions in the last three years (ie, contributions of €4 million or more per third country). If at least one of the notifying parties has received notifiable financial contributions, all must submit a notification.

  First, the parties must confirm that they are entitled to submit a declaration. For this purpose, Section 7 requires the parties to include the following specific statement: 'None of the notifying parties have received foreign financial contributions notifiable under Chapter 4 of Regulation (EU) 2022/2560'.

  Second, in Section 7 and Table 2, the notifying parties must provide information about financial contributions received in the last three years preceding the declaration. The following principles apply:

  All financial contributions of €1 million or more must be listed in Section 7. Form FS-PP does not provide a specific format in which this information must be provided. Because parties submitting a declaration must not complete Section 3, even any presumptively distortive subsidies would have to be reported in Section 7.

  Financial contributions below €1 million but above €200,000 must be declared in Table 2 in an aggregated form, without indicating their values. Importantly, the exemption from reporting obligations applicable in Table 1 does not apply in respect of Table 2. This means that non-selective tax benefits and buy/sell relationships at market rates must be reflected in the Table 2 overview (which also means that information about them must be gathered).

  Financial contributions below €200,000 do not have to be reported in the declaration.

  The Commission maintains, nonetheless, the right to request the parties to provide more detailed information about any financial contribution reported in Section 7.

- *Section 8*: Attestation
  Section 8 requires each notifying party to sign an attestation confirming that the information provided is, to the best of its knowledge and belief, true, correct, and complete, including in terms of documents attached, estimates, and opinions expressed, and that it is aware of the provisions and fines.

Completing Form FS-PP will frequently require notifying parties to gather and submit a considerable amount of information and documentation. Not all of this might be accessible to the parties, and potentially a significant share of all information might be irrelevant for the Commission's investigation. This highlights the importance of engaging with the Commission in pre-notification discussions early, with a view toward obtaining waivers from certain reporting obligations.[463]

---

[463] See Chapter III B1.

4. Review Process and Timeline

The review process consists of two formal phases that occur once an FSR notification has been filed: a mandatory preliminary review, and a second phase in-depth review for cases that are more complex and/or raise substantive concerns. These phases have statutory timelines prescribed under Article 30 FSR. In addition, the Commission encourages transaction parties to engage in informal 'pre-notification' discussions with the FSR case team before a formal notification is submitted.

A. *The FSR Review Timeline*

As in the case of the M&A tool, the review under the FSR's public procurement tool consists of two formal phases that occur once a complete notification or declaration has been filed: a mandatory preliminary review, and a second phase in-depth review for cases that raise more complex concerns. These phases have statutory timelines prescribed under Article 30 FSR. In addition, the Commission encourages parties to engage in informal 'pre-notification' discussions with the FSR case team before a formal notification is submitted.

The general timeline for the FSR review process in the context of public procurement projects is thus as follows:

- a pre-notification phase coinciding with the economic operator's preparation of its request to participate or of its tender;
- a preliminary review carried out by the Commission lasting, in principle, 20 working days (extendable by 10 days) after the Commission has received a complete notification or declaration (which occurs twice in the case of multi-stage procurement projects); and
- (potentially) an in-depth investigation that should be concluded, in principle, within 110 working days (extendable by 20 working days) after the Commission's receipt of the complete notification or declaration.

These phases are discussed in greater detail below. In keeping with the Commission's standard practice, the relevant time limits begin on the working day following that of the receipt of the complete notification by the Commission (and not by the contracting authority or entity) or on the working day following that of the adoption of the relevant Commission decision.[464]

During the FSR review process, contracting authorities or entities must notify the Commission of any decisions relating to the cancellation of the public procurement procedure, the rejection of a tender or participation request from the relevant economic operator, the submission of a new tender by that economic operator, or the award of the public contract subject to the specific conditions set out in Article 32(3) FSR.[465]

---

464 FSR Regulation 2022/2560 [2022] OJ L330/1 (n 1), art 32(8).

465 ibid, art32(6).

B. The FSR Review Process, Stage-By-Stage

B.1 Pre-Notification

Notifying parties are encouraged to participate in pre-notification discussions well in advance of the actual notification, ideally using a draft Form FS-PP as a starting point.[466] Pre-notification discussions start after the notifying parties have submitted a CTAR which informs the Commission about a forthcoming notification or declaration.

Experience in the context of the EUMR strongly suggests that pre-notification discussions, although not mandatory, are important to ensure a smooth outcome of a public procurement filing. These discussions can help determine various aspects, including the precise amount of information required in a notification, and ensure the completeness of the notification.

Moreover, engaging in pre-notification discussions can lead to a substantial decrease in the amount of information that parties must include in their notification. In particular, parties have the opportunity during the pre-notification phase to seek waivers from the obligation to submit specific information in Form FS-PP. The Commission will evaluate waiver requests in light of the following criteria:

- the economic operators can justify that relevant information is not available. When applicable and to the best extent possible, the economic operators should offer their most accurate approximations for the missing data, along with references to the sources of these estimates. Additionally, they should indicate where the Commission could access any of the requested information that is not accessible to the economic operators; and/or
- the economic operators can persuade the Commission that information is not essential for evaluating their notification.

However, the Commission's acceptance of the omission of specific information requested in Form FS-PP does not preclude the Commission from subsequently still requesting that information at any time during the review process, in particular via an RFI.[467]

Pre-notification discussions are of particular importance in the public procurement context. FSR procurement notifications have a hard stop: at the latest on the day the notifying parties' bid in a procurement project is due, they must be in a position to submit a complete FSR notification. Failure to submit a complete FSR notification risks exclusion from the procurement project.[468] The FSR provides for two ten-day periods during which the parties can cure the lack, or incompleteness, of a notification. But relying on these two periods, which cannot be extended, would appear to be very risky. Thus, notifying parties have a strong incentive to prepare their draft notifications early and engage with the Commission well ahead of the date on which they must submit their bid.

---

466 If there are multiple economic operators or consortia, each aiming to submit a separate tender within the same public procurement procedure, pre-notification discussions will take place separately and in full confidentiality with each economic operator or group of economic operators.

467 FSR Regulation 2022/2560 [2022] OJ L330/1 (n 1), art 13.

468 ibid, art 29(3) and (4).

It is not entirely clear at what point the Commission would be willing to commence pre-notification discussions. In principle, public procurement projects do not exist until they are published on TED. The Commission could therefore take the position that the TED publication is the earliest date to engage in pre-notification discussions. But in public procurement projects with short deadlines, this would create serious problems for notifying parties, in particular if they have not previously submitted FSR notifications or if the facts have materially changed since their last notification. Multi-stage procurement projects, for example, might have very short deadlines during which parties must express their interest in participating in a project, which can be as short as 30 or 45 days (or even 15 days in case of urgency). It could be unrealistic for a notifying party to give the Commission sufficient time to review a draft notification, gather all additional information and documentation the Commission might require, reply to Commission RFIs, and yet complete the notification on time. This problem would only be exacerbated if the Commission would seek additional information related to or from a third country that is less than eager to cooperate.

Therefore, the Commission will hopefully accept pre-notification discussions even before a project is published on TED. Typically, market participants will be aware of upcoming large procurement projects long before they are officially published, in particular when contracting authorities publish a program of purchases or prior information notices. If the basic elements of a procurement project are already sufficiently determined, including the project's estimated value, the parties can already anticipate whether an FSR filing would be required and could engage with the Commission. Contracting authorities or entities should have every incentive to support parties in those efforts, for example, by informing the Commission about the upcoming project and confirming the relevant elements. This would allow potential participants to get a head-start with the Commission, smoothen the notification process, and reduce the risk that FSR review could interfere with their public procurement project.

B.2 Preliminary Review Phase

The preliminary review period starts when the Commission receives a complete notification or declaration from the contracting authority or entity. If the Commission considers that a notification or declaration is incomplete, it must inform both the contracting authority or entity and the notifying party. In that case, the Commission must give the notifying party 10 working days to complete the notification or declaration, a period that cannot be extended. If the economic operator does not comply, the Commission must adopt a decision declaring the request to participate or tender irregular, and request the contracting authority or entity to adopt a decision rejecting such an irregular request to participate or tender.[469]

The aim of the Commission's preliminary review is to identify if there are sufficient indications that the notifying party has received financial contributions that distort competition in the internal market, which warrants further examination during an

469 If the notifying party submits a completed notification, the preliminary review period will start when the Commission has received the completed notification. See FSR Implementing Regulation 2023/1441 [2023] OJ L177/1 (n 30), art 7(1).

in-depth investigation.[470] The Commission has 20 working days to carry out this review, although it may in justified cases extend this period by an additional 10 working days.[471]

Throughout the preliminary review, the Commission's case team will examine Form FS-PP and any accompanying documentation. The case team may seek clarifications by posing questions and issue RFIs. Given the brief review period, these formal RFIs are likely to come with tight response deadlines.[472] Unlike the FSR's M&A tool, the procurement tool does not give the Commission the power to 'stop the clock' during its review if the parties fail to respond in a timely manner to an RFI. This increases the pressure to respond to Commission RFIs as rapidly as possible because otherwise the Commission might find itself forced to push the notification into an in-depth investigation.

If the Commission decides at the end of the preliminary review that an in-depth investigation is not warranted, it does not adopt a formal 'clearance' decision. As per the context of the M&A tool, this has the advantage that the Commission is not required to gather sufficient information to support a formal clearance decision which should be helpful particularly in notifications that clearly do not raise any substantive issues. But the lack of a formal decision also means that the Commission cannot adopt a conditional clearance decision at the end of the preliminary review, whereby it would accept commitments to address any concerns it has identified. Thus, any concerns that the Commission has identified can be addressed only during an in-depth investigation.

If the Commission has closed a preliminary review without opening an in-depth investigation and subsequently receives new information that raises concerns about the completeness of the already 'cleared' notification, the Commission may request additional information and reopen a preliminary review based on the new information it received. In that case, a new preliminary review period starts when the Commission has received the new notification or declaration.[473]

B.3 In-Depth Investigation

If the Commission concludes at the end of the 20-working day preliminary review that there are sufficient indications that an economic operator has received financial contributions that distort the internal market, it will adopt a formal decision to initiate the in-depth investigation. This decision should summarise the relevant issues of fact and law, and include a preliminary assessment of the existence of a foreign subsidy and of the actual or potential distortion in the internal market.

The Commission must also inform the notifying party, the contracting authority or entity, and the Member States of the decision. Moreover, it must publish a notice of its decision in the *Official Journal,* inviting the submission of written comments within a prescribed

---

470 FSR Regulation 2022/2560 [2022] OJ L330/1 (n 1), art 10.

471 ibid, art 30.

472 ibid, art 13(4).

473 ibid, art 30(4).

period of time.[474] Considering the practice under the EUMR, the notifying parties can be expected to submit a paper or other comments responding to the views expressed in the Commission's decision. The Commission can fix a deadline for receiving those comments, which should normally not exceed one month from the issuance of the decision.[475] The parties' reply to the decision has no formal effect, but – as in the merger control process – doing so might be useful to help address the case team's concerns and/or shape their views during the in-depth investigation. Third parties might also wish to submit their views.

The decision starts the 110-working day in depth review period (90 working days if the notifying party submitted an updated notification in the context of a multi-stage procedure). The Commission may extend this period once by 20 working days in exceptional cases. During the in-depth investigation, the Commission will closely examine the financial contributions identified in its decision, aiming to verify if they genuinely cause distortion within the internal market and to assess whether these distortions are outweighed by positive effects. In addition to issuing additional RFIs, the Commission may also conduct interviews[476] and/or inspections[477] as means of obtaining additional information.

Article 42(1) FSR provides that the Commission should issue a formal charge sheet outlining the grounds on which it intends to take a decision before adopting a negative decision. The Commission's ultimate decision must be based only on the grounds presented to the parties and on which they have had an opportunity to comment.[478] Once this charge sheet is issued, the parties have a right to gain access to the case file (including any supporting documents on which the decision will be based) and to submit a written response.[479]

During the in-depth review, the parties can also consider whether commitments might address the Commission's concerns and indicate their willingness of presenting commitments to the Commission. According to Article 14 FSR Implementing Regulation, the deadline to submit proposals for commitments is on working day 50. The FSR Implementing Regulation allows the Commission to consider commitments offered after this deadline in exceptional cases. However, any extension of this deadline must take into account the need to comply with the advisory procedure under Article 48(2) FSR that precedes the issuance of a formal decision.[480] As a consequence, notifying parties should not expect that the Commission will accept commitments submitted too late in the process.

Pursuant to Article 31 FSR, the Commission must issue a formal decision at the conclusion of the in-depth investigation. This decision can prohibit the notifying party from participating in the procurement project, or can allow participation subject to commitments or unconditionally.

474 ibid, art 10(3).
475 FSR Implementing Regulation 2023/1441 [2023] OJ L177/1 (n 30), art 8(1).
476 FSR Regulation 2022/2560 [2022] OJ L330/1 (n 1), art 13(7).
477 ibid, art 14.
478 ibid, art 42(3).
479 ibid, art 42(4).
480 ibid, art 11(3); FSR Implementing Regulation 2023/1441 [2023] OJ L177/1 (n 30), art 14(3). See Chapter IV 4.B.3.

General timeline for an FSR review

- a pre-notification phase of indeterminate length
- a preliminary review phase lasting up to 20 working days (extendable by 10 working days) from the time of notification which applies twice in the case multi-stage procedures
- (potentially) an in-depth investigation that should be concluded within 110 working days after notification

5. Scope of the Commission's Powers

The FSR confers extensive investigative powers on the Commission, which apply also in the context of procurement reviews.

The Commission's powers include:

- issuing RFIs and conducting interviews to obtain information needed to assess the transaction[481]
- carrying out inspections within and/or outside the EU[482]
- issuing decisions prohibiting participation in procurement projects or accepting commitments in order to remove distortion concerns[483]
- imposing fines for failing to observe the FSR's notification obligations or for providing incomplete or misleading information in the context of the Commission's review[484]

A. *RFIs, Interviews, and Inspections*

The FSR grants the Commission broad powers to request additional documentation and evidence needed to complete its review of a public procurement-related notification, to interview parties and to conduct inspections inside and outside the EU. These powers are discussed in more detail in Chapter VII and, in particular in the context of notifications, in Chapter III.

481 FSR Regulation 2022/2560 [2022] OJ L330/1 (n 1), art 13. See Chapter VII 3.A.
482 ibid, arts 14 and 15. See Chapter VII 3.B.
483 ibid, art 31. See Chapter VI 5.
484 ibid, art 17. See Chapter VII 4.A.

B. Interim Measures

The FSR empowers the Commission to issue a decision ordering interim measures to temporarily protect competition, pending the issuance of a final decision on a transaction.[485] However, according to Article 12(2) FSR, the Commission may not adopt interim measures in the context of public procurement reviews. This presumably reflects the legislator's decision that interim measures are neither necessary nor suitable in public procurement procedures.

C. Fines and Periodic Penalties

The FSR empowers the Commission to impose fines or periodic penalties to ensure compliance. Those fines or periodic penalties apply also under the public procurement tool. Fines are one-off punitive measures whereas periodic penalty payments continue until the recipient adopts the particular conduct that the Commission requires.

For example, according to the generally applicable provisions under the FSR, the Commission may impose fines on notifying parties of up to 1% of their aggregate turnover if they intentionally or negligently provided incorrect or misleading information in response to RFIs or failed to respond in a timely manner to such a request, or, during an inspection, provided incorrect or misleading information, failed to rectify incorrect or misleading answers, or refused to provide answers.[486]

Article 33 FSR gives the Commission additional powers to impose fines that are specific to public procurement notifications. These include the power to impose fines of up to 1% of the aggregate turnover of an economic operator for intentionally or negligently providing false or misleading information in a notification or declaration.[487] Moreover, the Commission may impose fines of up to 10% of the aggregate turnover of an economic operator for failure to notify and for actual or attempted circumvention of notification obligations.[488]

6. Substantive Review

Article 29 FSR tasks the Commission to determine whether, in the context of a specific public procurement project, foreign subsidies have enabled an economic operator to submit an 'unduly advantageous tender' and resulted in a distortion of competition in the internal market. In addition, Article 6 FSR prescribes a balancing test to weigh the distorted effects against positive effects of the subsidy.

---

485 ibid, art 12.
486 ibid, art 17(1).
487 ibid, art 33(2).
488 ibid, art 33(3). See Chapter III 5.C.

For a more detailed discussion on how these tests could be applied under the FSR, both in general and in the context of an FSR public procurement review, see Chapter II.

7. Outcomes of the Review Process

A. *Potential Outcomes*

The possible outcomes of the Commission's preliminary review depend on the type of public procurement procedure that the contracting authority or entity has chosen:

- multi-stage procedure: the Commission will not take any decision at the end of the first preliminary review. The review is essentially paused until the notifying parties submit an updated notification when they submit their bid in the public procurement project.
- open (one stage) procedure, or at the end of the second preliminary review in the context of a multi-stage procedure: the Commission may either close the preliminary review without decision or adopt a decision to initiate an in-depth investigation.[489]

Pursuant to Article 31 FSR, after completing its in-depth investigation, the Commission must issue an implementing act in the form of a decision to:

- raise no objections (no objection decision), if the Commission does not find that an economic operator benefits from a foreign subsidy distorting the internal market.[490]
- accept commitments (decision with commitments), if the Commission finds that an economic operator benefits from a foreign subsidy distorting the internal market, but the economic operator offers commitments that fully and effectively remedy that distortion.
- prohibit the award of the public contract to the economic operator concerned (prohibition decision), if the Commission finds that an economic operator benefits from a foreign subsidy distorting the internal market, and the economic operator does not propose commitments, or the Commission considers that the proposed commitments do not fully and effectively remedy the distortion in the internal market.

If the Commission adopts a 'no objection decision' or a 'decision with commitments', the contracting authority or entity may award the contract to the recipient of the decision. When the Commission adopts a 'prohibition decision', the contracting authority or entity must reject the notifying party's bid.

---

489 ibid, art 30(2) and (3).

490 ibid, art 31(1). That implementing act must be adopted in accordance with the advisory procedure referred to in ibid, art 48(2).

B. Remedies and Commitments

Article 31 FSR enables the Commission to accept commitments offered by the notifying party following an in-depth investigation (commitments cannot be offered during the preliminary review phase). These commitments form part of the Commission's clearance decision and become binding on the party. The Commission can monitor compliance with the commitments, and, if needed, issue further decisions imposing fines or periodic penalty payments to ensure compliance.[491] However, in the public procurement context, the Commission may not revoke its decision after the contracting authority or entity has awarded the contract to the party that entered into commitments but later was found to be non-compliant.[492] This means that in the case of non-compliance, fines and periodic penalty payments are the only tools available to the Commission.

Article 7 FSR provides a non-exhaustive list of potential commitments that may be offered, under any of the FSR's three instruments, including:

- divestment of certain assets;
- offering FRAND access to infrastructure (for example, infrastructure, R&D or other essential facilities) that were acquired through or supported by foreign subsides;
- licensing under FRAND terms of assets acquired or developed with the help of foreign subsidies (ie certain types of 'behavioural remedies' in the EUMR context);
- publicising R&D results;
- repaying the foreign subsidy;
- requiring companies to adapt their governance structure;
- reducing capacity or market presence; and
- refraining from certain investments.

In principle, any of these remedies could also be used at the end of a public procurement review. However, it is unclear whether any of them would be suitable to remove distortion concerns in respect of a specific procurement project. In the context of a notification under the public procurement tool, the Commission's assessment must be limited to determining whether foreign subsidies enabled a notifying party to submit an unduly advantageous tender and distorted competition in the internal market.[493] Thus, a commitment would be effective only if it could remove this distortive 'undue advantage' in the specific procurement project. But almost none of the remedies in the above list would have these specific effects, as required by the FSR.

Moreover, given that commitments would be accepted after a lengthy review process, it could simply be too late to find any suitable and effective commitments. As distortion in the public procurement context would exist if foreign subsidies 'enabled' a bidder to

---

491 ibid, art 17(5).

492 ibid, art18(2).

493 ibid, art 27.

submit an unduly advantageous tender, a commitment would have to remove the bidder's ability to submit a tender that could be considered unduly advantageous. The commitment could thus be considered effective only if it would result in the bidder changing the terms of its tender to something that is no longer considered at least 'unduly' advantageous. But this would be prohibited by Article 31(4) FSR if these changes would be incompatible with other provisions of EU law. If the bidder could maintain the terms of its initial tender despite the commitment, the initial finding that the foreign subsidies 'enabled' the bidder to submit an unduly advantageous tender would be obviously false.

But such a commitment resulting in revised terms would become effective only many months after the deadline for submitting tenders in the public procurement project. Allowing the bidder to submit a revised tender with commitment-compliant terms would not be possible under procurement law. It would likely also be inconsistent with the requirement in Article 32(7) FSR that the application of the FSR may not result in outcomes that would infringe the principles of non-discrimination and equality governing EU procurement law.

In sum, it remains uncertain whether there is much room for commitments to resolve FSR concerns under the public procurement tool. In the end, prohibition decisions might be the only remedy available to the Commission for addressing a finding of distortion.

Outcomes of the review process:

- preliminary review without decision, or with decision to open an in-depth investigation
- in-depth investigation with three potential outcomes:
  - no objection decision
  - decision with commitments (although it is not clear whether there could be any remedies that could adequately address distortion concerns related to specific procurement projects)
  - prohibition decision

Chapter V
Practical Compliance with the FSR's Notification Obligations

1. Introduction

The FSR poses practical compliance challenges for companies participating in large-scale EU M&A and public procurement projects that could trigger notification obligations.[494] Meeting these – novel – challenges requires advanced planning and substantial internal coordination.

This chapter discusses:

- how to approach gathering the information relevant to an FSR assessment;
- creating a risk profile for any financial contributions a company receives;
- the role of FSR compliance in the lifecycle of an M&A transaction; and
- the role of FSR compliance in public procurement projects.

Finally, while this chapter focusses on the due diligence actions companies should take to prepare for a notification or declaration under the FSR's M&A and public procurement tools, some of the considerations discussed in this chapter might also be helpful in guiding companies to identify relevant information if they are targeted in an investigation under the FSR's ex officio tool.

2. Gathering Relevant Information

As discussed in greater detail in Chapters III and IV, companies will need to gather a considerable amount of information to comply with the FSR's mandatory notification requirements when engaging in M&A and public procurement projects that meet – or

494 Once the Commission begins launching investigations under the ex officio tool, companies under investigation will also face substantial information gathering and compliance challenges. At this point, however, it is uncertain when the Commission will start to launch these investigations, which sectors it will target, and how the investigations will be conducted. Therefore, it currently remains difficult to anticipate effective compliance and risk mitigation strategies. However, we note that, eg, the European Commission has already expressly asked the European wind industry to submit evidence of 'foreign distorting subsidies allow[ing]wind manufacturers receiving them to be successful in public procurement procedures or in concentrations involving EU target companies'. See Commission Communication COM (2023) 669 final (n 88) 17.

might meet – the relevant FSR thresholds. As outlined below, there is preliminary work that companies anticipating large scale M&A or procurement projects in the EU can already undertake before a specific transaction or procurement project is contemplated.

Starting the process of gathering FSR-related information only once a company has decided to go ahead with a specific transaction or public procurement project would create material risks, particularly as companies will typically not collect and store relevant information in the ordinary course of business. Such a wait-and-see strategy would not only lead to significant delays; it could even endanger participation in a public procurement project or prevent the successful completion of a transaction.

To gather information required for FSR notifications most efficiently, companies should be strategic in identifying which information is needed to determine: (i) whether a notification obligation arises in the first place, and then (ii) what additional detail will be needed to produce a complete notification form.

Key considerations when gathering information for FSR compliance:

- start the information-gathering and organisation process early
- develop workable information-gathering structures tailored to the specific needs of the company
- consider what information needs to be gathered based on the type of notification process (M&A or public procurement tool) in which the company anticipates participating
- use pragmatic methods to quickly identify whether transactions with public or State-affiliated private entities are considered contributions from a foreign State
- use extra caution when assessing contributions from high-risk jurisdictions (notably China)

A. *Information-Gathering Preparations*

Any M&A deal in which the merging parties, target or JV generates at least €500 million in EU turnover raises the possibility that an FSR notification will be required. Moreover, any public procurement project worth at least €250 million will require a notification (if the foreign contributions thresholds under Article 28(b) FSR are also met) or a declaration (if they are not). As discussed below, companies that anticipate participating in such large-scale EU M&A or tender activities should not wait until a deal or tender opportunity has become concrete to begin preparations and begin to develop internal structures to gather and store relevant information.

A.1 The Importance of Starting Early

The FSR's notification thresholds and reporting requirements are based on a company being granted a 'financial contribution', which, as discussed in Chapter II, is a broad concept. Information on all contributions is unlikely to be stored in a central, easily reviewable manner. Gathering information on financial contributions from all relevant entities within the control group (potentially involving many jurisdictions) might involve considerable time and effort, particularly in the context of M&A notifications. The number and complexity of questions needed to correctly identify financial contributions will typically increase with the company's scale and number of subsidiaries operating outside the EU.

The number of entities that are relevant as potential recipients of financial contributions will likely be smaller in the public procurement context (see Chapter IV). Nevertheless, although this might affect the scale of the information-gathering process, it will not reduce the complexity of the questions that are likely to arise.

The FSR's M&A tool takes into account the aggregate financial contributions received by other parties involved in the deal (though the contributions received by each party individually might not be sufficient to trigger a notification). The public procurement tool, by contrast, requires at least one notifying party to meet the contributions threshold individually. However once one party has met this threshold, the notification rules apply to all notifying parties. Consequently, the notification obligations under both tools might, in some cases, depend on the contributions received by other parties. Nevertheless, even without information on contributions received by other parties, companies can complete a substantial amount of preparatory work in advance on a unilateral basis.

Early preparatory work will provide additional advantages beyond meeting transaction or tender timetables:

- *Risk assessment*: advance preparatory work allows dealmakers to better assess the likelihood of the transaction becoming mired in a lengthy Commission assessment, of clearance necessitating remedies affecting the value of a deal, or of a prohibition being issued. Without advance preparation, potential risks might not be readily apparent to the business arm leading the M&A or tender participation. For example, if a European subsidiary of a global business is negotiating an acquisition, it might not be aware of subsidies received by the parent company through a separate subsidiary operating in Asia.
- *Developing arguments concerning potentially distortive subsidies*: it is to a company's advantage to be aware of whether it has received contributions that are likely to be considered distortive subsidies. Early awareness will provide extra time to prepare well-substantiated arguments that the subsidy does not distort competition and to collect supporting documents for a notification. Advance preparations might be especially helpful if certain relevant information or documents reside with the government entity that granted a subsidy and the process to obtain that information is lengthy.

- *Enhancing a company's attractiveness as a potential partner in a transaction or public procurement project*: FSR compliance might well become part of routine due diligence in European M&A and public procurement projects. If a company is not prepared to provide an overview of the levels of its financial contributions and the likelihood of potential substantive clearance concerns, it might risk losing a deal opportunity to a better-prepared rival. Likewise, tender participants that consider bidding for projects in groups and/or rely on suppliers or sub-contractors that would fall under the FSR's definition of 'main' subcontractors or suppliers likely would want to ensure that their subcontractors and suppliers are ready to submit FSR documentation swiftly and will not raise substantive FSR concerns. They might prefer to work with those that can demonstrate that they have already completed most of the preparatory work.

A.2 Establishing FSR Information-Gathering Structures

The FSR requires gathering data sets that are not usually collected in the course of ordinary deal-planning and that might reach across different business functions lines (tax, legal, sales, accounting, HR, etc) and across various subsidiaries and geographies. Depending on the size and activities of the company in question, it is advisable to establish internal mechanisms to make collecting and updating the information needed for an FSR notification more routine and streamlined. Companies might wish to consider the following when designing mechanisms adapted to their individual needs:

- *Consider whether the company will likely be active in both public procurement and M&A projects*: the company entities whose contributions are relevant to the notification thresholds are different under each tool. If the company plans to engage in M&A, all contributions received by its control group will be relevant, necessitating a group-wide approach to data collection. Under the public procurement tool, contributions from a narrower set of company entities would be relevant. This might reduce the need for an extensive group-wide data collection mechanism if a company can focus only on future procurement projects and can identify which entities most likely would participate in tenders. At the same time, a procurement project-focused information-gathering exercise may need to collect more information about smaller financial contributions.
- *Nominate a task force/group with information collection responsibilities*: establishing such an internal body could assist in preventing duplication of effort or inconsistency where a company controls multiple entities that each participate in M&A or tenders. It is also helpful for a defined person or group to understand which entities or reporting lines hold information relevant to an FSR assessment, which do not, and who the contact points are.
- *Create a repository for information and updates*: organising FSR-relevant information into a central hub as a preparatory measure would avoid dealmakers or tender organisers within a company needing to reach into each of the various subsidiaries and pockets of relevant data every time a transaction is contemplated.

- *Tag information that is invariably FSR-relevant*: certain data that will always be relevant to calculating FSR contributions (for example, buy/sell relationships with State entities, land grants) could be routinely 'tagged' in the ordinary course of business or regularly reported to the central FSR hub to make data collection easier.
- *Establish information updating cycles*: depending on the size and structure of the company, the speed and difficulty involved in data gathering, and how active it plans to be in large-scale EU M&A or public procurement, consider how often centrally gathered FSR data should be updated. It might be possible to devise a pragmatic approach that does not overburden the business during routine updates but that still improves notification readiness.
- *Consider how active the company plans to be*: more active companies might require a more formally structured and regular information-gathering process. Less active companies might instead benefit from a simpler preparatory exercise consisting of mapping out the information available and its location within the company so that it can be more easily retrieved if and when a notification is needed.

Regardless of the specifics of the data-collection approach a company ultimately implements, establishing and documenting a clear process is important to demonstrate best efforts at compliance. Given the breadth of information falling under the FSR's concept of a 'financial contribution', it is likely that a company might inadvertently omit certain data in a notification. It is therefore important to be able to show the Commission that the company took credible, good-faith efforts to comply.

B. What Information Needs to Be Gathered

The approach to information gathering depends on whether the company intends to participate in large-scale M&A, or public procurement projects, or both. Differences in the notification thresholds and disclosure requirements under each tool mean that different data-gathering approaches will likely be more efficient if a company can prioritise one or the other. Companies should also develop an efficient method to quickly assess what financial interactions are likely to be considered contributions, particularly when assessing interactions with public or private entities with an affiliation to a third country that is difficult to define. Finally, during the information-gathering phase, it is recommended to take special care when considering financial contributions from entities in non-market economies, and in particular from China.

B.1 M&A Tool

A step-by-step approach may reduce the information-gathering burden. In particular, although all financial contributions that a company receives are relevant to assessing the application of the mandatory notification requirement, not all contributions must be declared in the respective notification forms. As a consequence, companies should consider gathering information for M&A compliance in two phases as described below.

Suggested two-phase information-gathering approach under the M&A tool:

- first, companies should assess financial contributions to the extent necessary to determine whether the overall amount of contributions received is sufficient to meet the relevant notification thresholds set out in Article 20(3)(b) FSR
- second, only if this threshold is met (or is likely to be met), companies will need to identify the specific subset of information that will need to be declared in the relevant notification form

B.1.1 Calculating the Notification Threshold

As set out in greater detail in Chapter III, the €50 million threshold is met by aggregating all subsidies received by – depending on the type of transaction concerned – both the acquirer and target, the merging companies, or the companies creating a JV as well as the JV itself. The financial contributions that should be calculated for each relevant entity include those received by its entire control group (including any/all companies that: (i) the entity controls, (ii) control the entity, and (iii) are controlled by a company controlling the entity).

The FSR requires that all financial contributions received should be taken into account to determine whether the relevant FSR notification thresholds are met, regardless of whether these contributions are likely to be considered subsidies (much less distortive subsidies). As discussed in Chapter II, the concept of a financial contribution includes any touchpoints where benefits could flow from any public authority (of a third country) to the company (including situations where the public authority forgoes revenues that would be due).[495]

Form FS-CO requires the notifying party/parties to certify that the relevant contribution threshold has been reached. However, it does *not* require the notifying party/parties to specify the total amount of aggregated contributions received or the basis for a company's determination that it meets the €50 million threshold. As a consequence, it is useful to determine as a first step whether the threshold is met at all (regardless of the amount of financial contributions received by their other deal partners), so as to concentrate further efforts on identifying only those contributions that will need to be declared in the notification.

When conducting this first step analysis, it is advisable to be strategic and to conduct a first screening looking for the most readily identifiable financial contributions, in order to see whether the threshold is easily met by virtue of those contributions alone. This approach would involve compiling the list of the financial contributions a company

---

495 Foreign financial contributions received in currencies other than the euro should be calculated using the yearly average European Central Bank (ECB) exchange rate for the calendar year in which the contribution was granted. For foreign contributions granted in the same year as the notification, the Commission has instructed parties to use the average ECB exchange rate for the ongoing year (up until the date of calculation).

receives starting with those that are the easiest to identify in a company's accounting system. These could include, for instance:

- large government contracts with third countries' public authorities or public companies;
- utility bills;
- other purchases of goods and services from public authorities or public companies;
- social security/pension contributions;
- tax exemptions or deferrals; or
- significant direct transfers of funds (such as grants, loans, capital injections or direct contributions, etc).

Only if the threshold is not reached by virtue of these contributions that are easiest to identify, contributions that are more difficult to spot must be considered. Once the €50 million threshold is deemed to be met, there is no added value in identifying or itemising every contribution received globally. Rather, it is advisable to move on to the second stage of the information-gathering process, to identify the information that would need to be disclosed in the notification in a more targeted way.

On the other hand, if the thresholds are not met even after a more thorough search (taking into account the broad definition of contributions and all the relevant entities whose contributions should be considered), this does not mean that the company will not be subject to FSR notifications obligations. Rather, it means that any contributions received by its future deal partners will have to be taken into account when determining whether a notification is required.

It is prudent to consider how close the company is to meeting the thresholds on its own based on a more granular information-gathering process. In particular, if the total amount of financial contributions identified is already very close to the threshold, any potential deal target/partner would be likely to push the future concentration or tender over the thresholds. In this type of situation, it is advisable to proceed as if they were met and to engage in the second step of information gathering. Conversely, if the company is not close to meeting a threshold, deep diving into the particular types of contribution received before a specific transaction is on the horizon might not be a priority.

B.1.2 Gathering Information in Light of M&A Reporting Requirements

After determining that the notification threshold will be met (or is almost certain to be met), it is advisable to begin identifying more carefully the financial contributions that will need to be included in the notification form (Form FS-CO). This process should be guided by the reporting requirements set forth in Form FS-CO, which distinguishes contributions received in the past three years[496] into three categories as listed below. These categories

---

[496] For concentrations, the relevant three-year period prior to the conclusion of the agreement, the announcement of the public bid or the acquisition of a controlling interest.

require the notifying parties to provide different levels of detail and supplementary information, which should in turn be reflected in the information-gathering process.

B.1.2.1 *Likely Distortive Subsidies*

The FSR Implementing Regulation requires notifying parties to provide detailed information on financial contributions that the Commission considers most likely to distort the internal market. These likely distortive subsidies are any contributions that fall into any of the categories listed in Article 5(1) FSR, points (a) to (d), namely: (a) subsidies to ailing companies, unless there is a credible restructuring plan to which the company will contribute, (b) unlimited guarantees for debts or liabilities, (c) export financing measures not in line with the OECD Arrangement, or (d) subsidies directly facilitating a concentration. As described in greater detail in Chapter III, the questions in Section 5 of Form FS-CO are designed to identify the presence of these subsidies.

Any financial contribution of over €1 million granted to the parties that fits into the above-mentioned categories must be declared individually. The parties must also provide additional documentation concerning each of these contributions, as outlined in Sections 8.1 and 8.2(a) of Form FS-CO. This includes both supporting documentation relating to the subsides as well as documents prepared by or for or received by any member of the board of management, the board of directors or the supervisory board discussing the purpose, use, and economic rationale of the subsidies. Section 7 of Form FS-CO also invites parties to explain why these contributions are in line with broader EU policy goals.

Many companies might be able to determine that they have not received Article 5 subsidies. If these subsidies have been identified, however, it is advisable to start gathering all relevant information and consider arguments that they are not distortive and, where possible, aligned with EU policy goals, well in advance of any notification. In addition to developing arguments against the presumption of distortion in light of the factors set forth in Article 4 FSR, it would also be advisable to verify whether certain subsidies fall into a category of subsidies that cannot be remedied under the FSR (see Chapter II). Certain documentation or information might reside with the public entity (of the third country) granting the subsidies, and significant time might be required to obtain all helpful documentation/information in this case.

B.1.2.2 *Reportable Contributions*

Contributions that are not considered likely distortive subsidies but that are not exempt from reporting should be reported in a summary format with aggregated value estimates if they are above €45 million per country. Contributions below these thresholds (that do not meet the definition of likely distortive subsidies) do not need to be declared in the notification form. Form FS-CO provides tables for the parties to list these contributions. The tables require parties to list, for each third country, each type of financial contribution received as well as a brief description of the purpose of the contribution and the granting entity. For each third country, the parties are required to list estimates of the total amount of contributions received in ranges.[497]

---

[497] The ranges provided in the form are €45–100 million, €100–500 million, €500–1,000 million and above from €1,000 million.

B.1.2.3 *Non-Reportable Contributions*

The FSR Implementing Regulation expressly identifies certain types of financial contribution that do *not* need to be included in the notification at all. These include: (i) deferrals of payment of taxes or social security contributions, tax amnesties and tax holidays that are of general application (ie, non-selective), (ii) tax relief measures to avoid double taxation in line with – or based on the logic of – the provisions of bilateral or multilateral agreements for avoidance of double taxation, and (iii) the provision or purchase of goods and services (except financial services) at market terms.

Because these financial contributions occur on market terms, the Commission considers that they will not meet the definition of subsidies – much less ones that could distort competition on the internal market. This means that a substantial volume of financial contributions from third countries do not need to be further investigated – much less quantified – once the notification thresholds are determined to be met.

The list of financial contributions in the FSR Implementing Regulation is exhaustive, but the Commission may grant a waiver for other, similar market-rate financial contributions that do not expressly fall into the above-mentioned categories. However, as the notifying parties cannot count on a waiver being granted in any particular situation, they should be prepared to report any contributions not expressly exempted.

Gathering the information needed to satisfy the extensive reporting obligations for likely distortive subsidies and the less onerous obligations for reportable contributions will involve significant effort, even though this is considerably less than would be required if all contributions needed to be declared.

It is the Commission's expectation that large companies meeting the FSR turnover thresholds will normally also meet the FSR's modest contribution thresholds and will have received at least some contributions that are sufficiently large as to be reported in the notification. In the first months since the notification regime became effective, the Commission has received several blank FSR notification forms, submitted by parties that might have met the notification thresholds but who did not believe that any contributions received fell into a reportable category. The Commission has treated such submissions with scepticism. Further questioning revealed that while some parties submitting blank notifications had indeed applied a coherent methodology when designating their contributions as non-reportable, it became clear that others had merely done so through a lack of diligence.[498] In short, normally a large company will have at least some contributions that fall into the "Reportable Contributions" category and so notifying parties should take care not to designate all or nearly all contributions as non-reportable (unless they can confidently justify such designations under further questioning) as this will draw added Commission scrutiny to the notification.

---

[498] Remarks made by Commission officials at the 137th GCLC Lunch Talk, 'FSR merger tool – first experiences' (8 December 2023).

B.2 Public Procurement Tool

The two-step information-gathering process that is recommended for the M&A tool does not translate readily to the public procurement tool. The public procurement tool's notification threshold and disclosure requirements differ from those of the M&A tool in a few significant ways.[499]

Nevertheless, the approach toward gathering information for the three types of financial contribution, as outlined above for the M&A tool, would apply to a large extent also in respect of the procurement tool. Companies must keep in mind, however, that the per country exemption threshold for reportable contributions is only €4 million (and not €45 million as under the M&A tool). Moreover, companies expecting that they might be able to submit a declaration will have to capture information about smaller contributions that must be reported in Table 2 of Form FS-PP.

Suggested information-gathering approach under the public procurement tool:

- identify the entities within the corporate structure whose contributions are relevant to determining whether the notification threshold would be met
- establish a mechanism to itemise contributions received by the relevant entities, given the granularity required in the public procurement notification process

B.2.1 Calculating the Notification Threshold

The assessment of whether the notification threshold is reached is quite different under the public procurement tool as compared to the M&A tool. As outlined in Chapter IV, the €4 million threshold is reached by examining financial contributions received by the economic operator submitting the bid, including its subsidiaries without commercial autonomy, its holding companies, and, where applicable, its main subcontractors and suppliers involved in the same tender. This means that the relevant thresholds for procurement (unlike for M&A) do not extend to all contributions received by the economic operator's whole control group. Notably, the threshold excludes contributions received by the economic operator's subsidiaries that do have commercial autonomy, as well as any companies that, while also controlled by the economic operator's same holding company/companies, do not control the economic operator.

Consequently, the most relevant first step in a public procurement process is identifying which entities within an economic operator are relevant for calculating contributions. As the economic operator's holding companies (but not those holding companies' other subsidiaries) are included in the calculation of contributions, the closer the economic operator is to the ultimate parent company, the fewer intermediate entities will need to be taken into account. If the same entity within a company is usually the one participating in public procurement processes, it should be easier to identify and aggregate the

499 See Chapter III 2.A.

contributions that it, its parent companies, and its subsidiaries without commercial autonomy receive, even on a global scale. As discussed in Chapter IV, it might be advisable to include all subsidiaries of the economic operator in which it holds (*de jure*) control rights and not rely on arguments, which are uncertain to be accepted by the Commission, that some of these subsidiaries should be deemed 'commercially independent'.

The same considerations apply to all members of a bidding consortium, as each member would be considered an economic operator. Companies that expect to become notifying parties as main suppliers or subcontractors, are affected differently. This is the case because within the supplier's or sub-contractor's control group, only the entity that enters into a (supply or sub-contracting) agreement with an economic operator would be considered a relevant recipient of financial contributions, and not any of the entity's corporate affiliates. This applies irrespective of whether corporate affiliates would actually produce and deliver the products or provide the services to the economic operator (subject to the FSR's anti-circumvention provision).[500] This should provide main suppliers and sub-contractors some flexibility to decide through which entity or entities they would likely enter into contractual arrangements with economic operators in future procurement projects and focus procurement-related information-gathering efforts on them.

Under the public procurement tool, the financial contributions received by each of the relevant entities are not aggregated to determine whether the threshold is met. Only if a single party's contributions exceed the threshold is the tender notifiable. For instance, if an economic operator receives €2 million in foreign contributions and one of its main subcontractors also receives €2 million in the same country, the €4 million notification threshold is not reached. On the other hand, if the economic operator itself receives the full €4 million, the threshold would be reached and a notification by all notifying parties would be required.

Finally, if the contribution threshold is not reached, parties must nevertheless submit a declaration in any public procurement process that exceeds the FSR's value threshold of €250 million. Determining whether the contribution threshold is met does not carry nearly as much weight as a first step in the public procurement process as compared to the M&A process, as information for a submission will need to be gathered in any case. And even if a declaration requires less detailed information (Table 2 requires only a narrative for contributions below €1 million and no value estimates), the relevant information must nevertheless be collected and analysed to complete a declaration.

B.2.2 Completing the Notification

The notification in a public procurement process follows the same basic structure as the M&A tool, except that more small-scale contributions need to be reported. Combined with the requirement to submit a – fairly detailed – declaration (instead of a notification) if the contribution threshold is not met, the detailed procurement requirements mean that more contributions at smaller levels will need to be taken into account (see Chapter IV).

---

500 See Chapter VII 6.

As a result of these differences from the M&A notification process, it is recommended that parties regularly participating in public procurement projects identify the entity that will be considered the 'economic operator' (ie, the tender participant) and already establish a mechanism to catalogue all contributions received by it, its holding companies, and its subsidiaries without commercial autonomy, regardless of whether the contribution thresholds are met or not. This will allow a company to pivot relatively easily between submitting a full notification or a declaration.

B.3 Identifying Financial Contributions

When undertaking a data-collection exercise in the context of either the M&A or the public procurement tool, it is critical to identify all entities whose contributions are relevant to the assessment, and all financial contributions they have received. The identification of the relevant entities differs under each FSR tool.

The identification of foreign contributions is complex and is discussed in detail in Chapter II. Before identifying a foreign contribution within the meaning of Article 3 FSR, a crucial first step will be to determine whether the entity which granted the contribution is considered a government entity or a private entity whose actions are attributable to the State. If so, each contribution received from such an entity would be relevant under the FSR. If not, contributions by that entity (and all financial exchanges) can be excluded entirely.

The FSR captures contributions by public entities and private entities whose actions can be attributed to a third country. As discussed in Chapter II, disentangling the relationship between those entities and a third country can be a complex exercise, requiring an analysis of multiple factors, with reference to how similar entities are treated under both WTO and State aid law. Undertaking such an in-depth analysis is likely necessary when assessing high-value contributions, contributions that are considered likely distortive subsidies under Article 5(3) FSR, or contributions from entities in high-risk jurisdictions. However, conducting such an entity-by-entity assessment for all contributions can be overly burdensome in the context of global data gathering.

Instead, parties might be better served by assessing whether the entity granting the financial contribution has the following characteristics, and if so, treating the entity as one whose actions are attributable to a foreign State. This may result in an overly inclusive approach to data collection, but will err on the side of caution and avoid pausing data gathering to conduct an in-depth legal analysis for every such entity. It is recommended to consider entities as ones whose actions are attributable to the State for FSR purposes where:

- the State has a 50% or greater interest in the entity or otherwise exercises control rights; and
  - the entity acts not merely to maximise shareholder value (as a private entity would); or
  - the State's approval or input is required to grant the contribution in question.

Although the above criteria are not dispositive, they should provide a good and more concise framework to ensure that contributions that are attributable to the State are captured in most instances. Where the contributions concerned might fall under the subsidies listed in Article 5(3) FSR, are very large, or are from a high-risk jurisdiction, it is advisable to conduct a more detailed individualised assessment of the relationship between the State and the entity in question.

B.4 Specific Steps for High-Risk Third Countries

Although the FSR is country-agnostic, the Commission is likely to subject companies receiving subsidies from certain specific 'high-risk' third countries to heightened scrutiny. This will generally apply to any country where the government is involved to a high degree in the economy and in respect of which the Commission may assume that the government directs actions of market participants in light of its overall policy goals. The most obvious target for increased FSR scrutiny likely will be the People's Republic of China, as Chinese subsidies have often been considered as a source of rising concern, due to their allegedly distortive effect on the competition in the EU.[501] Certain sovereign wealth funds that might be considered to act, at least partially, in light of their governments' economic and policy goals might also fall into this group.

When gathering information related to these contributions, it is advisable to take a more comprehensive approach to all data-gathering for several reasons:

- first, a far wider pool of entities can be considered as public entities or authorities for the purposes of the FSR (for example, privately owned banks) in jurisdictions like China where the economy is State directed. Even entities that are considered 'private' might have very close ties with and receive directions from the State.
- second, the Commission might conclude that China should not be considered as a market economy for FSR purposes. In trade cases, this has allowed the Commission to conclude that transactions seemingly at (domestic) 'market rates' involved a subsidy by benchmarking the transactions against like transactions in other economies.[502] Thus, a company should take into account that there would be a greater risk that contributions would be considered subsidies, even if they are arguably consistent with domestic 'market rates'.
- third, for Chinese State-owned companies it might be very difficult to determine which entities should or should not be included in the company's overall control group (for M&A) or would be considered to be its 'holding companies' (for public procurement). Companies might form part of wider economic structures, such as a State-owned Assets Supervision and Administration Commission of

---

501 See Chapter II 2.B.3.

502 Regulation (EU) 2017/2321 of the European Parliament and of the Council of 12 December 2017 amending Regulation (EU) 2016/1036 on protection against dumped imports from countries not members of the European Union and Regulation (EU) 2016/1037 on protection against subsidised imports from countries not members of the European Union [2017] OJ L338/1, amended both the Anti-Dumping and Anti-Subsidy Regulations to grapple with the particularities of certain non-market economies against the backdrop of the expiry of s 15 of China's Accession Protocol. Article 2(6a) of the now amended Anti-Dumping Regulation allows the Commission to take account of 'significant distortions' in those non-market economies. At the same time, increased due process and transparency provisions were inserted into the Anti-Subsidy Regulation.

the State Council (SASAC) or similar, which might also comprise a range of other companies. Control relationships within (and potentially above) those groups would need to be investigated and documented to ensure that the full control group is captured, especially in the M&A context. Although the concept of the control group under the FSR's M&A tool is the same as under EU merger control, the analysis required is likely more extensive to comply with the FSR. For EU merger control purposes, it might be sufficient for companies to show that they exceed the turnover thresholds and to confirm that no other entities are engaged in overlapping product markets, regardless of the precise group structure. For FSR purposes, the group structure must be clearly defined in order to accurately notify all relevant contributions received from what the Commission likely would consider the full group (for M&A) or all holding companies (for public procurement). Similar issues might arise in other third countries where a State-owned holding company holds controlling interests in a range of operating companies.

This stricter approach would appear advisable especially for companies headquartered in a third country likely to attract greater scrutiny. But it could also be relevant for foreign companies with subsidiaries or joint ventures operating in these countries.

3. Creating an FSR Risk Profile

After completing an internal investigation into the financial contributions received, a company might want to consider whether the contributions it – or a deal partner – receives are likely to raise substantive FSR concerns that could create obstacles in achieving deal or tender clearance.

The risk presented by financial contributions generally follows the categorisation used in Forms FS-CO and FS-PP. The most high-risk contributions will be the likely distortive subsidies. This said, other reportable contributions might also pose a substantive risk of distorting competition if they provide a selective benefit and could be considered to facilitate the transaction. Therefore, any substantial subsidies falling into this category should be considered carefully.

Generally, the further removed a subsidy is operationally from the transaction or tender, or the clearer the evidence that a subsidy could only have local effects in a third country, the stronger the argument that its effects are likely to be non-distortive. However, even if a subsidy has no direct connection to the transaction or tender, the Commission may consider that a subsidy to one entity frees up capital that can be used by another entity in the same control group to strengthen its bargaining or bidding position. For these contributions, it would be advisable to document whether funds can, and in fact do, flow within the company from the entity receiving the subsidy to the entity participating in the transaction or tender process. Doing so will enable the parties to better assess how strong a case the Commission might make that those subsidies are capable of producing distortive effects in the EU.

After considering the types of contribution received, the parties will be better able to assess whether they have received any subsidies that are likely to pose a substantive clearance risk and/or more liable to draw follow-on questions from the Commission during its review. This will help the parties decide how to best address those financial contributions in the notification form and in discussions with the Commission. Depending on the individual situation, the parties might want to consider whether it would be a more effective strategy to provide additional explanations upfront for contributions that risk triggering questions from the Commission. Parties should consider preparing any additional arguments and documentation regarding financial contributions flagged during their internal risk assessment. Doing so can also help parties better budget the length of time it might take to achieve clearance. Transaction parties are advised to include such a discussion as part of the deal due diligence process, to ensure that all parties are aware of potential FSR risks and agree on a realistic clearance timeframe.

4. FSR in M&A Planning

The FSR will have a significant impact on the dealmaking process across the EU. Specifically, the FSR requires companies contemplating mergers, acquisitions, or the formation or entry into JVs to take FSR compliance obligations and potential Commission investigations into account at each stage of a deal's lifecycle.

Stages of the M&A lifecycle impacted by FSR reporting and clearance requirements:

- the initial decision-making process of identifying potential acquisition targets or potential buyers for a business
- the due diligence needed to prepare for a deal
- deal negotiations
- transaction notification and timing decisions

The FSR M&A tool's impact on these steps in the deal-making lifecycle is discussed in greater detail below.

A. The Initial Decision-Making Process

The notification thresholds under Article 20(3) FSR consider financial contributions received by all 'undertakings concerned' in the transaction. As a result, transaction parties are required to consider any financial contributions received not only by themselves but also by potential deal partners when considering the feasibility of potential transactions.

A.1 Sellers

When considering potential buyers for a business that meets the €500 million EU turnover threshold, sellers should evaluate the likelihood of potential deal partners raising FSR clearance concerns (just as sellers routinely consider whether a buyer is likely to pose merger control concerns). A seller should consider whether a potential buyer is likely to be the recipient of substantial financial contributions from third countries that might trigger a notification requirement or create a substantial risk of the Commission reviewing the transaction (assuming the target itself has not received enough contributions on its own to require a notification). It should also assess whether these contributions are likely to pose a problem in achieving a swift clearance.

The presence or extent of financial contributions might not be as readily apparent, and sellers might ask potential buyers to provide information outlining the general types and amounts of financial contributions received. It is particularly important that the seller identifies whether a potential counterparty is the recipient of subsidies likely to be considered distortive as outlined in Article 5(1)(a)–(d) FSR (and discussed in Chapter III), as these are most likely to trigger an in-depth investigation. In sum, sellers should ensure that they receive adequate disclosure from counterparties to accurately assess the FSR burden and risk, and factor this into their selection of a deal partner.

A.2 Buyers

Buyers should carefully consider the role foreign subsidies might play in their acquisitions. In particular, buyers of distressed companies or assets should be wary of whether these have received any foreign subsidies to keep them afloat. The FSR expressly lists subsidies granted to an ailing company to be problematic, unless there is a restructuring plan in place that can result in the long-term viability of such a target and includes significant contributions by the target itself.[503]

In addition to evaluating the viability of potential targets, buyers should be prepared to disclose their own financial contributions to potential counterparties. If a buyer engages in frequent acquisitions, it might be advisable to create and keep an updated account of all financial contributions over the past three years that can be reviewed by deal partners in the course of a bid process. Buyers that do not benefit from substantial subsidies that might trigger the FSR notification thresholds – or that are able to demonstrate upfront that any financial contributions received are likely not to be seen as having distortive effects on the EU internal market – might enjoy a significant advantage in positioning themselves as desirable buyers.

B. Deal Negotiations

Transaction agreements will need to take the FSR notification and review into account, much as they already include provisions addressing merger control and other necessary

---

503 FSR Regulation 2022/2560 [2022] OJ L330/1 (n 1), art 5(1)(a).

regulatory clearances. In particular, transaction parties might wish to ensure that deal documents address the FSR in conditions precedent, best efforts provisions, and allocation of risk clauses.

B.1 Conditions Precedent

Achieving FSR clearance should be included as a condition precedent to closing where the relevant notification thresholds are met. However, parties should bear in mind that the FSR empowers the Commission to request a notification of any deal, even if it falls under the notification thresholds. Consequently, parties should continue including flexible condition precedent clauses that apply if the deal is reviewed at the Commission's initiative (similar to clauses adapted to jurisdictions with 'voluntary' merger control notification regimes, such as the United Kingdom). Depending on the structure of the agreement and the certainty of notification, parties might prefer clauses that specifically address FSR review over general 'all regulatory clearances' clauses.

B.2 Best Efforts Provisions

As the FSR notification takes into account financial contributions received by all deal parties, there will need to be substantial coordination and collaboration between these parties to submit a timely notification. The parties will also need to respond to potentially extensive Commission RFIs under tight timelines throughout the review process. As in merger control, it is advisable for agreements to include best efforts provisions to ensure that all deal parties are actively engaged in securing clearance.

B.3 Allocation of Risk

Transaction parties should consider who will bear the risk of a potential prohibition decision and/or of the Commission calling in a deal falling below the FSR notification thresholds. The overall level of risk will depend on whether any party has received subsidies that are likely to be seen as problematic. While it can be expected that the vast majority of notified cases will not pose a substantive concern under the FSR, the parties should nevertheless carefully consider whether to include 'hell or high water' clauses (ie, a clause obliging a party to fulfil a condition regardless of the degree of difficulty).

Even if the parties do not appear to have received problematic foreign subsidies, the lack of Commission precedent makes determining the risk of a negative outcome more difficult than in the merger control context. Moreover, because of the wide range of remedies potentially at the Commission's disposal (see Chapter III), it might be much more difficult to predict the extent of the commitments that may be necessary to achieve clearance if a competitive concern is identified. If the transaction involves parties that have received extensive State assistance, those transactions should be considered inherently high-risk under the FSR and particular care should be exercised in risk allocation regardless of whether the FSR notification thresholds are met.

C. Deal Timing

In addition to a longer and more complex preparatory phase of the deal, transaction parties should also take into account the time needed for completing the FSR notification and the clearance procedure. Even if a company has prepared for the FSR in advance, putting together a notification and going through the pre-notification process until the Commission deems a notification complete will require considerable time and effort. This should be taken into account in any commitments to submit all required regulatory notifications within a certain period.

Thorough due diligence by all parties involved in a transaction should reduce uncertainties about the types of foreign subsidy that might be at issue and enable parties to reasonably anticipate whether a notification is required and the level of FSR risk a transaction will entail (including the likelihood that an in-depth investigation will be launched). Nonetheless, as the Commission has the ability to investigate transactions that do not meet the formal notification thresholds and to examine already-closed deals using its ex officio investigative powers, it might be difficult to eliminate all risks if the transaction parties receive sizeable financial contributions.

D. Coordination with other Regulatory Processes

The FSR introduces another regulatory obligation into the M&A process that is already subject to multiple different clearance processes. A transaction involving an EU target can trigger a number of different regulatory filings: FSR, EUMR, FDI, and potentially others depending on the jurisdiction, business structure and industry.[504]

D.1 Merger Control

An M&A deal large enough to trigger an FSR notification will often – but not always – be caught by the EUMR and require an EU merger control filing. The EU merger control notification forms require the parties to indicate whether they will also require FSR approval. Moreover, the Commission has established an internal control mechanism whereby any EU merger notification submitted (including drafts at the pre-notification stage) that indicates that the parties' turnover also meets the FSR thresholds will generally trigger a prompt from the Commission's FSR team to inquire as to whether a filing will be made. Therefore, it would not be feasible to attempt seeking merger control approval but bypass the EU FSR notification requirements. If a transaction does not

504 Eg, the Member States might each have a different set of applicable regulatory frameworks and some administrative processes might be required at regional or municipal level. These might differ depending on whether the company in question is publicly held or is engaged in certain regulated industries (eg, healthcare, media, and defence); processes might be managed by different regulatory bodies at various administrative levels.

meet EU merger notification thresholds, it will likely meet the notification thresholds in at least one Member State, necessitating one or more national merger filings.

The FSR's merger instrument is drawn from the EUMR in terms of process and many of the underlying conceptual frameworks. It is also the Commission-level structure with which many large companies will already be familiar from previous M&A activities in Europe. Consequently, the parallels and differences between the FSR and EUMR have been outlined in the course of this chapter. As noted in Chapter III, in theory it is possible for the timeline of an FSR and EUMR review by the Commission to sync very closely in terms of timing, particularly in unproblematic cases.

However, while the Commission has sole authority to review transactions under the FSR, the same deal might not necessarily meet the EU notification thresholds for a merger notification. If the deal does not meet the EU merger notification thresholds, it will still be subject to the merger control regimes of the Member States and could therefore undergo several national merger review processes in parallel with the FSR investigation. While national merger reviews generally follow the EUMR in terms of substance and, to a lesser extent, structure, these processes do not follow a synchronous timeline and can proceed at different speeds.

The outcome of an FSR review of a given transaction has the potential to significantly differ from the outcome of any merger control review(s) in both substance and timing.

Substance. The EUMR and the FSR envisage similar outcomes and remedies at the conclusion of the investigation of a transaction. As discussed in detail in Chapter III, the standard of review and the competition problems identified are different under the FSR and under a traditional merger control assessment. If the transaction substantially impedes effective competition (for merger review) or a financial contribution distorts the market (for FSR review) then it must be prohibited or may be approved only subject to remedies or commitments that remove these concerns.

Therefore, there is a real risk that a competitive problem might be identified in one process and not in the other. Likewise, it is possible that the remedies required to resolve competitive concerns under one instrument are insufficient – or potentially irrelevant – to resolving concerns in the other.

Timing. Timing of outcomes under the FSR and applicable merger control review might exacerbate any differences in outcome. As noted in Chapter III, although the FSR M&A tool and EUMR's timelines are aligned on paper, there is a significant potential for each review process to proceed according to a diverging schedule based on the length of the pre-notification process, the timing of the notifications, the complexity of the review, and other factors. If the transaction at issue requires merger control review in one or more Member States rather than at EU level, the timelines involved can be expected to diverge even more significantly.

The timelines of the FSR and EUMR processes might further diverge if remedies are offered in both cases. Notably, the FSR does not envisage the possibility of transaction parties offering commitments to resolve a potential competitive concern during the Commission's preliminary review phase. The FSR does not grant the Commission power to issue any form of clearance decision (conditional or otherwise) during the preliminary review phase. Absent such a decision accepting the parties' commitments, the Commission would have no way to ensure that the remedies offered are a required condition of clearance.

This differs markedly from the EUMR, as under the EU merger control process, commitments may be offered in either Phase 1 or in Phase 2. Indeed, it is common for transaction parties to offer commitments (even informally as early as pre-notification) where the transaction gives rise to a clearly identifiable competitive concern from the outset. The Commission welcomes those upfront remedy proposals early in the process, as it avoids the need to open a time-intensive and costly Phase 2 investigation to resolve potentially problematic transactions.

Although transaction parties might be able to propose remedies informally during FSR preliminary review phase, the fact that any conditional clearance can only be resolved at the close of an in-depth investigation might substantially increase the workload of the Commission and the parties (as even the decision to open such an investigation must be accompanied by a reasoned decision outlining the basis for the decision). Nonetheless, it might be that the EU legislator concluded that – particularly given the lack of a well-developed case practice and the complexity of remedying foreign subsidies – it would simply not be practicable for the FSR case team to evaluate the suitability of proposed remedies during the short preliminary review phase.

As a result, if the FSR and merger control timelines significantly diverge, there is a risk that remedies proposed in the course of one process ultimately prove to be incompatible with those offered later on to secure clearance in the other. Certain remedies offered to obtain one clearance might also change the competitive profile of the transaction as reviewed by the other authority (for example, remedies offered to scale back capacity offered under the FSR would directly affect the competitive situation of the parties under the EUMR). Transaction parties will need to carefully consider the compatibility and potential knock-on effects of remedies offered under either process.

D.2 FDI Control

The regulation of FDI takes place at the national level. As a result, whether one or more FDI filings arise will depend on the industry and jurisdictions involved. Deal documents should take into account any necessary FDI filings and the timing involved in obtaining clearance. However, there is little coordination between an FDI review and the FSR review process.[505]

5. FSR in Public Procurement Planning

The FSR will also have a significant impact on companies participating in large scale procurement projects in the EU and require them to take FSR compliance obligations

505 See Chapter I 4.E.

and potential Commission investigations into account when planning their participation in a public procurement project. However, the appropriate preparatory steps will depend on the form in which a company will participate in a public procurement project. For example, if the company anticipates that it will be the sole notifying (or declaring) party because it will not be part of a bidding consortium and not use main suppliers or sub-contractors, due diligence and negotiations related to other partners will not be relevant. They would become relevant, however, if a future FSR notification would be expected to include more than one notifying party.

A. The Initial Decision-Making Process and Due Diligence

If a company anticipates partnering with other bidders in a consortium or using suppliers or subcontractors that would qualify as 'main' suppliers or sub-contractors under the FSR, it is advisable to evaluate the likelihood of potential partners raising FSR clearance concerns. This would include considering whether a potential partner is likely to be the recipient of substantial financial contributions from third countries that might slow down the notification process and likely pose a problem in achieving a swift clearance.

In certain situations, a company might have the option of working with another partner, for example by switching to another supplier. This will not always be an option, however, as a particular supplier might be uniquely positioned to provide a certain input. Even in this scenario, initial due diligence would be helpful because it could signal early the need to fully engage with the supplier on FSR compliance.

Similar to what has been said above about buyers in the M&A context, due diligence could also be helpful for companies competing to become sub-contractors or suppliers to a bidder in a public procurement project. Companies that can confirm that they do not benefit from financial contributions or that are able to demonstrate upfront that any financial contributions received are likely not to be seen as distortive subsidies might enjoy a significant competitive advantage in positioning themselves as potential suppliers or sub-contractors.

B. Negotiations

In scenarios with several notifying parties – for example, a bidding consortium or the bidder relying on main suppliers or sub-contractors – it is advisable to consider including provisions related to FSR compliance in agreements between them. These could include clauses related to disclosing potential FSR risks, best effort clauses for the preparation and timely submission of notifications, consequences for parties that fail to prepare a notification on time, and arrangements for the handling of each party's confidential information to be included in a notification.

Parties might also consider including provisions on the consequences of potential non-compliance with the FSR. If there is a concern that certain parties might be the recipient of financial contributions that would be considered distortive subsidies, it is advisable to possibly resort to a mechanism for excluding them from the project in case the Commission signals during the review that it has serious concerns.

C. Timing Considerations

Timing concerns play a particular role in public procurement notifications. In the M&A context, delays in pre-notification discussions due to the notification being incomplete and the Commission demanding additional information would result in some frustration. By contrast, in the public procurement context, delays during pre-notification that prevent the parties from the timely submission of a complete FSR notification or declaration means exclusion from the public procurement project (unless the parties can cure any deficiencies during the grace periods provided by the FSR, see Chapter IV). In other words, a notification or declaration that the Commission will accept as complete must be ready on the day the tender is due. Moreover, this hard stop applies not only to the company submitting the bid, but to all notifying parties. The notifying party that is slowest in completing its notification determines whether the entire notification or declaration can be submitted on time.

As discussed in more detail in Chapter IV, this puts a premium on early preparations and early engagement with the Commission. Extra time might also be required to engage with suppliers or subcontractors that the main bidder identifies as 'main' suppliers or subcontractors and therefore as notifying parties, because they might be less aware of the FSR implications than the main bidder.

Chapter VI
The Ex Officio Control Tool

1. Introduction

The ex officio tool allows the Commission, on its own initiative and independently of any notification, to initiate investigations into any allegedly distortive foreign subsidies. This tool in many ways resembles trade defence investigations. Many concepts introduced by the FSR and certain of the Commission's investigatory powers – such as third-country inspections – are more suitable under this instrument than under the FSR's notification-based M&A and public procurement tools. Some of the fundamental concerns about the design of the FSR are less relevant under this tool than under the two notification-based tools.

The ex officio tool allows the Commission to open investigations on its own motion. Nevertheless, it can be expected that – as suggested by the recent complaint against football club PSG[506] and past practice in respect of trade defence investigations – the Commission will heavily rely on (informal) complaints submitted by parties claiming that foreign subsidies granted to their competitors are distorting the internal market. Still, the Commission is not obliged to undertake an investigation for each and every complaint it receives and enjoys broad discretion in defining its enforcement priorities.

In addition, recital 36 FSR highlights that '[b]elow the notification thresholds, the Commission [...] should also have the possibility to carry out a review on its own initiative of already implemented concentrations or awarded public contracts in an ex officio review'. The ex officio tool thus also allows the Commission to investigate transactions and bids in public procurement projects where the relevant notification thresholds in Articles 20(3) and 28(1) FSR, respectively, are not met and where the Commission has not received (or requested) a notification.[507] The Commission could also use the ex officio tool to investigate transactions that do not meet the definition of a 'concentration', such as the acquisition of minority interests without control rights.

As with other tools under the FSR, the remedies that the Commission may impose in the context of the ex officio tool can be substantial. Except in public procurement reviews where the status quo cannot be re-established because the Commission cannot cancel the award decision or terminate the contract, the Commission may impose the full range of measures available under the FSR. This includes the dissolution of the concentration

---

506 See 'LaLiga files complaint against PSG with European Commission' (*LaLiga*, 12 August 2023) <www.laliga.com/en-GB/news/laliga-files-complaint-against-psg-with-european-commission> accessed 18 December 2023.

507 See Chapters III 2 and IV 2 for further details.

or any suitable structural or non-structural remedy (for example, the repayment of the subsidy, inclusive of accrued interests, or sharing R&D results with other parties). These measures could have a significant impact on the entity subject to remedies.

An additional measure that the Commission may impose is the obligation to inform the Commission, for a limited period of time, of its participation in concentrations or public procurement procedures.[508] This obligation has the effect of subjecting that entity to the risk of additional scrutiny in the future because the Commission might open ex officio investigations (or require notifications) for any subsequent activity.

2. Scope of the Ex Officio Tool

A. Introduction

Under the ex officio tool, the Commission may investigate foreign subsidies distorting the internal market granted to an 'undertaking'. Unlike the FSR's two notification-based tools, the FSR does not provide a specific definition of the term 'undertaking' for the purpose of the ex officio tool, ie, the entity or control group that can be targeted in an investigation. As the ex officio tool uses the same term 'undertaking' as the M&A tool – whereas under the public procurement tool the relevant entity is the 'economic operator' and certain corporate affiliates – it can be assumed that the interpretation of this concept in ex officio will be the same as under the M&A tool.

Accordingly, ex officio investigations may cover the global activities of a firm, including all its subsidiaries, even if not directly related to activities in the EU. This could result in a broader reach of the FSR compared to trade defence instruments, where the investigated entity is the 'exporting producer', ie, the entity that is both producing the goods under investigation and exporting them to the EU, including its subsidiaries and other related entities. In trade remedies investigations, that type of entity qualifies as an interested party in the investigation (required to provide a questionnaire response) if it is: (i) an exporting producer, or (ii) involved in the sales or marketing of the product concerned destined for the EU.

B. Subsidies and Activities that May Be Investigated under the Ex Officio Tool

Under the ex officio tool, the Commission may investigate foreign subsidies granted to the recipient in the previous 10 years.[509] This ten-year period will become fully effective over time, as the FSR applies only to subsidies granted since 12 July 2018.[510]

---

508 FSR Regulation 2022/2560 [2022] OJ L330/1 (n 1), art 8.

509 ibid, art 38(1).

510 FSR Regulation 2022/2560 [2022] OJ L330/1 (n 1), art 53(1).

There is no restriction as regards the economic activities that may be targeted by the ex officio tool. In fact, the FSR empowers the Commission to investigate any foreign subsidy allegedly distorting the internal market. It follows that this instrument may be used in respect of a broad range of activities, including, for example:

- investments in infrastructure or assets within the EU (for example, purchasing land or assets, or building a factory);
- capital provided to companies which are already active in the internal market (for example, covering of operational costs);
- procurement processes by private entities;
- services provided over the internet by providers outside of the EU;
- the provision of services (for example, construction, financial services, insurance or sports competitions);[511] and
- sales of goods (if not covered by the trade defence instruments).

However, as regards this last category, and as noted in Chapter II, the FSR expressly provides that 'no action shall be taken under this Regulation which would amount to a specific action against a subsidy within the meaning of Article 32.1 of the [SCM Agreement]'.[512] This means that subsidies benefitting goods imported into the EU may be examined under the FSR – also through ex officio investigations – but may not be remedied under the FSR.[513]

From a practical perspective, ex officio investigations might focus on services and the movement of capital because the subsidised importation of goods can be addressed through the existing toolkit found in EU trade defence legislation.[514] However, the possibility cannot be excluded that the Commission might consider a subsidy theoretically covered by the SCM Agreement and the Basic Anti-Subsidy Regulation as being *de facto* covered by the FSR (for instance, because it is linked to or facilitates a concentration).

---

511 As noted above (n 506), the first publicly announced complaint under the FSR concerns football.

512 FSR Regulation 2022/2560 [2022] OJ L330/1 (n 1), art 44(9).

513 Moreover, as detailed in Chapter II, the recent Commission practice to consider so-called 'transnational subsidies', namely that financial contributions granted by a foreign government conferring a benefit on a producer located in a third-country (outside of the EU) are countervailable subsidies within the scope of the SCM Agreement (and the corresponding Basic Anti-Subsidy Regulation) entails the exclusion of those subsidies from the scope of the remediable foreign subsidies under the FSR (and the ex officio tool). In contrast to the SCM Agreement and the Basic Anti-Subsidy Regulation, the FSR seeks to remedy the distortions caused by foreign subsidies inside the internal market. That territorial dimension – by definition – falls outside the scope of the SCM Agreement and existing EU trade defence instruments because no subsidised goods are imported into the EU.

514 In this context, Commission Executive Vice-President Dombrovskis (Commissioner for Trade) declared that the subsidies granted by the US Government pursuant to the Inflation Reduction Act (IRA) might 'create adverse effects in Europe and could lead to trade defence instruments being used [against subsidized goods imported into the EU] to protect our internal market' (see European Commission, 'Statement by Executive Vice-President Dombrovskis' (n 90).

C. *Ex Officio Tool and the Notification-Based Tools under the FSR*

The ex officio tool is a generic instrument (not limited to a particular event) and therefore might overlap with the notification-based FSR tools. As a starting point, even if the ex officio tool is principally designed to deal with activities that are not notifiable, all concentrations and procurement projects may be investigated under the ex officio tool, regardless of whether they are notifiable.[515] As a result, this instrument might also be used to address distortions caused in the context of notifiable concentrations or public procurement tenders. This appears to be confirmed by recital 25 FSR, which refers to the instance '[w]here the concentration has already been implemented, *in particular* in cases where no prior notification was required because the notification thresholds were not reached' (emphasis added).

However, in practice, an ex officio review of a previously notified transaction or procurement project appears unlikely, as the previous review would already have remedied (if needed) any distortive effect on the internal market. Therefore, unless new information has emerged requiring intervention after the closing of the concentration or awarding of the contract, there would be no reason to review the same transaction under more than one tool. What is perhaps more realistic is the possibility that the Commission launches an ex officio review where a previously notified transaction becomes one of the elements of a broader investigation of potential distortive effects of foreign subsidies.

Contrary to the ex officio review of concentrations, the Commission's toolbox to remedy the distortive effects on a tender awarded to a specific company benefitting from distortive foreign subsidies is more limited. Awarded contracts are final, but closed transactions are not. The difference might result from the EU legislator's intention to create legal certainty and not to overburden public administrations in reopening tender procedures to replace the terminated contract with a new one. Such a scenario would be excessively costly, particularly if the contract has already been performed. This explains why, in such an instance, the legislator favoured other – less restrictive – remedies, such as, for instance, repayment or sharing obligations.

There is no definitive coordination framework governing the relationship between the ex officio tool and the M&A and public procurement tools. The only provision addressing this issue concerns the assessment of financial contributions. In particular, Article 34 FSR states that financial contributions notified in the context of a notifiable concentration or public procurement falling within the scope of the FSR's notification-based tools may be relevant and assessed in relation to different economic activities. Conversely, financial contributions assessed in the framework of the ex officio tool may be relevant and assessed in relation to different economic activities.

---

515 FSR Regulation 2022/2560 [2022] OJ L330/1 (n 1), recital 36. Under the notification-based tools, the Commission may also request prior notification of below-threshold transactions.

3. Review process

A. Starting the Investigation

The investigation is triggered if the Commission becomes aware of the possibility that foreign subsidies are distorting the internal market. From a practical perspective, this information can come 'from any source'.[516] Thus, it can be the result of investigative activities autonomously conducted by the Commission or – more likely – information or complaints submitted to the Commission by third parties or a Member State.

Specifically, Article 35 FSR requires the Member States to inform the Commission about potentially distortive foreign subsidies. This could include information gathered by observing the market or information that a Member State has received from third parties. Despite the broad information sharing obligation under Article 35 FSR, it is not clear under what circumstances a Member State would be able to share confidential (ie, non-public) information about potentially distortive subsidies that it has obtained in the context of national investigations. This might depend on the national law or the applicable EU regulation governing the national procedure. For example, the FDI Screening Regulation provides that the information received by a Member State as a result of its application may be used only for the purpose for which it was requested.[517] This would appear to preclude a Member State from sharing confidential information obtained in the course of FDI screening procedures. Likewise, Regulation 1/2003[518] as well as Regulation 773/2004[519] contain provisions limiting the use of information obtained in antitrust investigations. Under Article 28 Regulation 1/2003, and without prejudice to the provisions on the exchange of information among competition authorities and cooperation with the courts of the Member States, information collected during antitrust investigations pursuant to Articles 101 and 102 TFEU can be used only for the purpose for which it was acquired.[520] Under these provisions, competition authorities would appear to be prevented from sharing confidential information on potentially distorting foreign subsidies gathered during the enforcement of EU competition law.

Ultimately, the EU Courts might have to resolve this apparent tension between the broad information sharing obligation in Article 35 FSR and prohibitions from sharing confidential information obtained in other enforcement proceedings.

In addition to information transmitted by the Member States, the FSR envisages the possibility for any natural legal person or association to communicate to the Commission any information it might have regarding foreign subsidies that might distort the internal market. This can include, for example, European competitors of the

---

516 ibid, art 9(1). See Commission Communication COM (2023) 669 final (n 88). See Chapter VII 2.A.1.

517 FDI Screening Regulation 2019/452 [2019] OJ LI79/1 (n 75), art 10(1).

518 Regulation 1/2003 of 16 December 2002 on the implementation of the rules on competition laid down in Articles 81 and 82 EC Treaty (Regulation 1/2003) [2003] OJ L1/1 (as amended).

519 Commission Regulation (EC) 773/2004 of 7 April 2004 relating to the conduct of proceedings by the Commission pursuant to Articles 81 and 82 EC Treaty [2004] OJ L123/18 (as amended).

520 Regulation 1/2003 [2003] OJ L1/1 (n 518), art 28(1).

beneficiaries of the foreign subsidy or players placed either upstream or downstream of the targeted company.

Contrary to State aid law, the FSR does not envisage a specific procedure for submitting and analysing third party complaints.[521] At the time of writing, the FSR legal framework only includes a Commission Communication setting out the technical details (for example, file's format and size, electronic signature etc) for the transmission of information to the Commission.

When the Commission receives information on potentially distortive foreign subsidies, it is free to decide whether to examine those allegations. Receiving this information does not require the Commission to proceed with an investigation or reject a complaint. Moreover, the FSR does not expressly confer any specific rights to third parties (such as complainants) during the pre-investigation phase (ie, the phase dedicated to the examination of the information provided) or the investigation itself.

Consistently with complaints lodged with the Commission in respect of other areas of EU law,[522] the Commission has a general duty of informing the complainant of the result of its assessment of the information provided. Moreover, the FSR allows any party to present its views to the Commission following the decision to initiate an in-depth review.[523] The submission of information or a fully-fledged complaint, however, do not give rise to a specific right of that party to intervene in the investigation, or to the right of a decision rejecting a formal complaint.

Other potential sources for the Commission to gather information are market investigations conducted under Article 36 FSR and information collected by the Commission in the exercise of other powers under EU law.

Information that might trigger an ex officio investigation:

- information collected by the Commission on its own motion
- information or complaints submitted by third parties (including competitors of the beneficiaries of foreign subsidies)
- information submitted by the Member States
- limitations apply to sharing information collected in the context of a separate national procedure
- no formal complaints mechanisms and no formal third party rights

---

521 Commission Communication pursuant to Articles 4(2), 8(1), 15, 17(2) and 25 of Implementing Regulation (EU) 2023/1441 on detailed arrangements for the conduct of proceedings by the Commission pursuant to Regulation (EU) 2022/2560 of the European Parliament and of the Council on foreign subsidies distorting the internal market OJ [2023] OJ C246/2.

522 Other provisions of EU law (and, notably, Commission Communication EU law: Better results through better application [2017] OJ C18/10) might apply to this phase, obliging the Commission to at least provide a response to the complainant within a reasonable period of time.

523 For a discussion on the involvement of third parties in FSR proceedings, see L Hornkohl, 'The Role of Third Parties in the Enforcement of the Foreign Subsidies Regulation: Complaints, Participation, Judicial Review, and Private Enforcement' (2023) 8 *Competition Law & Policy Debate* 30–43.

B. Preliminary Review

Ex officio investigations begin with a preliminary review which is subject to Article 10 FSR. The FSR does not set any limit regarding the duration of the preliminary review phase.

The Commission may launch a preliminary investigation when information in its possession indicates the possibility of a foreign subsidy distorting the internal market. The wording of the FSR suggests that there is no requirement that the information must meet certain qualitative criteria. In particular, unlike the requirements applicable in anti-subsidy investigations, the FSR does not require 'sufficient evidence' that a distortion exists, but merely information 'indicating' the 'possibility' of distortive effects. Therefore, the evidentiary threshold is lower than in trade defence investigations.

As things stand, under the FSR, the Commission may initiate ex officio reviews on the basis of mere allegations that: (i) financial contributions granted by a third country amount to foreign subsidies, and (ii) those subsidies distort the internal market. However, in practice, resource restraints make it likely that the Commission will start the process only when 'sufficient' information is available, meaning that the Commission possesses prima facie evidence that the two conditions are satisfied.

Upon initiation of a preliminary review, the Commission is empowered to 'seek all the information it considers necessary to assess, on a preliminary basis, whether the financial contribution under examination constitutes a foreign subsidy and whether it distorts the internal market'.[524]

For this purpose, the FSR grants the Commission powers similar to those it enjoys in other fields of EU law, notably in trade defence investigations. In particular, as described in detail in Chapter VII, the Commission may request information from the companies under investigation, third parties or associations, the Member States or third countries (Article 13), interview any natural or legal persons (subject to their consent, Article 13(7)) or carry out inspections in the EU or third countries (Articles 14 and 15, respectively).

At the stage of the preliminary review, Article 10(2) FSR requires the Commission to inform: (i) the Member States that have notified the Commission of pending or envisaged relevant national reviews (for instance, pursuant to FDI screenings investigations),[525] and (ii) the national contracting authorities or contracting entities concerned in the event that the review is initiated in relation to a public procurement procedure. Therefore, the Commission is not obliged to inform all the Member States of each and every ex officio review it has started.

---

524 FSR Regulation 2022/2560 [2022] OJ L330/1 [2022] OJ L330/1 (n 1), art 10(1).

525 Under the FDI Regulation, the Member States must inform the Commission (and other Member States) as soon as possible about FDI in their territory that is undergoing screening. This notification includes details about, amongst others, the ownership structure of the foreign investor and the target company, the approximate value of the FDI, the activities of the foreign investor and of the target company, and the funding of the investment and its source.

The FSR does not specify whether a 'relevant' national procedure includes, apart from FDI screening procedures (that are explicitly mentioned), any procedures conducted under EU or national law concerning the same company under investigation by the Commission (for FSR purposes).[526] Therefore, it is unclear whether Article 10(2) FSR will have any implications beyond FDI proceedings. In other words, there is a question of whether – arguably, in accordance with the principle of sincere cooperation[527] – national authorities would have to inform the Commission in other proceedings, such as investigations conducted pursuant to national merger control legislation or Regulation 1/2003 (where notifications are sent to the European Competition Network).

Initiation of the preliminary review stage:

- no 'sufficient' evidence standard
- the Commission may seek information from the Member States, third countries, companies, etc
- limited obligation to notify the Member States and, in respect of public procurement procedures, the contracting authorities or entities

At the end of the preliminary review, the Commission may either close the investigation or initiate an in-depth investigation.

Closure of the investigation is called for if, following the preliminary review, the Commission concludes that an in-depth investigation is not warranted because there is no evidence of foreign subsidies within the meaning of the FSR, or there are insufficient indications of an actual or potential distortion in the internal market. This would likely also occur if the foreign subsidies granted to a specific company cannot be remedied under the FSR (for example, subsidies for imports of goods).[528]

Contrary to, for example, merger control rules, the FSR does not allow the Commission to terminate the preliminary review with commitments or redressive measures because it cannot adopt a decision ending the preliminary review. The target of an investigation can therefore not effectively offer any remedies before the initiation of an in-depth investigation.

---

526 Cases where the Member States could encounter information relevant for the purposes of the FSR are varied. For instance, decisions concerning capital increase or capital injection by foreign shareholders entailing a foreign contribution under the FSR could be subject to publication procedures by national registries or be investigated by regulatory or financial authorities of the Member States. An obligation on the authorities of the Member States to notify to the Commission of any investigation where they might learn of foreign subsidies being granted to an undertaking would be a significant burden for both the authorities and the Commission. The former would be required to carry out a prospective analysis on whether they might come across information that is 'relevant' for the purposes of the FSR, while – if the Member States follow this approach – the Commission would likely be inundated with information on any proceedings they carry out (or plan to do so) in anticipation of a possible initiation of an ex officio investigation pursuant to the FSR against the same undertaking.

527 TEU, art 4(3).

528 See Chapter II 3.A.2.4

When terminating the investigation, the Commission must inform: (i) the company under investigation, (ii) the Member States that were already informed of the preliminary review (notably, those that notified the – actual or planned – opening of a national procedure), and (iii) the contracting authorities or entities concerned if the preliminary review was initiated in relation to a public procurement procedure.[529]

C. *Initiation of an In-Depth Investigation*

The Commission must initiate an in-depth investigation if it considers that is has 'sufficient indications' that a company has been granted foreign subsidies that distort the internal market.[530] The reference to 'sufficient indication' entails a higher evidentiary threshold as compared to the mere 'possibility' standard applicable to the initiation of a preliminary review.

That decision must include both a summary of the relevant issues in fact and in law and a preliminary assessment of the existence of a foreign subsidy and of the actual (or potential) distortion caused by the subsidy in the internal market.[531]

When opening an in-depth investigation, the Commission must inform: (i) the target of the investigation, (ii) the Member States, and (iii) if the investigation is initiated in relation to a public procurement procedure, the contracting authority or entity concerned.

The Commission must also publish a notice in the *Official Journal* of the EU.[532] The notice will include a general invitation to submit written observations. Any natural or legal person, the Member States or the third country that granted the foreign subsidy may submit written observations. There is no legal requirement for third parties to demonstrate a concrete interest in the case.

Article 8 FSR Implementing Regulation specifies that the time limit to provide comments following the opening of an in-depth investigation will be set by the Commission and will typically not exceed one month from the date on which the company under investigation has been informed of the decision. For third parties, the one-month comment period starts from the date of publication of the summary notice in the *Official Journal* of the EU. The Commission may extend this time limit in justified cases.

Pursuant to Article 35(3) FSR, the decision to initiate an in-depth investigation will also be published in the database of decisions established pursuant to the FSR that the Commission will make available to the Member States and contracting authorities or entities concerned.

---

529 FSR Regulation 2022/2560 [2022] OJ L330/1 (n 1), art 10(4).

530 ibid, art10(3).

531 ibid.

532 In addition, pursuant to ibid, art 40, the Commission must publish a summary notice of its decision to initiate an in-depth investigation (likely on its own website). As with the notice in the *Official Journal*, this summary includes the same invitation for comments.

> *Initiation of an in-depth investigation*:
>
> - 'sufficient evidence' standard
> - publication, in the *Official Journal* and FSR database, of initiation decision and invitation to submit comments (typically one month for submitting comments; no interest requirement applies)
> - obligation to notify the Member States and, in respect of public procurement procedures, the contracting authority or entity

D. In-Depth Investigation

During the in-depth investigation, the Commission has powers identical to those in the preliminary review. Accordingly, it can seek to obtain all the information it deems necessary to further assess the foreign subsidy that had been identified in the decision to initiate the in-depth investigation by means of RFIs or inspections in accordance with Articles 13, 14 and 15 FSR, respectively.[533]

Similar to the statement of objections in competition law cases and the final disclosure in trade defence investigations, Article 42(1) FSR obliges the Commission to inform the target about the grounds on which it intends to adopt the decision to conclude the in-depth investigation. The company under investigation may submit observations on these grounds.

As set out in Article 17 FSR Implementing Regulation, the time limit for the target of the investigation to provide observations will be no less than 10 working days. Although consistent with the minimum deadline envisaged under Article 30(5) Basic Anti-Subsidy Regulation, the minimum period granted to companies is particularly short (considering that in antitrust cases the minimum time granted to companies under investigation is four weeks).[534] This short (minimum) time envisaged by the FSR might prevent parties under investigation from fully exercising their rights of defence, particularly considering the complex nature of the assessment of foreign subsidies.

In addition to the right to submit comments on the disclosure, the company under investigation has the right to access the Commission's file, subject to the protection of confidentiality or legitimate interests.[535]

---

533 ibid, art 11(1).

534 Regulation 773/2004 [2004] OJ L123/18 (n 519), art 17(2). See also Van Bael & Bellis, *Competition Law of the European Union* (6th ed. Wolters Kluwer 2019) 1092.

535 FSR Regulation 2022/2560 [2022] OJ L330/1 (n 1), art 42(4). The right of access to the file may not extend to confidential information or internal documents of the Commission or the Member States or, in particular, to correspondence between the Commission and the Member States. The right of access to the file is subject to the legitimate interest of companies or associations of companies in the protection of their business secrets and other confidential information. The Commission may ask the company under investigation and the associations

The disclosure obligation applies to all decisions concluding the in-depth investigation or imposing interim measures or fines.[536] Exceptionally, however, a decision imposing interim measures pursuant to Article 12 FSR may be taken provisionally ex parte (ie, without the target of the investigation being given the opportunity to submit its observations beforehand). In that case, the Commission must disclose the relevant information as soon as possible after it has adopted its decision.[537]

Main features of an in-depth investigation:

- broad investigatory powers
- disclosure of grounds for the decision to terminate the in-depth investigation – exception: decision imposing interim measures
- company under investigation may comment on the disclosure (at least 10 working days period for submitting comments) and access the Commission's case file
- overall length: approximately 18 months

4. Scope of the Commission's Powers

The general investigatory powers conferred by the FSR on the Commission apply also in the context of ex officio reviews. For a more comprehensive analysis, see Chapter VII.

The toolkit at the Commission's disposal when using the ex officio tool is similar to that in trade defence investigations. In fact, although powers such as inspections or RFIs are also found in competition law procedures, it can be expected that the Commission will conduct ex officio investigations similarly to anti-subsidy investigations. This would mean that companies would be required to respond to an extensive questionnaire detailing the subsidies received and undergo inspections, including in third countries. Because third-country inspections can take place only if the government of those countries do not object, these investigations likely will look more like trade defence verifications than antitrust dawn raids.

In terms of the length of the procedure, the Commission is not bound by specific deadlines (without considering the limitation period affecting the Commission's powers to investigate and/or to impose remedies or fines). The FSR merely indicates that it should 'as far as possible, endeavour' to conclude the in-depth investigation within 18 months

of companies that provided information to the Commission to agree on terms to disclose that information. If they object to those terms, the Commission has the power to impose the terms on which the information is to be disclosed. See Chapter VII 2.B.6.

536 For the sake of completeness, this provision also applies to decisions under ibid, art 18.

537 ibid, art 42(2).

from the opening of that phase of the review.[538] The wording of the FSR makes it clear that this limit is only indicative as there is no precise obligation on the part of the Commission to terminate the investigation within that timeframe. Moreover, this provision only concerns the in-depth investigation, and not the preliminary review. As a result, not only are there no statutory deadlines, but the FSR does not provide guidance on the preferred duration of the preliminary review.

5. Outcomes of the Review Process

At the conclusion of the ex officio investigation, the Commission has different options.

First, if the in-depth investigation does not confirm the Commission's preliminary assessment that a distortive foreign subsidy exists, or if the distortion of the internal market is outweighed by positive effects in the sense of Article 6 FSR, the Commission will adopt an implementing act in the form of a 'no objection decision', resulting in no further actions or measures.[539]

Second, if the in-depth investigation confirms that a foreign subsidy exists and that it distorts the internal market, two alternative avenues are available depending on the availability of suitable commitments to restore the level playing field in the internal market.

If the company under investigation offers commitments which the Commission deems appropriate and sufficient to fully and effectively remedy the distortion in the internal market, the Commission may adopt an implementing act in the form of a 'decision with commitments', making these commitments binding.[540] The FSR specifies that a decision accepting the repayment of the foreign subsidy concerned (including interest) in accordance with Article 7(6) FSR[541] is considered to be a decision with commitments.

If no commitments are offered, or if the Commission does not deem them appropriate and sufficient to remedy the distortion in the internal market, the Commission may adopt an implementing act in the form of a 'decision with redressive measures'.[542] Redressive measures include, but are not limited to, offering access under FRAND conditions, reducing market presence, repayment of the foreign subsidy, and divestment of certain assets. Further details on commitments and redressive measures are provided in Chapter VII. As far as public procurement procedures are concerned, the Commission's decision may not result in the cancellation of a decision awarding a contract or in the termination of such a contract.

The wording of the FSR (may adopt) makes it clear that the Commission is not required to adopt redressive measures – or accept commitments – as a condition for terminating

---

538 ibid, art 11(5).

539 ibid, art 11(4).

540 ibid, art 11(3).

541 See Chapter VII 2.B.4.1 for further details.

542 FSR Regulation 2022/2560 [2022] OJ L330/1 (n 1), art 11(2).

an investigation, even if it has found distorting foreign subsidies. In other words, even if the Commission finds evidence of a distortion in the internal market, it would not be legally required to take any further action. Even if the Commission finds that distortive foreign subsidies cannot be outweighed by positive effects, it is not obliged to issue a decision imposing redressive measures or accepting commitments.

The adoption of all decisions at the end of the in-depth investigation phase must follow the advisory procedure referred to in Article 48(2) FSR. Under the advisory procedure, the Commission must present a draft decision to a committee composed of Member State representatives. The committee must adopt an opinion, if necessary by majority vote, which the Commission must take into account (although not necessarily follow).[543] Moreover, pursuant to Article 40(2) FSR, all decisions at the conclusion of the in-depth investigation phase[544] must be published in the *Official Journal* of the EU.

543 Regulation (EU) 182/2011 laying down the rules and general principles concerning mechanisms for control by Member States of the Commission's exercise of implementing powers [2011] OJ L55/13.

544 These decisions are expressly qualified as 'implementing acts' by the FSR.

Chapter VII
Investigatory and Enforcement Powers

1. Introduction

The FSR confers on the Commission strong investigatory and enforcement powers, which are similar to the rules governing antitrust investigations, merger control and trade remedies investigations. This chapter discusses the investigatory stages of an FSR review, the investigatory powers and tools available to the Commission, as well as the fines and periodic penalty payments that the Commission may impose.

The investigatory stages, the investigatory powers available to the Commission and the fines and periodic penalty payments that the Commission may impose apply, in principle, equally to all three FSR tools: (i) the notification-based M&A tool, (ii) the notification-based public procurement tool, and (iii) the general ex officio tool.

However, the investigatory powers likely will not be equally relevant for each tool. For example, in M&A and public procurement investigations following notifications, it would appear to be less likely, due to time constraints, that the Commission would consider conducting a foreign inspection. Conversely, some of the enforcement powers are specific to the two notification tools.

2. Investigation Stages

As is the case in State aid and merger control investigations,[545] the Commission's investigations under the FSR are divided into two stages. During the preliminary review, the Commission is to assess whether there are indications that the financial contributions constitute foreign subsidies and whether these subsidies at least potentially distort the EU internal market. If so, the Commission can decide to initiate an in-depth investigation. The Commission may also adopt interim measures and, under certain circumstances, revoke previous decisions.

---

545 See more on State aid and merger control investigations in Van Bael & Bellis (n 534)

A. *Preliminary Review*

A.1 Sources of Information

In addition to information that the Commission receives through notifications under the M&A and public procurement tools, it may receive information concerning the existence of potentially distortive foreign subsidies from various other sources, including:

- *the Member States*: the Member States must transfer relevant information to the Commission when they consider that a foreign subsidy might exist and distort the internal market, with a corresponding obligation on the Commission to inform the Member State that has transferred the information;[546]
- *natural or legal persons or associations*: a natural or legal person or association may also communicate to the Commission any information it might have about foreign subsidies that potentially distort the internal market;[547]
- *other sources*: the Commission might obtain information on potentially distortive foreign subsidies from any other available source, including by conducting market surveillance and monitoring activities of market conditions and trends, and WTO notifications of subsidies. The Commission also can rely on its agreements or relationships with third countries to obtain information related to subsidies.[548]

The Commission may decide to establish a contact point to facilitate the provision of information concerning potentially distortive foreign subsidies in a confidential manner.[549]

Contrary to trade defence,[550] competition,[551] and State aid investigations,[552] the FSR does not establish a formal complaints procedure granting third parties that provide information to the Commission with specific rights or an official status (with corresponding rights) in the investigation. This approach will allow the Commission to focus on the substantive merits of information it has received, rather than conducting and continuing an investigation merely with a view towards establishing sufficient support for a decision rejecting a complaint.

> *Sources of information relating to potentially distortive foreign subsidies*:
>
> - notifications under the M&A and public procurement tools
> - the Member States

546 FSR Regulation 2022/2560 [2022] OJ L330/1 (n 1), art 35(1) as well as recital 27. See Chapter VII 2.A.3

547 ibid, art 35(2).

548 ibid, recitals 8 and 27, as well as art 9(1).

549 ibid, recital 27.

550 See Regulation (EU) 2016/1037 [2016] OJ L176/55 (n 32), art 10 55–91.

551 See Regulation 2015/1589 [2015] OJ L248/9 (n 43), art 12(1).

552 See Regulation 1/2003 [2003] OJ L1/1 (n 518), Chapter V.

- natural or legal persons or associations
- other sources (for example, market surveillance and monitoring activities of market conditions and trends, together with national authorities, WTO notifications of subsidies, agreements or relationships with third countries)

A.2 Object and Purpose of the Preliminary Review

During the preliminary review, the Commission considers whether there are sufficient indications that a company has received a foreign subsidy that distorts the internal market. This is a lower evidentiary threshold than establishing, and supporting with the requisite evidence, that there has been a distortion. In essence, the Commission must decide at the end of the preliminary review whether there are sufficient facts deserving a closer look in the form of an in-depth investigation.

The Commission is not required to carry out the balancing test during the preliminary review, whereby the negative effects of a foreign subsidy in terms of distortion are balanced against the positive effects on the development of the relevant subsidised economic activity, or the broader positive effects in relation to the relevant policy objectives.[553]

A.3 Obligation to Inform the Member States and the National Contracting Authority or Entity

If Member States have previously notified the Commission of relevant national procedures that are envisaged or that have been opened (such as an FDI screening procedure or another type of procedure not otherwise regulated by the FSR),[554] the Commission must inform them of the initiation of the preliminary review.[555] Similarly, if a preliminary review is initiated in relation to a public procurement procedure, the Commission must inform the national contracting authority or entity concerned.[556]

A.3.1 Timeframe for Preliminary Investigations

The length of a preliminary investigation depends on the FSR tool under which the Commission has launched the investigation. For preliminary investigations under the ex officio tool, the FSR provides for no time limits. This is different from ex officio in-depth investigations, where the FSR indicates that the Commission should seek to reach a decision within 18 months.

For preliminary investigations under the two notification tools, investigations have fixed time limits – 25 working days under the M&A tool, and 20 working days (extendable by 10 working days) under the procurement tool.

---

553 FSR Regulation 2022/2560 [2022] OJ L330/1 (n 1), art 6.

554 See FDI Screening Regulation 2019/452 [2019] OJ LI79/1 (n 75).

555 FSR Regulation 2022/2560 [2022] OJ L330/1 (n 1), art 10(2).

556 ibid, art 10(2).

A.3.2 End of the Investigation

If the preliminary review does not provide sufficient indications of the existence of a foreign subsidy and/or of an actual or potential distortion of the internal market, the Commission must close its preliminary review. Practice will show whether the Commission might also be willing to conclude that a company has received subsidies with potentially distortive effects, but that they do not merit an in-depth investigation because the subsidies cannot be remedied under the FSR.

The company under investigation and any of the Member State(s) that have been notified of the preliminary review, as well as the national contracting authority or entity concerned (if the preliminary review was initiated in relation to a public procurement procedure) must be informed of this decision.[557]

Possible outcomes of the preliminary review:

- there are sufficient indications that a company has received a foreign subsidy that distorts the internal market which deserve a closer look in the form of an in-depth investigation
- there are sufficient indications that a company has received foreign subsidies, but there are insufficient indications of distortion and therefore there is no need for an in-depth investigation
- there are sufficient indications that a company has received subsidies with potentially distortive effects, but they do not merit an in-depth investigation because these subsidies could not be remedied under the FSR

A.3.3 Start of the In-Depth Investigation

If there are sufficient indications of the existence of a distortive foreign subsidy, the Commission must adopt a decision initiating an in-depth investigation.[558] The decision must contain a summary of the relevant factual and legal issues, as well as the preliminary assessment regarding the existence of the alleged distortive foreign subsidy.

The Commission must also publish a notice of initiation in the *Official Journal* of the EU, inviting the submission of views by natural or legal persons, the Member States, and the third country granting the foreign subsidy.[559] The time limit for those submissions is set by the Commission but may not exceed one month from the date on which the target of the investigation has been informed of the decision, or from the date of publication of the summary notice of the decision in the *Official Journal* of the EU in all other cases.[560] In addition, if the in-depth investigation is initiated in relation to a

[557] ibid, art 10(4).

[558] ibid, art 10(3).

[559] ibid, arts 10(3) and 40(1). If the submission contains confidential information, the submitting person is requested to provide a non-confidential version of the submission at the same time as the confidential version (see FSR Implementing Regulation 2023/1441 [2023] OJ L177/1 (n 30), art 8(3).

[560] FSR Implementing Regulation 2023/1441 [2023] OJ L177/1 (n 30), art 8(1).

public procurement procedure, the Commission must inform the national contracting authority or entity at issue.

Taking into account that the Commission decision opens an administrative investigation, eventually the EU Courts might be asked to decide whether the corresponding initiation decision is a reviewable act within the meaning of the fourth paragraph of Article 263 TFEU, and who benefits from legal standing to initiate a direct action against that decision of the Commission. That assessment depends on whether the investigation is considered more akin to State aid cases (where the opening decision is considered a challengeable act)[561] or trade defence investigations where, on the contrary, the EU Courts have consistently declared the corresponding action for annulment to be inadmissible.[562]

Admissibility of actions for annulment against decisions initiating in-depth investigation ultimately depends on whether starting such a phase produces legal effects on the target of the investigation. There are similarities with the opening of State aid investigations because investigations under the FSR can potentially lead to a repayment of the subsidy received (if already disbursed). There are, however, at least two important differences: (i) contrary to Article 108(3) TFEU, the FSR does not envisage a suspension obligation in relation to foreign subsidies, and (ii) under the FSR, repayment is only one of the available remedies, while in State aid law reimbursement of incompatible or illegal aid is mandatory. These differences might prompt the EU Courts to decide against an analogy with State aid law, and that a direct action against FSR initiation decisions is inadmissible.

B. In-Depth Investigation

B.1 Object and Purpose of the In-Depth Investigation

During the in-depth investigation, the Commission seeks to obtain all information necessary[563] in order to further assess: (i) the foreign subsidies identified in the notice of initiation, (ii) their potential distortive impact on the internal market, and (iii) whether

---

561 Joined Cases T-80/06 and T-182/09 *Budapesti Erőmű Zrt v European Commission* EU:T:2012:65, paras 37–39. Contrary to existing aid, decisions to initiate a formal procedure in relation to new aid produces legal affects as it 'necessarily alters the legal implications of the measure under consideration and the legal position of the recipient firms' because of the suspension obligation imposed on Member States pursuant to TFEU, art 108(3). For further details, see K Lenaerts, I Maselis and K Gutman, *EU Procedural Law* (Janek Tomasz Nowak ed, 2nd edn, OUP 2023) 302 ff.

562 See, eg, Case T-134/95 *Dysan Magnetics Ltd and Review Magnetics (Macao) Ltd v Commission of the European Communities* EU:T:1996:38, paras 21–23 and the case-law cited; Case T-267/97 *Broome & Wellington v Commission of the European Communities* EU:T:1998:108, paras 26–29; Case T-744/20 *Airoldi Metalli SpA v European Commission* EU:T:2021:853, para 23. However, in the event of expiry reviews, an action directed against the initiation of the review has been declared admissible because it produces the legal effect of maintaining the validity of the measure (Case T-45/06 *Reliance Industries Ltd v Council of the European Union* EU:T:2008:398, paras 40–43).

563 In accordance with FSR Regulation 2022/2560 [2022] OJ L330/1 (n 1), arts 13, 14 and 15.

the distortion caused in the internal market is outweighed by positive effects on the development of the relevant subsidised economic activity on the internal market or by other positive effects (the balancing test).[564]

What is assessed during the in-depth investigation?
– the existence of foreign subsidies
– their potential distortive impact
– the balancing test

B.2 Possible Outcomes of the In-Depth Investigation

The in-depth investigation can have the following outcomes:[565]

- *no objection decision*: if the Commission does not confirm that a distortive foreign subsidy exists, or concludes that the distortion of the internal market is outweighed by positive effects (the balancing test),[566] it must adopt a 'no objection decision' resulting in no further actions or measures;[567]
- *decision with redressive measures*: if the in-depth investigation confirms that a foreign subsidy exists which distorts the internal market and is not justified in light of the balancing test, the Commission must adopt a 'decision with redressive measures'.[568] Those measures are aimed at remedying the distortion of the internal market which is caused by the foreign subsidy, and can include a prohibition of a transaction or a prohibition to participate in a public procurement project;[569] and
- *decision with commitments*: if the Commission finds that a distortive foreign subsidy exists and is not justified in light of the balancing test, the company under investigation may offer commitments. If the Commission concludes that these commitments are appropriate and sufficient to fully and effectively remedy the distortion, it will adopt a 'decision with commitments', making these commitments binding.[570]

B.3 Timeframe to Adopt a Decision Following the Start of the In-Depth Investigation

The FSR does not provide a maximum time limit for the adoption of a decision in an ex officio review. As far as possible, taking into account the complexity of the case as well as the level of cooperation of the targets and third countries concerned, the Commission

564 ibid, art 6 and 11(1). See Chapter II 4, on the 'balancing test'.
565 These decisions must be adopted in accordance with the advisory procedure of Regulation 182/2011 according to which the Commission must consult a committee comprising of representatives of the Member State on the draft decisions that it proposes. Regulation (EU) 182/2011 [2011] OJ L55/13 (n 543).
566 FSR Regulation 2022/2560 [2022] OJ L330/1 (n 1), art 6. See Chapter II 4, on the 'balancing test'.
567 ibid, art 11(4).
568 ibid, art 11(2).
569 ibid, art 7(1).
570 ibid, art 11(3).

will aim to adopt a decision within 18 months from the opening of the in-depth investigation under the ex officio tool.[571]

This is different from trade defence investigations which should, whenever possible, be concluded within one year from the opening of the investigation but which must, in all cases, be concluded within 13 months of initiation (in the case of anti-subsidy investigations)[572] and within 15 months of initiation (in the case of anti-dumping investigations).[573] In in-depth investigations under the M&A tool, the Commission has 90 working days to adopt a final decision on the compatibility of the planned transaction with the EUMR.[574] Under the public procurement tool the Commission has 110 working days from the date of notification to adopt a final decision. This means that the in-depth investigation will also continue for 90 working days unless the preliminary review has been extended by 10 working days, leaving only 80 working days for the in-depth investigation. The Commission can, however, extend the in-depth period by 20 working days.

B.4 Commitments and Redressive Measures

The FSR distinguishes between commitments and redressive measures to remedy any distortion caused by a foreign subsidy in the internal market. Commitments are offered by the target of the investigation.[575] Redressive measures are imposed by the Commission on the target of the investigation.[576]

B.4.1 Types of Commitments and Redressive Measures

The FSR provides for an extensive list of possible commitments and redressive measures, including, for example:[577]

- offering access under FRAND conditions to infrastructure that was acquired or supported by the foreign subsidies at issue;
- reducing capacity or market presence, including by means of a temporary restriction on commercial activity;
- refraining from making certain investments;
- the licensing on FRAND terms of assets acquired or developed with the help of the foreign subsidies at issue;
- the publication of R&D results;
- the divestment of certain assets;
- the prohibition or dissolution of the concentration concerned;
- the adaptation of a company's governance structure; or
- the repayment of the foreign subsidy, including an appropriate interest rate.

---

571 ibid, art 11(5) and recital (31).
572 Regulation (EU) 2016/1037 [2016] OJ L176/55 (n 32), art 11(9).
573 Regulation (EU) 2016/1036 [2016] OJ L176/21 (n 237), art 6(9).
574 EUMR Regulation 139/2004 [2004] OJ L24/1 (n 35), art 10(3).
575 FSR Regulation 2022/2560 [2022] OJ L330/1 (n 1), recital 23 and art 7.
576 ibid, recital 22 and art 7.
577 ibid, art 7(4).

Some of these remedies are familiar from EU State aid law and merger control cases. Others are novel and have not been tested in other enforcement regimes, and their effective implementation in practice would raise formidable challenges. For example, it might appear attractive to require a company which was able to successfully engage in an R&D project due to a foreign subsidy to share or license the results on FRAND terms. However, the design of such a remedy effectively would be fraught with difficulties. Those remedies would also require long-term monitoring, which is usually, and for good reasons, disfavoured in other enforcement regimes.

Repayment is a standard remedy in EU State aid cases.[578] It is unclear whether this remedy will have the same relevance under the FSR, as verification will likely be more challenging in relation to third countries as compared to the EU Member States. The FSR recognises this challenge. It provides that the Commission should accept a repayment offered as a commitment only if it can ascertain that the repayment fully remedies the distortion, is executed in a transparent and verifiable manner and is effective in practice, while taking into account the risk of circumvention of the FSR's objectives.[579] If the Commission considers repayment of a subsidy to be a viable option, it might have to be paired with other measures in order to fully restore the level playing field, because the recipient might have already obtained a competitive advantage due to the foreign subsidy at issue.

B.4.2 Conditions Applicable to Commitments and Redressive Measures

Commitments and redressive measures must be proportionate and fully and effectively remedy the distortion caused on the internal market by the foreign subsidy at issue.[580] This means that if the Commission considers different, equally effective remedy options, it must choose the measure which is the least burdensome for the target of the investigation.[581] Moreover, if the Commission accepts commitments, it should not impose redressive measures.[582]

> *Conditions to impose commitments/redressive measures*:
>
> - proportionality
> - effectively remedy the distortion
> - no redressive measures if commitments are accepted

B.4.3 Monitoring of Compliance with Commitments and Redressive Measures

A company's compliance with the commitments and remedies must, where appropriate, be monitored.[583] The Commission must, where appropriate, impose reporting and

578 See Regulation 2015/1589 [2015] OJ L248/9 (n 43), art 16.
579 FSR Regulation 2022/2560 [2022] OJ L330/1 (n 1), recital 24.
580 ibid, art 7(3) and recital 22.
581 ibid, recital 22.
582 ibid, recital 23.
583 ibid, art 7(2).

transparency requirements with regard to the implementation of commitments and remedies it has imposed.[584] Similarly, in the trade defence context, the Commission requires any country or exporter from which undertakings have been accepted to periodically provide information relevant to the fulfilment of that undertaking, and to permit verification of pertinent data.[585] The Commission might follow the example of merger and antitrust cases, and appoint monitoring trustees to ensure full and continuing compliance with remedies.

B.4.4 Comparison with Voluntary Undertakings in Trade Defence Cases

Similar to the possibility of offering commitments under the FSR, in the trade defence context, voluntary undertakings can be offered whereby: (i) the country of origin and/or export agrees to eliminate or limit the subsidy at issue or take other measures concerning its effects, or (ii) any exporting producer undertakes to revise its prices or to cease exports in the area in question as long as those exports benefit from countervailable subsidies, if the injurious effect of the subsidies is thereby eliminated.[586]

The Commission has, however, been reluctant to accept undertakings in the trade defence context.[587] Moreover, as a general rule, the Commission does not accept undertakings from exporting producers that did not (sufficiently) cooperate in the course of the investigation.[588]

B.5 Right to Submit Observations

As is the case in the EUMR and in the trade defence regulations, the FSR provides that, at the end of its in-depth investigation, the Commission should issue a formal charge sheet outlining the grounds on which it intends to take a decision before issuing a negative decision. It must give the target of an investigation the opportunity to submit observations in writing on the grounds on which the Commission intends to adopt its decision.[589] Although not explicitly envisaged under the FSR, it can be assumed that the target would also have the opportunity to comment on proposed remedies, at least where they include more complex behavioural elements.

---

584 ibid, art 7(5).

585 Regulation (EU) 2016/1037 [2016] OJ L176/55 (n 32), art 13(7).

586 ibid, art 13(1).

587 See, eg, Commission Implementing Decision (EU) 2015/87 of 21 January 2015 accepting the undertakings offered in connection with the anti-dumping proceeding concerning imports of citric acid originating in the People's Republic of China [2015] OJ L15/75 in the anti-dumping context and Commission Implementing Regulation (EU) 2019/244 of 11 February 2019 imposing a definitive countervailing duty on imports of biodiesel originating in Argentina [2019] OJ L40/1 in the anti-subsidy context.

588 See, eg, Council Implementing Regulation (EU) 856/2010 of 27 September 2010 terminating the partial interim review of Regulation (EC) 661/2008 imposing a definitive anti-dumping duty on imports of ammonium nitrate originating in Russia [2010] OJ L254/5, recital 21; Council Regulation (EC) 803/2009 of 27 August 2009 imposing a definitive anti-dumping duty on imports of certain tube and pipe fittings, of iron or steel, originating in the People's Republic of China and Thailand, and those consigned from Taiwan, whether declared as originating in Taiwan, or not, and repealing the exemption granted to Chup Hsin Enterprise Co Ltd and Nian Hong Pipe Fittings Co Ltd [2009] L233/1, recital 125.

589 FSR Regulation 2022/2560 [2022] OJ L330/1 (n 1), art 42(1).

The Commission may base its decision only on grounds on which the company concerned has been given an opportunity to submit its observations.[590] In the merger control context, such a submission of observations rarely sways the Commission from its intended decision. While this is likely to be the case in the FSR context as well, the arguments which the parties raise in such a reply might prove useful should they appeal the Commission's final decision.

The Commission must set a time limit of no less than 10 working days for this purpose, and it is not obliged to take account of written submissions received after the expiry of that time limit.[591] However, where appropriate and upon a reasoned request made by the company under investigation before the expiry of the original time limit, the Commission may extend that time limit.[592]

Contrary to competition[593] and trade defence proceedings,[594] the FSR does not envisage the possibility of conducting oral hearings as part of the in-depth investigation.

B.6 Confidentiality

B.6.1 Principle of Confidentiality under the FSR

To ensure the protection of confidential information, the FSR states that information acquired in the context of the FSR may only be used for the purposes for which it was acquired, unless the provider of the information agrees otherwise in accordance with Regulation 2022/2560.[595] Moreover, the Member States and the Commission, their officials and other persons working under their supervision, may not disclose information covered by the obligation of professional secrecy that they have acquired in an FSR procedure.[596]

B.6.2 Obligation to Inform about the Use of Information Provided

In the context of an RFI,[597] when conducting an interview[598] or requesting oral explanations during an inspection,[599] the Commission must inform the persons or companies providing information that they agree that access to that information may be granted in the context of the right of access to file.[600] Where the Commission otherwise receives information,

---

590 ibid, art 42(3).

591 FSR Implementing Regulation 2023/1441 [2023] OJ L177/1 (n 30), art 17(1).

592 ibid, art 17(4).

593 EUMR Regulation 139/2004 [2004] OJ L24/1 (n 35), art 18; Commission Implementing Regulation (EU) 2023/914 of 20 April 2023 implementing Council Regulation (EC) 139/2004 on the control of concentrations between undertakings and repealing Commission Regulation (EC) 802/2004 [2023] OJ L119/22, arts 13–15.

594 Regulation (EU) 2016/1037 [2016] OJ L176/55 (n 32), art 11(5) and Regulation (EU) 2016/1036 [2016] OJ L176/21 (n 237), art 6(5).

595 FSR Regulation 2022/2560 [2022] OJ L330/1 (n 1), art 43(1) and FSR Implementing Regulation 2023/1441 [2023] OJ L177/1 (n 30), art 18.

596 ibid, art 43(2) and FSR Implementing Regulation 2023/1441 [2023] OJ L177/1 (n 30), art 19.

597 FSR Regulation 2022/2560 [2022] OJ L330/1 (n 1), art 13. See Chapter VII 3.A.

598 ibid, art 13(7). See Chapter VII 3.C.

599 ibid, arts 14 and 15. See Chapter VII 3.B.

600 FSR Implementing Regulation 2023/1441 [2023] OJ L177/1 (n 30), art 19(2). See also FSR Regulation 2022/2560 [2022] OJ L330/1 (n 1), art 42(4) and FSR Implementing Regulation 2023/1441 [2023] OJ L177/1 (n 30), art 20.

it must also inform the parties providing that information that access to the information may be granted in the context of the right of access to file.[601]

To facilitate access to the file, parties must, if requested by the Commission, provide non-confidential versions of the documents submitted or of statements made during interviews. Similarly, the Commission must require a company under investigation to identify, within a specified time limit, confidential parts of decisions adopted at the end of a preliminary review or an in-depth investigation, before the decision is published.

Where a party or the company under investigation fails to identify the information that it considers to be confidential, the Commission may assume that the information concerned does not contain confidential information.[602]

B.6.3 Disclosure of Information Identified as Confidential

If the Commission considers that certain information that is claimed to be confidential may be disclosed, because either it does not constitute a business secret or confidential information, or there is an overriding interest in its disclosure, it must inform the party or the company under investigation of its intention to disclose that information.

If the party or the company under investigation objects within five working days after it has been informed of the Commission's intention, the Commission may adopt a decision specifying the date after which the information will be disclosed or published. This date may not be less than five working days from the date of notification of the Commission's decision. The decision must be notified to the natural or legal person concerned.[603]

B.6.4 Publication of Statistics and Reports and Information Showing the Existence of a Distortive Foreign Subsidy

The protection of confidential information does not prevent:

- the publication of statistics and reports which do not contain information allowing the identification of specific companies or associations of companies;[604] and
- the Commission from using and disclosing, to the extent necessary, information showing the existence of a distortive foreign subsidy.[605]

B.7 Access to the File

In order to be able to exercise the right to submit observations, a company under investigation or a notifying party may request access to the Commission's file after being informed of the grounds on which the Commission intends to adopt a decision.[606]

---

601 ibid.

602 FSR Implementing Regulation 2023/1441 [2023] OJ L177/1 (n 30), art 19(5).

603 ibid, art 19(6).

604 FSR Regulation 2022/2560 [2022] OJ L330/1 (n 1), art 43(3).

605 FSR Implementing Regulation 2023/1441 [2023] OJ L177/1 (n 30), art 19(7).

606 FSR Regulation 2022/2560 [2022] OJ L330/1 (n 1), art 42(4) and FSR Implementing Regulation 2023/1441 [2023] OJ L177/1 (n 30), art 20(1). This right also exists in the context of trade defence investigations (see Regulation (EU) 2016/1036 [2016] OJ L176/21 (n 237), art 6(7) and Regulation (EU) 2016/1037 [2016] OJ L176/55 (n 32), art 11(7).

B.7.1 Right to Access Non-Confidential Versions of the File

When providing access to the file, the Commission must provide the company with a non-confidential version of all documents mentioned in the grounds on which the Commission intends to adopt a decision.[607] Moreover, the Commission may give access to some or all documents in a redacted form[608] at any time during the procedure, in order to avoid a disproportionate delay or administrative burden.[609]

The scope of the right of access to the file is more limited under the FSR than in trade defence investigations. In trade defence investigations, interested parties may, subject to certain limitations, 'inspect all information made available by any party to an investigation, […] which is relevant to the presentation of their cases […] and is used in the investigation'.[610] The term 'information' used in this context is broader than the concept of 'documents' used in the FSR, and information 'used in the investigation' is likely to encompass more than only 'documents mentioned in the grounds on which the Commission intends to adopt a decision'. In fact, the Appellate Body in *EC – Fasteners (China)* clarified that whether information is 'used' by an investigating authority does not depend on whether the investigating authority specifically relied on that information in its determinations.[611]

The FSR remedies this more limited access to file by fuller access rights within the framework of confidentiality rings.

B.7.2 Rights to Access Confidential Versions of the File (Confidentiality Rings)

As is the case in merger control,[612] and trade defence investigations,[613] the right of access to the file is subject to the legitimate interest in the protection of business secrets and other confidential information.[614] However, the Commission may ask the company under investigation and third parties that have provided information to the Commission to agree on terms to disclose that information.[615]

The FSR allows the Commission to organise access to file with confidentiality rings, thereby avoiding the burdensome need to create a non-confidential version of the entire file on record. The terms governing confidentiality rings are set forth in Article 20 FSR Implementing Regulation. They specify that a party's external legal counsel, economic advisors, and external technical experts may be granted access to the file. Those with

---

607 FSR Implementing Regulation 2023/1441 [2023] OJ L177/1 (n 30), art 19(3).

608 ibid.

609 ibid, art 20(9).

610 Regulation (EU) 2016/1036 [2016] OJ L176/21 (n 237), art 6(7) and Regulation (EU) 2016/1037 [2016] OJ L176/55 (n 32), art 11(7).

611 WTO Appellate Body Report, *EC – Fasteners (China)* (2016), WT/DS397/AB/R, para 479.

612 EUMR Regulation 139/2004 [2004] OJ L24/1 (n 35), art 18(3).

613 Regulation (EU) 2016/1036 [2016] OJ L176/21 (n 237), art 6(7) and Regulation (EU) 2016/1037 [2016] OJ L176/55 (n 32), art 11(7).

614 FSR Regulation 2022/2560 [2022] OJ L330/1 (n 1), art 42(4) and FSR Implementing Regulation 2023/1441 [2023] OJ L177/1 (n 30), art 19(1).

615 ibid and FSR Implementing Regulation 2023/1441 [2023] OJ L177/1 (n 30), 19(4).

access rights are prohibited from disclosing confidential information to persons outside the confidentiality ring.[616]

Members of the confidentiality ring may, within one week of receiving access to the file under the terms of disclosure, make a reasoned request to the Commission for:

- access to a non-confidential version of any document in the Commission's file not already provided to the company under investigation, with a view to making that document available to that company; or
- an extension of the terms of disclosure to additional specified external legal and economic counsel or external technical experts.

That additional access to the non-confidential version of documents or extension to other individuals may only be granted if it is essential for the proper exercise of the rights of defence of the target of an investigation.[617] If the Commission considers that such a request is well-founded, the Commission must either make a non-confidential version of the document available to the company under investigation or adopt a decision extending the terms of disclosure for the documents in question.[618]

B.7.3 *Limitations of the Right to Access the File*

B.7.3.1 *Certain Documents Are Excluded from the Right to Access*

As is the case in trade defence investigations,[619] the right to access the file does not extend to the following documents: (i) internal documents of the Commission, (ii) internal documents of the authorities of the Member States or third countries, including competition authorities and contracting authorities or entities, (iii) correspondence between the Commission and the authorities of the Member States or third countries, including competition authorities and contracting authorities or entities, and (iv) correspondence between the authorities of the Member States and between the Member States and third countries.[620]

B.7.3.2 *Harm to the Information Provider*

In exceptional circumstances, the Commission may decide not to grant access under the terms of disclosure to certain documents or to grant access to partly redacted documents if it determines that the harm that the information provider would likely suffer from disclosure would, on balance, outweigh the importance of the disclosure for the exercise of the rights of defence.[621]

The Commission must perform a similar assessment when it considers that it needs to disclose or partly disclose correspondence between the Commission and public authorities

---

616 FSR Implementing Regulation 2023/1441 [2023] OJ L177/1 (n 30), art 20(5).

617 ibid, art 20(6).

618 ibid, art 20(8).

619 Regulation (EU) 2016/1036 [2016] OJ L176/21 (n 237), art 6(7) and Regulation (EU) 2016/1037 [2016] OJ L176/55 (n 32), art 11(7).

620 FSR Regulation 2022/2560 [2022] OJ L330/1 (n 1), art 42(4) and FSR Implementing Regulation 2023/1441 [2023] OJ L177/1 (n 30), art 20(2).

621 FSR Implementing Regulation 2023/1441 [2023] OJ L177/1 (n 30), art 19(5).

of the Member States or of third countries and other types of sensitive documents provided by the public authorities of the Member States or of third countries. Prior to the disclosure of that correspondence or documents, the Commission must consult the authorities of the Member State or of the third country.[622]

C. Interim Measures

C.1 Circumstances in which Interim Measures May Be Imposed

The Commission may order interim measures when: (i) there are 'sufficient indications' that a financial contribution constitutes a foreign subsidy and distorts the internal market, and (ii) there is a risk of serious and irreparable damage to competition in the internal market.[623]

However, it remains uncertain whether interim measures based on substantive concerns will play any role under the FSR. Given the fact that the foreign subsidies would have been granted by third countries in the past, it might be exceedingly difficult for the Commission to establish a prima facie FSR violation (which would also require a balancing exercise) and the urgency justifying an interim measure after an initial investigation.[624]

It appears more likely that the Commission might be able to use interim measures on procedural grounds. In particular, in the context of the M&A tool, the Commission may order interim measures where: (i) a concentration has been implemented in breach of the standstill requirement under Article 21 FSR, or (ii) a concentration has been implemented in breach of a conditional clearance decision imposing commitments under Article 25(3)(a) FSR.[625] Interim measures cannot be adopted in the context of public procurement projects.[626]

Conditions to impose interim measures:

- sufficient indications that a financial contribution constitutes a foreign subsidy and distorts the internal market
- risk of serious and irreparable damage to competition in the internal market

---

622 ibid.

623 FSR Regulation 2022/2560 [2022] OJ L330/1 (n 1), art 12(1).

624 Case T-44/90 *La Cinq SA v Commission of the European Communities* EU:T:1992:5, para 60, fn 246. See also Case T-23/90 *Automobiles Peugeot SA v Commission of the European Communities* EU:T:1991:45, para 61, fn 799, where the General Court stated that 'in proceedings relating to the legality of a Commission decision imposing provisional measures, the requirement of a finding of a *prima facie* infringement cannot be placed on the same footing as the requirement of certainty that a final decision must satisfy'. On urgency, see also *La Cinq* (above), para 28, fn 246. The Commission had strictly interpreted this notion to mean that only damage that could not be remedied by any subsequent decision, such as cessation of activities, could be considered as 'irreparable'. Furthermore, according to DG Competition's Antitrust Manual of Procedures, module 17, point 17, financial loss is not regarded as irreparable unless the survival of the undertaking concerned is threatened.

625 FSR Regulation 2022/2560 [2022] OJ L330/1 (n 1), art 25(7).

626 ibid, art 12(2).

- interim measures cannot be adopted in the context of public procurement projects

Circumstances in which interim measures may be imposed:

- a concentration has been implemented in breach of the standstill requirement under Article 21 FSR
- a concentration has been implemented in breach of a conditional clearance decision imposing commitments under Article 25(3)(a) FSR

C.2 Types of Interim Measure

Interim measures may include, but are not limited to:[627]

- offering access under FRAND conditions to infrastructure, including research facilities, production capabilities or essential facilities, which were acquired or supported by foreign subsidies distorting the internal market;[628]
- refraining from certain investments;[629]
- licensing on FRAND terms assets acquired or developed with the help of foreign subsidies.[630]

C.3 Timing, Renewal and Provisional Interim Measures

Interim measures are by definition temporary and of a conservatory nature (ie, they are limited to maintaining the status quo ante).[631] As is the case in the context of merger investigations,[632] interim measures may be applied either for a specific period of time, which may be renewed in so far as it is necessary and appropriate, or until the Commission takes a final decision.[633]

---

627 ibid. Interim measures have rarely been used in competition law cases in recent years. *NDC Health/IMS Health*: *Interim measures* (Case COMP/D3/38.044) [2002] OJ L59/18; Commission Decision of 16 October 2019, *Broadcom* (Case COMP/AT.40608) [2019] OJ C81/23.

628 FSR Regulation 2022/2560 [2022] OJ L330/1 (n 1), art 7(4)(a).

629 ibid, art 7(4)(c).

630 ibid, art 7(4)(d).

631 See, in the merger control context, Case 792/79R *Camera Care Ltd v Commission of the European Communities* EU:C:1980:18, para 19, fn 797; Case T-184/01R *IMS Health Inc v Commission of the European Communities* EU:T:2001:200, para 25. In *Broadcom* (n 627) see European Commission, Press Release, 'Antitrust: Commission imposes interim measures on Broadcom in TV and modem chipset markets' (16 October 2019) <https://ec.europa.eu/commission/presscorner/detail/en/IP_19_6109> accessed 18 December 2023, the measures were imposed for three years or until the adoption of a final decision on the substance or the closure of the investigation.

632 Regulation 1/2003 [2003] OJ L1/1 (n 518), art 8. See also *Camera Care* (n 631), paras 12–21.

633 FSR Regulation 2022/2560 [2022] OJ L330/1 (n 1), art 12(3).

C.4 Right to Be Heard, Access to File and Provisional Interim Measures

C.4.1 Right to Be Heard and Access to File

As is the case in merger and antitrust investigations,[634] before adopting a decision imposing interim measures, the Commission must give the company under investigation the opportunity to submit observations on the grounds on which the Commission intends to adopt its decision.[635] In order to be able to exercise this right, the company under investigation has the right to access the Commission's file.[636]

The Commission must set a time limit of no less than 10 working days within which the company under investigation may submit its observations in writing and may not take account of any written submissions received after the expiry of the time limit.[637] The Commission may base its decision only on grounds on which the companies concerned have been given the opportunity to submit their observations.[638]

This means that while interim measures are supposed to be an expeditious measure to preserve the status quo, in practice their adoption will require a significant amount of time.

C.4.2 Provisional Interim Measures

A decision to impose interim measures can also be taken ex parte, without the company under investigation being given the prior opportunity to submit its observations. In this case, however, the Commission must give the target that opportunity as soon as possible after having taken its decision.[639]

If the Commission adopts a provisional decision imposing interim measures, it must set a time limit within which the company under investigation may submit its observations in writing.[640] After receiving observations, the Commission must take a final decision on the interim measures repealing, amending or confirming the provisional decision. Where the company under investigation has failed to submit observations within the time limit set by the Commission, the provisional decision becomes final upon the expiry of that time limit.[641]

---

634 Regulation 1/2003 [2003] OJ L1/1 (n 518), art 27.

635 FSR Regulation 2022/2560 [2022] OJ L330/1 (n 1), art 42(1).

636 ibid, art 42(4). See Chapter VII 2.B.7.

637 FSR Implementing Regulation 2023/1441 [2023] OJ L177/1 (n 30), art 17(1).

638 FSR Regulation 2022/2560 [2022] OJ L330/1 (n 1), art 42(3).

639 ibid, art 42(2).

640 Where appropriate and upon reasoned request made by the undertaking under investigation before the expiry of the original time limit, the Commission may extend this time limit (see FSR Implementing Regulation 2023/1441 [2023] OJ L177/1 (n 30), art 17(4)).

641 ibid, art 17(3).

D. Revocation

According to Article 18 FSR, the Commission may revoke a decision taken at the end of an in-depth investigation (decision with redressive measures, decision with commitments, or no objection decision),[642] and adopt a new decision instead if:

- the company to which a decision was addressed fails to respect its commitments or the redressive measures imposed;[643]
- the initial decision was based on incomplete, incorrect or misleading information;[644] or
- the redressive measures or commitments are not effective.[645]

Article 18 FSR grants the Commission significant powers to intervene in markets ex post on the grounds that a remedy has been deemed to be 'not effective'. This would mean that the Commission could in principle re-open any investigation if market conditions have not developed as envisaged at the time of the initial decision. Thus, the Commission could adopt an incremental approach to remedies, starting with less intrusive remedies and increase their scope if it does not see the expected results. The broad discretion the Commission enjoys under Article 18 FSR raises concerns about the lack of legal certainty, as the Commission could in principle use an FSR decision to engineer market outcomes over time.

However, in the context of public procurement, the revocation and adoption of a new decision by the Commission will not affect the decision of a national contracting authority or entity awarding a procurement contract.[646]

E. Market Investigation and Third-Country Dialogue

E.1 Market Investigation

If information available to the Commission substantiates a reasonable suspicion that foreign subsidies in a particular sector, for a particular type of economic activity or based on a particular subsidy instrument might distort the internal market, the Commission may conduct a market investigation.[647]

During a market investigation, the Commission may require the companies or associations of companies to supply the necessary information and carry out the necessary

---

642 See Chapter VI 5.

643 FSR Regulation 2022/2560 [2022] OJ L330/1 (n 1), art 18(1)(a).

644 ibid, art 18(1)(b).

645 ibid, art 18(1)(c).

646 ibid, art 18(2).

647 ibid, arts 13, 14, 15, and 17 apply to market investigations (see ibid, art 36(4)).

inspections. The Commission may also request the Member States or the third country to supply information.[648]

Where relevant, the Commission must publish a report on the results of its market investigation and seek comments.[649] It may use the information obtained from those market investigations in the framework of the three tools under the FSR.[650] However, the FSR does not confer the power on the Commission to adopt measures based on the results of the market investigation similar to the powers competition authorities have in some Member States.

E.2 Third-Country Dialogue

Where, following a market investigation,[651] the Commission suspects the existence of repeated foreign subsidies distorting the internal market, or where several enforcement actions under the FSR identify foreign subsidies distorting the internal market granted by the same third country, the Commission may engage in a dialogue with the third country concerned. The purpose of that dialogue is to explore options for stopping or changing those subsidies, so as to eliminate their distortive effects on the internal market.[652]

Similarly, the Commission may engage with third countries to improve the multilateral rules on subsidies. This allows the Commission to fight the consequences of distortive subsidies in the EU and to attempt to address their root causes in third countries, while preserving openness and striving for multilateral solutions.[653] Third-country dialogues do not prevent the Commission from taking actions under the FSR.

Dialogues with third countries are also used in the trade defence context. However, in that context, engaging in a dialogue is an obligation and takes place during an investigation. The Commission is required, as soon as possible after the receipt of a properly documented complaint and, in any event, before the initiation of an investigation, to notify the government of the country of origin and/or export concerned and to invite it for consultations with the aim of clarifying the situation and arriving at a mutually agreed solution.[654] Throughout the investigation, the Commission must also afford the government of the country of origin and/or export a reasonable opportunity to continue the consultations.[655]

---

648 ibid, art 36(1).
649 ibid, art 36(2).
650 ibid, art 36(3).
651 ibid, art 36.
652 ibid, art 37(1).
653 European Parliament, Press Release, 'Agreement on foreign subsidies: ensuring equal competition in the EU' (30 June 2022) <www.europarl.europa.eu/news/en/press-room/20220627IPR33918/agreement-on-foreign-subsidies-ensuring-equal-competition-in-the-eu> accessed 18 December 2023.
654 Regulation (EU) 2016/1037 [2016] OJ L176/55 (n 32), art 10(7).
655 ibid, art 11(10).

F. *Limitation Period*

The powers of the Commission in the context of a preliminary and in-depth investigation, using the ex officio tool, are subject to a limitation period of 10 years, starting on the day on which a foreign subsidy is first granted. Any action taken by the Commission in the context of its preliminary investigation,[656] RFIs,[657] or actions taken in the context of investigations within or outside the EU,[658] interrupt that limitation period.[659] These rules are subject to the transition provision in Article 53(1) FSR, stating that the FSR applies to subsidies granted since 12 July 2018.

Under the FSR's notification-based tools, the Commission may investigate only financial contributions granted during the previous three years.

3. Investigatory Powers

The Commission's investigative powers under the FSR mirror the powers conferred on the Commission in antitrust[660] and merger control law.[661] The FSR also draws inspiration from the rules concerning EU trade defence investigations.[662] It grants far-reaching investigative powers to the Commission, empowering the Commission to issue binding RFIs, to conduct inspections either inside or outside the EU, and to conduct interviews.

Commission's investigatory powers and tools:

- binding RFIs
- inspections either inside or outside the EU
- interviews

A. *RFIs*

A.1 RFIs Addressed to the Company under Investigation

The Commission may issue binding RFIs, requiring the target of an investigation to provide all the information the Commission deems necessary[663] This is similar to the

---

656 FSR Regulation 2022/2560 [2022] OJ L330/1 (n 1), art 10.
657 ibid, art 13.
658 ibid, arts 14 and 15.
659 ibid, art 38(1).
660 See Regulation 1/2003 [2003] OJ L1/1 (n 518), arts 18–22.
661 See EUMR Regulation 139/2004 [2004] OJ L24/1 (n 35), arts 11–13.
662 See Regulation (EU) 2016/1037 [2016] OJ L176/55 (n 32), arts 10–15.
663 FSR Regulation 2022/2560 [2022] OJ L330/1 (n 1), art 13(2).

Commission's powers in trade defence investigations where 'questionnaires' can be sent to parties involved in the investigation.[664]

The Commission enjoys the same powers under the EUMR and in antitrust investigations. However, contrary to merger and antitrust cases, where the Commission may request information either by formal decision or, more commonly, by an informal request,[665] the Commission can only issue formal RFIs by way of a decision. This applies also when the Commission requests information from third parties.

RFIs are subject to the principle of proportionality.[666] Following the *Meta Platforms Ireland (Facebook Group)* judgment,[667] it can be expected that it will be difficult to challenge an RFI based on a lack of proportionality. In that case, after applying a proportionality test, the General Court found that the Commission's request for disclosure of information containing sensitive personal data was proportionate to achieving objectives of general interest.[668]

When issuing an RFI, the Commission must:

- indicate the legal basis and the purpose of the request, as well as the information required and set an appropriate time limit within which the information is to be provided;[669]
- provide a statement certifying that, if incorrect, incomplete or misleading information is provided, fines or periodic penalty payments may be imposed;[670] and
- provide a statement confirming that, in case of a lack of cooperation, the Commission is authorised to take a decision based on the facts that are available to it.[671]

A.2 RFIs Addressed to the Member States

At the Commission's request, the Member States must also provide all the information the Commission requires. When making such a request, the Commission must indicate the legal basis and purpose of the request, the information required and an appropriate time limit within which the information is to be provided.[672]

A.3 RFIs Addressed to Third Countries

The Commission may also request information from a third country. RFIs must indicate the legal basis and purpose of the request, the information required and a time limit within which the information is to be provided, as well as the fact that, in case of a lack of cooperation, the Commission is authorised to take a decision based on the facts that are available to it.[673]

---

664 Regulation (EU) 2016/1037 [2016] OJ L176/55 (n 32), art 11(2) and Regulation (EU) 2016/1036 [2016] OJ L176/21 (n 237), art 6(2).

665 EUMR Regulation 139/2004 [2004] OJ L24/1 (n 35), art 11.

666 FSR Regulation 2022/2560 [2022] OJ L330/1 (n 1), art 13(3).

667 Case T-451/20 *Meta Platforms Ireland Ltd v European Commission* EU:T:2023:276.

668 ibid, para 266 and following (appeal pending, Case C-497/23 P *Meta Platforms Ireland v European Commission*).

669 FSR Regulation 2022/2560 [2022] OJ L330/1 (n 1), art 13(4)(a).

670 ibid, art 13(4)(b). See also ibid, art 17.

671 ibid, art 13(4)(c). See also ibid, art 16.

672 ibid, art 13(5).

673 ibid, art 13(6).

However, the Commission cannot require third countries to comply. The Commission will likely rely on agreements concluded with third countries and/or on diplomatic relations in this context. In the context of anti-subsidy investigations, the Commission must also rely on cooperation from the country from which the products at issue in that investigation are exported. This has not raised particular issues in most instances because the requested information is usually directly available to the exporting country's government.[674]

Information provided by third countries is expected to be particularly relevant to the Commission's investigations under the FSR, because third-country governments are likely to have more detailed information about the financial contributions they might have provided. They can also provide more information about the structure of domestic laws which might be relevant to the assessment of the existence of a foreign subsidy, such as whether a certain tax measure is selectively provided to only certain beneficiaries. This might prompt the companies, at least under the FSR's notification-based tools, to encourage their governments to respond in a detailed manner to RFIs issued by the Commission.

A.4 Time Limit to Provide the Requested Information

The Commission could in principle reject any information submitted after the expiry of the deadline if the (late) information does not concern minor corrections of information already submitted and/or significantly alters the contents of the original response. It is possible that the submission of significant amendments to the original response is invoked as a reason to reject even the originally submitted response as unreliable.[675]

In trade defence investigations, parties that reply outside of the specified time limit are normally treated as non-cooperating parties by the Commission.[676] However, this does not mean that any information submitted after the set deadline will necessarily be disregarded. As explained by the WTO Panel in *Korea – Certain Paper*, if information is submitted after the deadline, but within a reasonable period, the investigation authority cannot disregard it and simply resort to facts available.[677] According to that

---

674 Van Bael & Bellis (n 110) 681.

675 See, eg, Council Regulation (EEC) 993/93 of 26 April 1993 imposing a definitive anti-dumping duty on imports of certain electronic weighing scale originating in Japan [1993] OJ L104/4, recital 27.

676 See, eg, Commission Implementing Regulation (EU) 2017/141 of 26 January 2017 imposing definitive anti-dumping duties on imports of certain stainless steel tube and pipe butt-welding fittings, whether or not finished, originating in the People's Republic of China and Taiwan [2017] OJ L22/14; Commission Implementing Regulation (EU) 1346/2014 of 17 December 2014 imposing a definitive anti-dumping duty on imports of sulphanilic acid originating in the People's Republic of China and repealing the definitive anti-dumping duty on imports of sulphanilic acid originating in India following an expiry review pursuant to Article 11(2) Council Regulation (EC) 1225/2009 [2014] OJ L363/82; Council Implementing Regulation (EU) 430/2013 of 13 May 2013 imposing a definitive anti-dumping duty and collecting definitively the provisional duty imposed on imports of threaded tube or pipe cast fittings, of malleable cast iron, originating in the People's Republic of China and Thailand and terminating the proceeding with regard to Indonesia [2013] OJ L129/1; Council Regulation (EC) 91/2009 of 26 January 2009 imposing a definitive anti-dumping duty on imports of certain iron or steel fasteners originating in the People's Republic of China [2009] OJ L29/1; Commission Regulation (EC) 553/2006 of 23 March 2006, imposing a provisional anti-dumping duty on imports of certain footwear with uppers of leather originating in the People's Republic of China and Vietnam [2006] OJ L98/3; Consolidated text: Council Regulation (EC) 1522/2000 of 10 July 2000 imposing a definitive anti-dumping duty on imports of synthetic staple fibres of polyester originating in Australia, Indonesia and Thailand and collecting definitively the provisional duty imposed [2000] OJ L175/10.

677 See WTO Panel Report, *Korea – Certain Paper* (2007), WT/DS312/R, para 7.49.

panel, in considering whether information is submitted within a reasonable period of time, investigating authorities should consider factors such as: (i) the nature and quantity of the information submitted, (ii) the difficulties encountered in obtaining the information, (iii) the verifiability of the information and the ease with which it can be used by the investigating authorities in making their determination, (iv) whether other interested parties are likely to be prejudiced if the information is used, (v) whether acceptance of the information would compromise the ability of the investigating authorities to conduct the investigation expeditiously, and (vi) the number of days by which the investigated exporter missed the time-limit.[678]

In *Kito Ceramics*, the General Court agreed that 'reasonableness should be defined on a case-by-case basis, in the light of the specific circumstances of each investigation'.[679] In that case, the required information was minor and accessible to the applicant, but nevertheless would have required an on-site visit to verify. Taking into account also that it was provided at a time when the Commission's essential determinations had already been made, the 10-month delay was considered unreasonable.[680]

B. Inspections within the Member States and Third Countries

Under the FSR, where necessary, the Commission may conduct inspections of companies, both within and outside the EU.[681] This is similar to the power of the Commission to undertake inspections in antitrust and merger cases, and to carry out 'verifications' (in third countries) in trade defence investigations.[682]

The EUMR also grants the Commission the power to conduct inspections in merger control review, but this is rarely used, in part due to the tight timeframes involved. It seems unlikely that this tool, and especially inspections outside the EU, will be frequently used in the context of the M&A or public procurement tools under the FSR (due to the applicable timeframes).

B.1 Inspections within the Member States

The Commission must notify a Member State of inspections to be carried out within that Member State in good time prior to the inspection, including the date on which the inspection will begin.[683] The Commission may require the assistance of national authorities. In that situation, officials and other persons authorised or appointed by the

---

678 See ibid, para 7.49.

679 Case T-633/11 *Guangdong Kito Ceramics Co Ltd and Others v Council of the European Union* EU:T:2014:271, paras 70–91.

680 ibid, paras 59–61 and paras 70–91.

681 FSR Regulation 2022/2560 [2022] OJ L330/1 (n 1), art 14(1).

682 Regulation (EU) 2016/1037 [2016] OJ L176/55 (n 32), art 26 and Regulation (EU) 2016/1036 [2016] OJ L176/21 (n 237), art 16.

683 FSR Regulation 2022/2560 [2022] OJ L330/1 (n 1), art 14(4).

Member State must, at the request of their national authorities (most likely competition authorities having experience with inspections) or the Commission, actively assist with the investigation, including providing police assistance where necessary.[684]

B.2 Inspections in Third Countries

The Commission may also carry out inspections on the territory of a third country, provided that the government of that third country was formally notified of the intended inspection and did not object to the inspection.[685]

In trade defence investigations, the Commission also must obtain the agreement of the firms concerned prior to carrying out investigations in third countries.[686] The FSR, however, merely states that the Commission '*may* also ask the undertaking or association of undertakings to give its consent to the inspection'[687] when conducting inspections in third countries.

B.3 Rights of Inspection

The Commission's rights of inspection are similar to its powers in the context of a suspected infringement of Articles 101 or 102 TFEU and trade defence investigations. They include the right to:[688]

- enter any premises, land and means of transport of the company or association of companies;
- examine books and other business records, irrespective of the medium on which they are stored, and to take or request copies;
- ask any representative or member of staff of the company or association of companies for explanations on facts or documents relating to the subject-matter and purpose of the inspection and to record their answers; and
- seal any business premises and books or records for the period of the inspection and to the extent necessary for that inspection.

The target of an inspection must comply when being presented with a Commission decision detailing:[689] (i) the subject matter and purpose of the inspection, and (ii) the fact that the Commission may take a decision based on the facts available in case of a lack of cooperation.[690] Where the inspection is carried out in the EU, the decision must also set out: (i) the possibility of fines and periodic penalty payments being imposed,[691] and (ii) the right to have the inspection decision reviewed by the General Court.[692]

---

684 ibid, art 14(5)–(7).
685 ibid, art 15.
686 Regulation (EU) 2016/1037 [2016] OJ L176/55 (n 32), art 26(2) and Regulation (EU) 2016/1036 [2016] OJ L176/21 (n 237), art 16(2).
687 FSR Regulation 2022/2560 [2022] OJ L330/1 (n 1), art 15 (emphasis added).
688 ibid, art 14(2).
689 ibid, art 14(3).
690 ibid, art 16.
691 ibid, art 17.
692 TFEU, art 263.

C. *Interviews*

The Commission may conduct interviews with any natural or legal person consenting to be interviewed for the purpose of collecting information relating to the company and/or the foreign subsidies under the investigation.

A Member State in the territory of which an interview will take place must be informed ahead of time. For interviews in a third country, the Commission must obtain the prior consent of that third country's government.[693] Interviews must be documented, and the person interviewed may submit comments within a time limit set by the Commission.[694]

The EUMR also grants the Commission the power to conduct interviews in merger control reviews, but this power is rarely used. It is unclear whether this tool will be more frequently used in the context of the FSR.

4. Fines and Periodic Penalty Payments

A. *Situations in which Fines and Periodic Penalty Payments May Be Imposed*

The Commission may impose fines and periodic penalty payments where a company intentionally or negligently:

- supplies incorrect, incomplete or misleading information in response to an RFI or does not supply that information within the prescribed time limit.[695] Before imposing a fine or periodic penalty payment for this reason, the Commission must set a final time limit of two weeks to receive the missing information;[696]
- produces the required books or other records related to its business in incomplete form in the context of inspections carried out within the EU;[697]
- (i) gives an incorrect or misleading answer, (ii) fails to rectify an incorrect, incomplete or misleading answer given by a staff member within the time-limit set by the Commission, or (iii) fails or refuses to provide a complete answer to questions relating to the subject-matter and purpose of an inspection when

693 FSR Regulation 2022/2560 [2022] OJ L330/1 (n 1), art 13(7).
694 ibid, art 9.
695 ibid, art 17(1)(a).
696 ibid, art 17(4).
697 ibid, arts 14 and 17(1)(b).

the Commission requests explanations of facts or documents in the context of inspections carried out within the EU;[698]

- refuses to submit to inspections within the EU[699] or has broken seals[700] affixed on business premises, books or records;[701]
- fails to comply with the conditions for access to the file or the terms of disclosure[702] imposed by the Commission.[703]

In addition, the Commission may impose fines for failure to comply with commitments,[704] a decision imposing redressive measures,[705] or with interim measures,[706] or if the company does not comply with a decision requiring it to inform the Commission of its future participation in concentrations or public procurement procedures.[707]

Finally, specific fines and periodic penalty payments may be imposed in the context of the M&A tool or the public procurement tool, and where a company does not comply with a decision with commitments,[708] a decision ordering interim measures,[709] or a decision imposing redressive measures.

B. Level of Fines and Periodic Penalty Payments

Where a company or association of companies intentionally or negligently does not cooperate in the investigation as specified in Article 17(1) FSR, the Commission may impose fines not exceeding 1% of the aggregate turnover of the company concerned in the preceding financial year.[710] Periodic penalty payments may not exceed 5% of the average daily aggregate turnover of the company concerned in the preceding financial year for each working day of delay, calculated from the day established in the decision, until the company submits complete and correct information as requested by the Commission, or until it submits to an inspection.[711]

---

698 ibid, arts 14(2)(c) and 17(1)(c).

699 ibid, art 14.

700 See ibid, art 14(2)(d). In a merger case for example, a company received a €8 million fine for breach of a seal during an inspection (see Commission decision of 24 May 2011 relating to a proceeding under Regulation 1/2003 [2003] OJ L1/1 (n 518), art 23.

701 FSR Regulation 2022/2560 [2022] OJ L330/1 (n 1), art 17(1)(d). See Case T-272/12 *Energeticky a prumyslovy holding as v European Commission* EU:T:2014:995; Case T-141/08 *E.ON Energie AG v European Commission* EU:T:2010:516.

702 FSR Regulation 2022/2560 [2022] OJ L330/1 (n 1), art 42(4).

703 ibid, art 17(1)(e).

704 ibid, art 11(3).

705 ibid, art 11(2).

706 ibid, art 12.

707 ibid, arts 8 and 17(5).

708 ibid, art 11(3).

709 ibid, art 12.

710 ibid, art 17(2).

711 ibid, art 17(3).

Where a company does not comply with a decision with commitments,[712] a decision ordering interim measures,[713] a decision imposing redressive measures,[714] or a decision imposing reporting obligations, the Commission may impose: (i) fines not exceeding 10% of the aggregate turnover in the preceding financial year, or (ii) periodic penalty payments not exceeding 5% of the average daily aggregate turnover in the preceding financial year for each day of non-compliance, starting from the day of the Commission decision imposing those penalty payments, until the Commission finds that the company complies with the decision.[715]

In fixing the amount of the fine or periodic penalty payment, the Commission must take into account the nature, gravity and duration of the infringement as well as the principles of proportionality and appropriateness.[716] It should also take into account cases of repeated non-compliance.[717] Where the company has satisfied the obligation which a periodic penalty payment was intended to enforce, the Commission may reduce the definitive amount of the periodic penalty payment compared to that under the original decision imposing periodic penalty payments.[718]

Level of fines and periodic penalty payments:

- a company intentionally or negligently does not properly cooperate in the investigation:
  - fines: maximum 1% of the aggregate turnover of the company in the preceding financial year
  - periodic penalty payments: maximum 5% of the average daily aggregate turnover of the company in the preceding financial year
- a company does not comply with a decision with commitments, a decision ordering interim measures, a decision imposing redressive measures, or a decision which obliged the company to inform the Commission of its future participation in concentrations or public procurement procedures:
  - fines: maximum 10% of the aggregate turnover of the company in the preceding financial year
  - periodic penalty payments: maximum 5% of the average daily aggregate turnover of the company in the preceding financial year

Aspects to take into account when imposing fines and periodic penalty payments:

- nature of the infringement
- gravity of the infringement

712 ibid, art 11(3).
713 ibid, art 12.
714 ibid, art 11(2).
715 ibid, art 17(5).
716 ibid, art 17(6).
717 ibid, recital 32.
718 ibid, art 17(7).

- duration of the infringement
- proportionality
- appropriateness
- repeated non-compliance

C. Limitation Period

The powers of the Commission to impose fines or periodic penalty payments is subject to a limitation period of three years, starting on the day when the infringement at issue took place. In the case of continuing or repeated infringements, the limitation period starts on the day on which the infringement ceases.[719] The powers of the Commission to enforce decisions imposing fines or periodic penalty payments is subject to a limitation period of five years, starting on the day on which the Commission decision imposing fines or periodic penalty payments is taken.[720]

5. Non-Cooperation

If parties fail to provide certain information or obstruct an investigation, the Commission may take its decision at the end of a preliminary review or at the end of an in-depth investigation on the basis of facts available. Relying on facts available also means that when a company has failed to provide the necessary information to determine whether a financial contribution confers a benefit on it, that undertaking may be deemed to have received such a benefit.[721]

The Commission may rely on best facts available if a party to an investigation or the third country that granted a foreign subsidy:

- provides incomplete, incorrect or misleading information in response to an RFI;
- fails to provide the information requested within the time limit prescribed by the Commission;
- refuses to submit to the Commission's inspection in a Member State or third country; or
- otherwise impedes the preliminary review or the in-depth investigation.[722]

---

719 ibid, art 38(2).
720 ibid, art 38(3).
721 ibid, art 16(3).
722 ibid, art 16(1).

The right to base a decision on available facts mirrors the Commission's rights in trade defence investigations.[723] This power is designed to incentivise cooperation in investigations, especially in third counties and to address the lack of information resulting from non-cooperation. When applying facts available, the result of the procedure may be (and will likely be) less favourable to the company than if it had cooperated with the Commission.[724]

The FSR does not specify which information the Commission should use when relying on the best facts available. The Basic Anti-Subsidy and Anti-Dumping Regulations expressly require the Commission to act with special circumspection[725] when basing findings on the facts available.[726] Where practicable, information from secondary sources such as the complaint are to be checked by the Commission by reference to information from other available independent sources. Similarly, the WTO Appellate Body has found that, when relying on facts available, an investigating authority must generally use, in the first instance, any information that the respondent did provide (if the respondent acted to the best of its ability).[727] The FSR does not impose similar requirements on the Commission.

In trade defence investigations, the Commission also relies on facts available in case a party has submitted false or misleading information or otherwise significantly impeded the investigation.[728] When false or misleading information is submitted, the Commission can either disregard all information provided by the party concerned or only that portion that was found to be false or misleading. This will depend on the circumstances of the case, in particular on the extent to which false or misleading information was submitted.[729] Similarly, under the FSR, the Commission must disregard the information

---

723 See WO Anti-Dumping Agreement, art 6.8 and SCM Agreement (n 2), art 12.7, Regulation (EU) 2016/1036 [2016] OJ L176/21 (n 237), art 18; Regulation (EU) 2016/1037 [2016] OJ L176/55 (n 32), art 28.

724 FSR Regulation 2022/2560 [2022] OJ L330/1 (n 1), art 16(4).

725 In *Korea – Certain Paper* (n 677), paras 6.16–6.58, the WTO Panel found that Korea had failed to exercise special circumspection in the use of information from secondary sources, in violation of the WTO Anti-Dumping Agreement, art 6.8 and Annex II para 7, when it used information obtained from a production company to construct missing cost information for a trading company, even though suitable cost information was also available from a trading company subject to the same investigation.

726 Regulation (EU) 2016/1036 [2016] OJ L176/21 (n 237), art 18(5); Regulation (EU) 2016/1037 [2016] OJ L176/55 (n 32), art 28(5).

727 WTO Appellate Body Report, *Mexico – Anti-Dumping Measures on Rice* (2005), WT/DS295/AB/R.

728 See, eg Commission Regulation (EC) 358/2002 of 26 February 2002 imposing a provisional anti-dumping duty on imports of certain tube and pipe fittings, of iron or steel originating in the Czech Republic, Malaysia, Russia, the Republic of Korea and Slovakia and accepting an undertaking offered by an exporting producer in Slovakia [2002] OJ L56/4, recital 35; Commission Regulation (EC) 390/2007 imposing a provisional anti-dumping duty on imports of peroxosulphates (persulphates) originating in the United States of America, the People's Republic of China and Taiwan [2007] OJ L97/6, recital 103; Commission Regulation (EC) 994/2007 of 28 August 2007 imposing a provisional anti-dumping duty on imports of ferro-silicon originating in the People's Republic of China, Egypt, Kazakhstan, the former Yugoslav Republic of Macedonia and Russia [2007] OJ L223/1.

729 See Regulation 390/2007 [2007] OJ L97/6 (n 728), recital 103; Commission Regulation (EC) 492/2008 of 3 June 2008 imposing a provisional anti-dumping duty on imports of monosodium glutamate originating in the People's Republic of China [2008] OJ L144/14, recitals 15–18; Commission Regulation (EC) 2005/2006 of 22 December 2006 imposing provisional anti-dumping duties on imports of synthetic staple fibres of polyesters (PSF) originating in Malaysia and Taiwan [2006] OJ L379/65; Council Regulation (EC) 1987/2005 of 2 December 2005 imposing a definitive anti-dumping duty and collecting definitively the provisional duty imposed on imports of granular polytetrafluoroethylene (PTFE) originating in Russia and the People's Republic of China [2005] OJ L320/1, recitals 28–35.

if a company, a Member State or a third country involved has supplied incorrect or misleading information.[730]

The FSR does not require the Commission to provide the party concerned an opportunity to submit further explanations, once the Commission has determined that the evidence or information presented is unacceptable or deficient.[731] Although the same rule applies in trade defence investigations, the Commission routinely provides interested parties with the opportunity to request a hearing with the Hearing Officer[732] when it has informed the interested parties of its intention to rely on the best facts available.[733]

However, the FSR does not provide for oral hearings or the involvement of a Hearing Officer. Therefore this practice might not be used in FSR investigations. While the use of facts available is likely to have a significant impact on the outcome of an investigation, the FSR appears to provide fewer protections for parties as compared with trade defence investigations.

In the context of trade defence investigations, obtaining information from third countries has sometimes proven to be difficult in case the third country is a non-transparent economy with a high percentage of SOEs and/or does not typically make information concerning their subsidy schemes publicly available.[734] Companies under FSR investigation will equally depend on the willingness of their government to provide information to the Commission and risk a decision based on facts available if their government refuses to cooperate.

6. Anti-circumvention and the FSR

Article 39(1) FSR prohibits circumvention of the notification requirements under the M&A and public procurement tools. It covers the mandatory notification requirements as well as the situation where the Commission requires notification under these tools, despite the relevant thresholds not being met.[735] In particular, companies must not arrange

---

730 FSR Regulation 2022/2560 [2022] OJ L330/1 (n 1), art 16(2).

731 Regulation (EU) 2016/1036 [2016] OJ L176/21 (n 237), art 18(4); Regulation (EU) 2016/1037 [2016] OJ L176/55 (n 32), art 28(4). See also *Mexico – Anti-Dumping Measures on Rice* (n 727), para 259.

732 In trade defence investigations, the Hearing Officer is a person to whom any of the parties in an investigation may turn for the safeguarding of their procedural rights.

733 In Commission Implementing Regulation (EU) 2016/1328 of 29 July 2016 imposing a definitive anti-dumping duty and collecting definitively the provisional duty imposed on imports of certain cold rolled flat steel products originating in the People's Republic of China and the Russian Federation [2016] OJ L210/1, recitals 30–31, the Commission organised two hearings for a Russian exporting producer following the use of facts available to establish the provisional dumping duties. The exporting producer was, however, not able to support its challenge to the use of Article 18 either with information contained in its questionnaire reply or information collected during verifications. The Commission therefore confirmed the use of facts available.

734 CP Bown and JA Hillman, 'WTO-ing a Resolution to the China Subsidy Problem' (October 2019) Peterson Institute for International Economics Working Paper, 12; M Frank, 'The EU's new foreign subsidy regulation on collision course with the WTO' (2023) 60 CML Rev 935–936.

735 FSR Regulation 2022/2560 [2022] OJ L330/1 (n 1), art 39(1) refers to the notification requirements in ibid, arts 21(1), (5), 29(1), (5) and (8).

financial operations or contracts to circumvent those requirements. Examples of such arrangements could include the situation, under the public procurement tool, where a front company has been set up for the sole purpose of shielding foreign subsidies received by the entity that acts *de facto* as the main supplier, taking into account that, for the contribution threshold under that tool, any financial contribution received by the subcontractor/supplier's parents or other corporate affiliates are not relevant for calculating the relevant thresholds.[736]

In the event that the Commission suspects that a company or economic operator has engaged in a circumvention practice or is engaging in such a practice, it may initiate a review into that circumvention and request further information from the relevant company or economic operator.[737] That review corresponds with the review in case of a failure to notify as required (Article 21(4) FSR, in respect of the M&A tool) or the re-opening of a preliminary review in case new information becomes available after closure of the initial preliminary review without a decision (Article 30(4) FSR, in respect of the public procurement tool).

Companies or economic operators intentionally or negligently circumventing or attempting to circumvent the notification requirements under the M&A and public procurement tools may be fined by the Commission. The level of the fine can be up to 10 % of their aggregate turnover in the preceding financial year when the (attempted) circumvention took place.[738]

Article 39(2) FSR expressly refers to the Commission's power under Articles 21(4) and 30(4) FSR to require parties to submit a notification if it considers that the parties might have circumvented their notification obligations. However, nothing would preclude the Commission from initiating an ex officio review in this situation. The Commission could use the ex officio tool without having to substantiate its concerns about circumvention.

Moreover, circumvention risks can, in essence, feature in any part of the Commission's review under the FSR. For example, where the proposed commitment is repayment of the subsidy, the Commission must accept that commitment 'only where it can ascertain that the repayment is transparent, verifiable and effective, while taking into account the risk of circumvention' of the objectives of the FSR.[739]

---

736 See Chapter IV 2.A.2.2.2.

737 FSR Regulation 2022/2560 [2022] OJ L330/1 (n 1), art 39(2).

738 ibid, arts 26(3)(d) and 33(3).

739 ibid, art 7(6) and recital 24.

Concurrences
Competition Laws Review

Concurrences Review

Concurrences is a print and online quarterly peer reviewed journal dedicated to EU and national competitions laws. It has been launched in 2004 as the flagship of the Institute of Competition Law in order to provide a forum for academics, practitioners and enforcers. Concurrences' influence and expertise has garnered contributions or interviews with such figures as Christine Lagarde, Bill Kovacic, Emmanuel Macron, Antonin Scalia and Magrethe Vestager.

Contents

More than 15,000 articles, print and/or online. Quarterly issues provide current coverage with contributions from the EU or national or foreign countries thanks to more than 2,500 authors in Europe and abroad.

Format

In order to balance academic contributions with opinions or legal practice notes, Concurrences provides its insight and analysis in a number of formats:

- Forewords: Opinions by leading academics or enforcers
- Interviews: Interviews of antitrust experts
- On-Topics: 4 to 6 short papers on hot issues
- Law & Economics: Short papers written by economists for a legal audience
- Articles: Long academic papers
- Case Summaries: Case commentary on EU and French case law
- Legal Practice: Short papers for in-house counsels
- International: Medium size papers on international policies
- Books Review: Summaries of recent antitrust books
- Articles Review: Summaries of leading articles published in 45 antitrust journals

Boards

The Scientific Committee is headed by Laurence Idot, Professor at Panthéon Assas University. The International Committee is headed by Frederic Jenny, OECD Competition Comitteee Chairman. Boards members include Douglas Ginsburg, Benoît Cœuré, Howard Shelanski, Richard Whish, Wouter Wils, Joshua Wright, etc.

Online version

Concurrences website provides all articles published since its inception, in addition to selected articles published online only in the electronic supplement.

Write for Concurrences

Concurrences welcome spontaneous contributions. Except in rare circumstances, the journal accepts only unpublished articles, whatever the form and nature of the contribution. The Editorial Board checks the form of the proposals, and then submits these to the Scientific Committee. Selection of the papers is conditional to a peer review by at least two members of the Committee. Within a month, the Committee assesses whether the draft article can be published and notifies the author.

www.ingramcontent.com/pod-product-compliance
Ingram Content Group UK Ltd.
Pitfield, Milton Keynes, MK11 3LW, UK
UKHW020214290926
15470UKWH00001B/185

9 781939 007773